ADVANCE PRAISE FOR

Asian/American Scholars of Education

"Nicholas D. Hartlep, Daisy Ball, and Kevin E. Wells and their second edition of *Asian/ American Scholars of Education: 21st Century Pedagogies, Perspectives, and Experiences* place their field-shifting perspectives on the engagements of Asian American faculty in Academe who have received named professorships. Hartlep, Ball, and Wells stand on the shoulders of the giants in the field—Derald Wing Sue, Robert Teranishi, and Mitchell Chang among others—to gain an aerial view of the higher education landscape that has been at best sparsely occupied, and at worst bereft of literature that speaks to the Asian American experience. Their tome unapologetically provides intellectual space to problematize pedagogical approaches, as well as experiential and perspectival engagements through the narratives shared by these named professors."

—Dr. Fred A. Bonner II,
Professor and Endowed Chair,
Whitlowe R. Green College of Education,
Prairie View A&M University

"Hartlep, Ball, and Wells present an incredible array of essays written by the world's foremost scholars on what it means to be Asian American and hold distinguished faculty appointments. These collected works will raise much needed consciousness on the trials, tribulations, and hopes of a racial group that has experienced tragic experiences of exclusion and xenophobia."

—Dr. René Antrop-González,
Dean and Professor of Education,
SUNY at New Paltz

"Improving the representation of Asian American endowed chairs, particularly in education, is of great importance because of their unusually low current representation relative to their achievements."

—Dr. Jonathan Wai (from the Foreword),
Assistant Professor of Education Policy and Psychology
and 21st Century Endowed Chair in Education Policy,
University of Arkansas

Asian/American Scholars
of Education

Narrative, Dialogue,
and the Political
Production of Meaning

Michael A. Peters & Peter McLaren
Series Editors

Vol. 22

The Education and Struggle series is part of the Peter Lang Education list.
Every volume is peer reviewed and meets
the highest quality standards for content and production.

PETER LANG
New York • Bern • Berlin
Brussels • Vienna • Oxford • Warsaw

Asian/American Scholars of Education

21st Century Pedagogies, Perspectives, and Experiences, Second Edition

Nicholas D. Hartlep, Daisy Ball,
and Kevin E. Wells, *Editors*

Foreword by Jonathan Wai
Afterword by Christian D. Chan

PETER LANG
New York • Bern • Berlin
Brussels • Vienna • Oxford • Warsaw

Library of Congress Cataloging-in-Publication Data

Names: Hartlep, Nicholas Daniel, editor. | Ball, Daisy, editor. |
Wells, Kevin E., editor.
Title: Asian/American scholars of education: 21st century pedagogies,
perspectives, and experiences / edited by Nicholas D. Hartlep,
Daisy Ball, Kevin E. Wells.
Description: 2nd edition. | New York: Peter Lang, 2022.
Series: Education and struggle: narrative, dialogue,
and the political production of meaning; vol. 22
ISSN 2168-6432 (print) | ISSN 2168-6459 (online)
Includes bibliographical references and index.
Identifiers: LCCN 2021016316 (print) | LCCN 2021016317 (ebook)
ISBN 978-1-4331-8679-0 (paperback) | ISBN 978-1-4331-8680-6 (ebook pdf)
ISBN 978-1-4331-8681-3 (epub) | ISBN 978-1-4331-8682-0 (mobi)
Subjects: LCSH: Asian American college teachers—Biography. |
Education—Study and teaching (Higher)—United States. | Minorities in
higher education—United States.
Classification: LCC LC2633.6 .A83 2022 (print) | LCC LC2633.6 (ebook) |
DDC 378.1/982995073—dc23
LC record available at https://lccn.loc.gov/2021016316
LC ebook record available at https://lccn.loc.gov/2021016317
DOI 10.3726/b18191

Bibliographic information published by **Die Deutsche Nationalbibliothek.**
Die Deutsche Nationalbibliothek lists this publication in the "Deutsche
Nationalbibliografie"; detailed bibliographic data are available
on the Internet at http://dnb.d-nb.de/.

© 2022 Peter Lang Publishing, Inc., New York
80 Broad Street, 5th floor, New York, NY 10004
www.peterlang.com

Nicholas dedicates this book to the many unnoticed Asian American faculty members who have not been given opportunities to lead in higher education. I hope that this book shows others that you deserve an opportunity. Continue to do good work!

Daisy dedicates this book to Noriko Ishibashi.

Kevin dedicates this book to contract faculty everywhere. You are worthy.

Table of Contents

Illustrations and Tables

Abbreviations

AACTE	American Association of Colleges of Teacher Education
AAPI	Asian American and Pacific Islander
AASC	Asian American Studies Center
AASCU	American Association of State Colleges and Universities
ABA	Applied Behavior Analysis
AERA	American Educational Research Association
AOP	Advanced Opportunity Program
ASHE	Association for the Study of Higher Education
BD	Behavior Disorders
BIP	Behavior Intervention Plan
BRT	Behavior Research and Training
CARE	National Commission on Asian American and Pacific Islander Research in Education
CBER	Center for Behavioral Education and Research
CEHD	College of Education and Human Development
CGU	Claremont Graduate University
CMSI	Center for Minority Serving Institutions
CPRE	Consortium for Policy Research in Education
CPS	Center for Postsecondary Success
CV	Curriculum Vitae

DE	Developmental Education
DMA	Dynamic Multilevel Analysis
DNA	Dialogic Narrative Analysis
DOJ	U.S. Department of Justice
DP	Distinguished Professor
EBS	Effective Behavior Support
EC	Endowed Chair
EdUHK	The Education University of Hong Kong
ELL	English Language Learner
ELPS	Department of Educational Leadership and Policy Studies
ETS	Educational Testing Service
FSU	Florida State University
FTIC	First-Time-In-College
GED	General Education Development
GMS	Gates Millennium Scholarship Program
GOA'L	Global Oversearch Adoptees' Link
GOLD	Graduate of the Last Decade
GRE	Graduate Record Examination
HHS	U.S. Department of Health and Human Services
HSI	Hispanic Serving Institution
IDEA	Individuals with Disabilities Education Act
IEP	Individualized Education Plan
IES	Institute of Education Sciences
IGE	Institute for Immigration, Globalization, and Education
IGLAS	Institute for Global-Local Action & Study
IHEP	Institute of Higher Education Policy
ISU	Illinois State University
KLICK!	Kids Learning In Computer Klubhouses
MDA	Multilevel Diffusion Analysis
MMSP	Model Minority Stereotype Project
MOU	Memorandum of Understanding
MSI	Minority Serving Institution
MSU	Metropolitan State University
MSU	Michigan State University
MTSS	Multi-Tiered Level of Systems of Support
NAPLeS	Network of Academic Programs in the Learning Sciences
NAYRE	National Association of Year-Round Education
NCLB	No Child Left Behind Act
NIE	National Institute of Education (see Singapore)
NIMH	National Institute of Mental Health
NORC	National Opinion Research Center

NSSE	National Survey of Student Engagement
NYC	New York City
NYU	New York University
OSEP	Office of Special Education Programs
PBIS	Positive Behavioral Interventions and Supports
PBS	Positive Behavior Support
PIRLS	Progress in International Reading Literacy Study
PISA	Programme for International Student Assessment
PKU	Peking University
PREPARE	Promoting Responsible, Empirical, and Proactive Alternatives in Regular Education for Students with Behavior Disorders
REAPA	Research on the Education of Asian and Pacific Americans, see also SIG
RQ	Research Question
SBI	Schema-Based Instruction
SDA	Statistical Discourse Analysis
SHU	Seton Hall University
SIG	Special Interest Group
SSCE	Social Science and Comparative Education
STEM	Science, Technology, Engineering, and Mathematics
SWPBIS	School-Wide PBIS
TC	Teachers College, Columbia University
TIMSS	Trends in International Mathematics and Science Study
TOEFL	Test of English as a Foreign Language
UCD	University of California at Davis
UCLA	University of California at Los Angeles
UCONN	University of Connecticut
UCR	University of California at Riverside
UCSB	University of California at Santa Barbara
UCSC	University of California at Santa Cruz
UH	University of Houston
UIUC	University of Illinois at Urbana-Champaign
ULM	University of Louisiana at Monroe
UMN	University of Minnesota, Twin Cities
UO	University of Oregon
URI	University Research Initiative
USDOE	U.S. Department of Education
UW	University of Washington
UWM	University of Wisconsin at Milwaukee
WSA	Washington State Achievers Program
WWII	World War II

Foreword

"Luck and Mentorship": Brief Reflections of a Chinese American in Higher Education

JONATHAN WAI
University of Arkansas

The Asian American actor John Cho, perhaps most widely known as the co-star of the movie *Harold and Kumar*, recently penned an op-ed for the *Los Angeles Times* aptly titled "Coronavirus reminds Asian Americans belonging is conditional" (Cho, 2020). And in *The Washington Post*, one of the most visible Asian Americans in politics and former presidential candidate, Andrew Yang, wrote an op-ed titled "We Asian Americans are not the virus, but we can be part of the cure" (Yang, 2020). That is, two high profile Asian Americans had to pen op-eds in order to remind the rest of America that Asians who are citizens of the U.S. are Americans, and that we had no responsibility for introducing the coronavirus on American soil. Although Cho and Yang are highly visible, they are anomalies: Asian Americans have extremely low representation, or a "low base rate," when it comes to reaching pinnacle positions in acting and politics. Another achievement in which Asian Americans are underrepresented, I learned recently, is the attainment of an endowed chair in the field of education, which is the topic of this volume.

As a Chinese American born in a community in which my sister and I always knew we didn't look the same as the other kids, even if we did share their American accent and cultural interests, I have long understood the feeling of being one of the few people of color. My parents, who grew up in Hong Kong and came to the U.S. as Chinese graduate students in biophysics and electrical engineering, have always reminded me how difficult it is to fit in when you are an outsider.

My mother shared with me recently advice given to her by her cousin (my "uncle" Tom), who took care of her when she first arrived in the U.S.: "You will face discrimination here, and you will simply have to be better."

When Nicholas Hartlep wrote to me about his book project honoring Asian American endowed chairs in education and asked me to write the foreword, I was very touched to do so. And so I am writing this foreword in the spirit of the person who wrote the foreword for the first edition of this book, who presciently wrote, "As scholars of color, it is imperative that we continue to be vigilant in telling our stories" (Freeman, 2018, p. xix). This foreword is a brief version of my own story as a person of color, and this edited volume shares the collective stories of so many distinguished scholars who also happen to be Asian American, told through the lenses of others who they have touched, inspired, and educated.

I am a scholar of education policy who was trained in differential psychology and measurement, and who also has expertise in a number of other subfields including gifted education, expertise, and intelligence. Thus, my work is highly interdisciplinary. And one strand of my research has focused on low base rate outcomes from two perspectives. One perspective is from the prospective angle, looking at early precursors to the development of exceptional achievement (e.g., Wai, Lubinski, & Benbow, 2005). The other perspective is from the retrospective angle, looking at multiple groups of people who have achieved numerous low base rate achievements and then looking back in their life course trajectories to understand how education and other qualities may have impacted their path to the top of these diverse domains (e.g., Wai, Anderson, Perina, Worrell, & Chabris, in progress). Longitudinal studies of highly gifted youths (e.g., Lubinski & Benbow, 2006) illustrate that trying to predict low base rate outcomes like earning doctorates, patents, publications, and even university tenure is possible to some measure. However, certain outcomes are so low base rate (e.g., the Nobel Prize) that prediction becomes enormously challenging (Lubinski, 2004) due to the multivariate nature of the variables involved, including luck or randomness in success and failure (Pluchino, Biondo, & Rapisarda, 2018).

At a time when university budgets are being hit hard by the coronavirus and hiring freezes take hold, it is never a better time to remember how lucky those of us who have academic jobs are. As a recent analysis of the faculty job market concluded, "Our findings suggest that there is no single clear path to a faculty job offer and that metrics such as career transition awards and publications in high impact factor journals were neither necessary nor sufficient for landing a faculty position" (Fernandes, Sarabipour, Smith, Niemi, Jadavji, Kozik, et al., 2020. Reinero (2019) provides an analysis of the faculty job market in psychology and also found that publication record does matter, but that mentorship matters much more than we think.

Luck and mentorship. I have had both in enormous measure. As someone who was not too long ago on the job market, I can attest that mentorship played a fundamental role in my success. My key undergraduate mentor was Diane F. Halpern at Claremont McKenna College who told me I was going to be a psychologist, opened the very first doors to graduate school, and collaborated with me on my very first scientific paper. Then there's David Lubinski and Camilla P. Benbow, my graduate school mentors at Vanderbilt University, who taught me how to develop my scientific taste, to seize upon important questions, and to work nonstop to see projects to completion. I am grateful to Martha Putallaz, my first postdoctoral advisor, who told me to think of my own ideas and research program, gave me resources and complete freedom to do so in a role as a research scientist for many years at Duke University, and provided me the opportunity to work remotely to support the career of my spouse and for the birth of our two young children. Finally, I deeply value Christopher F. Chabris at Geisinger Health System who not only allowed me to remotely work as a postdoc as I transitioned jobs, but who mentored me in interdisciplinary scientific thinking and in clarity of writing and expression. I have had numerous others who have mentored and helped me, but here I only mention those who were part of my formal educational training. And one important fact I wish to highlight is that none of these mentors were Asian American themselves and most were women, though they helped an Asian American.

Improving the representation of Asian American endowed chairs, particularly in education, is of great importance because of their unusually low current representation relative to their achievements (Hartlep, Ball, Theodosopoulos, Wells, & Morgan, 2016), and if nothing else to ensure that such individuals are recognized fairly, and not held to a different standard or discriminated against. This is something that Asian Americans know all too well in other areas of elite education (e.g., Arcidiacono, Kinsler, & Ransom, 2020). And though it is absolutely true that Asian Americans and those profiled in this volume are able to contribute new ideas because of their Asian backgrounds and this should not be forgotten, it is also important to ensure that diversity of all kinds are included at the table (e.g., Duarte, Crawford, Stern, Haidt, Jussim, & Tetlock, 2014) to ensure the field of education advances through a variety of research paradigms and questions asked (Singer, 2019).

I am honored to be able to write this foreword in honor of the Asian American scholars who are recognized here, and I am also honored to have the opportunity to thank all of my mentors—both those who I have mentioned here, and so many who I have not. I am also grateful to my students and to my colleagues past and present—especially those at the University of Arkansas in the Department of Education Reform where I am both an Assistant Professor of Education Policy and Psychology and the 21st Century Endowed Chair in Education Policy. I look forward to the continued opportunity to encourage and inspire students to pursue interesting and important questions in education and to bring those questions into the social sciences more broadly (and vice versa). I hope that the individuals profiled in this volume will inspire many scholars of color, including Asian Americans, to seek to achieve highly in academia and contribute to scientific knowledge and understanding in the pursuit of helping better educate children. At the same time, it is important to remember—as Cho and Yang reiterated in their op-eds— that as Asians we are as every bit American as anyone, and that we are worthy of being role models for our achievements, and nothing more. In higher education our belonging should not be conditional, and we most certainly can be a part of the cure.

REFERENCES

Arcidiacono, P., Kinsler, J., & Ransom, T. (2020). Asian American discrimination in Harvard admissions. *NBER Working Paper*. Retrieved from: http://public.econ.duke.edu/~psarcidi/realpenalty.pdf

Cho, J. (2020). Coronavirus reminds Asian Americans belonging is conditional. *Los Angeles Times*. Retrieved from: https://www.latimes.com/opinion/story/2020-04-22/asian-american-discrimination-john-cho-coronavirus

Duarte, J., Crawford, J. T., Stern, C., Haidt, J., Jussim, L., & Tetlock, P. E. (2014). Political diversity will improve social psychological science. *Behavioral and Brain Sciences*, *38*, e130.

Fernandes, J. D., Sarabipour, S., Smith, C. T., Niemi, N. M., Jadavji, N. M., Kozik, A. J., Holehouse, A. S., Pejaver, V., Symmons, O., Filho, A. W. B., & Haage, A. (2020). Insights from a survey-based analysis of the academic job market. *bioRxiv*. Retrieved from: https://www.biorxiv.org/content/10.1101/796466v1

Freeman, S. (2018). Foreword. In. N. D. Hartlep, A. K. Kahlon, & D. Ball (Eds.), *Asian/American scholars of education: 21ˢᵗ century pedagogies, perspectives, and experiences* (pp. xv–xxi). New York: Peter Lang.

Hartlep, N. D., Ball, D., Theodosopoulos, K., Wells, K., & Morgan, G. B. (2016). A national analysis of endowed chairs and distinguished professors in the field of education. *Educational Studies*, *52*(2), 119–138.

Lubinski, D. (2004). Introduction to the special section on cognitive abilities: 100 years after Spearman's (1904) "'General intelligence,' objectively determined and measured." *Journal of Personality and Social Psychology*, *86*, 96–111.

Lubinski, D., & Benbow, C. P. (2006). Study of Mathematically Precocious Youth after 35 years: Uncovering antecedents for the development of math-science expertise. *Perspectives on Psychological Science*, *1*, 316–345.

Pluchino, A., Biondo, A. E., & Rapisarda, A. (2018). Talent vs luck: The role of randomness in success and failure. *Advances in Complex Systems*, *21*, 1850014.

Reinero, D. A. (2019). The path to professorship by the numbers and why mentorship matters. *Nature*. Retrieved from: https://socialsciences.nature.com/users/325112-diego-a-reinero/posts/55118-the-path-to-professorship-by-the-numbers-and-why-mentorship-matters

Singer, J. D. (2019). Reshaping the arc of quantitative educational research: It's time to broaden our paradigm. *Journal of Research on Educational Effectiveness, 12*(4), 570–593.

Wai, J., Anderson, S., Perina, K., Worrell, F. C., & Chabris, C. F. (in progress). The most successful and influential "outlier" Americans come from a surprisingly narrow range of elite educational backgrounds.

Wai, J., Lubinski, D., & Benbow, C. P. (2005). Creativity and occupational accomplishments among intellectually precocious youths: An age 13 to age 33 longitudinal study. *Journal of Educational Psychology, 97*, 484–492.

Yang, A. (2020). We Asian Americans are not the virus, but we can be part of the cure. *The Washington Post*. Retrieved from: https://www.washingtonpost.com/opinions/2020/04/01/andrew-yang-coronavirus-discrimination/

Preface

NICHOLAS D. HARTLEP

I was convinced that a second edition of *Asian/American Scholars of Education: 21st Century Pedagogies, Perspectives, and Experiences* was needed as more of my colleagues and acquaintances in the field of education were receiving named professorships.[1] I was genuinely interested to see if racial and gender composition in the field had changed since our previous research (see Hartlep, Ball, Theodosopoulos, Wells, & Morgan, 2016; Hartlep, Kahlon, & Ball, 2018). This second edition of *Asian/American Scholars of Education* updates the data analysis of the national demographics of endowed and distinguished education professors. In addition to an updated national data analysis, it contains four new chapters:

1. Dr. Hua-Hua Chang who is the Charles R. Hicks Chair Professor of Educational Measurement and Research Methodology at Purdue University.
2. Dr. Nicholas Hartlep who is the Robert Charles Billings Chair in Education at Berea College.
3. Dr. Justin Perry who is Dean of the University of Missouri, Kansas City's School of Education and Ewing Marion Kauffman/Missouri Endowed Chair.
4. Dr. Kui Xie who is the Cyphert Distinguished Professor in the Department of Educational Studies at Ohio State University.

5. Dr. Guofang Li who is Canada Research Chair (Tier 1) in Transnational/ Global Perspectives of Language and Literacy Education of Children and Youth in the Department of Language and Literacy Education, Faculty of Education, University of British Columbia, Canada.

The book's foreword is written by Jonathan Wai, an Asian/American and an endowed Assistant Professor. Dr. Wai holds the 21st Century Endowed Chair in the Department of Education Reform at the University of Arkansas. There well could have been another chapter, as Zhihui Fang was recently (2019) named the Irving & Rose Fien Endowed Professor of Education at the University of Florida.

This second edition supports the first insofar as it confirms our central finding that oftentimes the road to securing an endowed or distinguished position happens unexpectedly, but it also shares suggestions for up-and-coming scholars and scholars interested in obtaining such positions. For example, Sheng-Lun Cheng and Vanessa W. Vongkulluksn's chapter shares how adaptability, collaboration, mentorship, and impact are important for scholars who wish to become endowed professors. In the first edition Sydney Freeman (2018) wrote about "the academy's lack of transparency related to the guidelines towards promotion to full professor" (p. XVII). Freeman (2018) pointed out that with the exception of Thompson, Bonner, and Lewis' (2016) edited book *Reaching the Mountaintop of the Academy: Personal Narratives, Advice, and Strategies from Black Distinguished and Endowed Professors*, "[t]here is a dearth of scholarship that addresses what it takes to become an endowed or distinguished professor [of education]" (p. XVIII). Importantly, since authoring that foreword, he has since published the article "The Paucity of Asian-American Distinguished Professors and Endowed Chairs: Toward a More Racially Integrated System of Advancement in the Professoriate" (Freeman & Forthun, 2019).

The purpose of this second edition remains the same as the first:

> It could be said that this book is a festschrift for Asian/American endowed education professors. The professors who are included in this book are luminaries. According to the dictionary, a luminary is "a person who inspires or influences others, especially one prominent in a particular sphere." The Asian/American professors included in this volume are inspiring, and their personal and professional stories in this book are equally enlightening. (Hartlep, Kahlon, & Ball, 2018, p. 2)

NOTE

1 LaGarrett J. King is the Isabelle Wade Lyda and Paul C. Lyda Professor at the University of Missouri; Bettina L. Love is the Georgia Athletic Association Professor in Education at the

University of Georgia; Gilbert Q. Conchas is the Wayne K. and Anita Woolfolk Hoy Endowed Professor in Educational Policy Studies at Pennsylvania State University; Enrique Aleman is the Lillian Radford Endowed Professor of Education at Trinity University.

REFERENCES

Freeman, S. (2018). Foreword. In N. D. Hartlep, A. K. Kahlon, & D. Ball (Eds.), *Asian American scholars of education: 21st century pedagogies, perspectives, and experiences* (pp. XV–XXI). New York: Peter Lang.

Freeman, S., & Forthun, G. (2019, Spring). The Paucity of Asian-American distinguished professors and endowed chairs: Toward a more racially integrated system of advancement in the professoriate. *eJournal of Education Policy*, 1–12. Retrieved from https://files.eric.ed.gov/fulltext/EJ1234496.pdf

Hartlep, N. D., Ball, D., Theodosopoulos, K., Wells, K., & Morgan, G. B. (2016). A national analysis of endowed chairs and distinguished professors in the field of education. *Educational Studies, 52*(2), 119–138.

Hartlep, N. D., Kahlon, A. K., & Ball, D. (Eds.). (2018). *Asian/American scholars of education: 21st century pedagogies, perspectives, and experiences.* New York: Peter Lang.

Thompson, G. L., Bonner, F. A. II, & Lewis, C. W. (2016). *Reaching the mountaintop of the academy: Personal narratives, advice, and strategies from Black distinguished and endowed professors.* Charlotte, NC: Information Age Publishing.

Introduction

NICHOLAS D. HARTLEP, DAISY BALL AND KEVIN E. WELLS

FIRST EDITION INTRODUCTION

Edited books are a saving grace for many writers I know. They provide editors space and opportunity to collate chapters, thoughts, and ideas that they couldn't generate by themselves. These book editors simply have an idea and lack sufficient content, or they have structured the book such that is necessitates the collaboration of multiple scholars. The idea for a book that focused on Asian/American endowed professors of education has been with me for quite some time. In 2014 I wrote, with a graduate assistant, a piece published by *The Journal of Blacks in Higher Education* that shared the names of African/Americans who held endowed and distinguished professorships in education. Because my research has focused on Asian/Americans, and being an urban teacher educator, naturally I was interested in studying the education field as a whole, and race disaggregated. In 2016, two years after my initial foray into African/American endowed professors of education, I co-authored with Daisy Ball, Kendra Theodosopoulos, Kevin E. Wells, and Grant B. Morgan, "A National Analysis of Endowed Chairs and Distinguished Professors in the Field of Education" published in *Educational Studies*. That article was illuminating for me and others based upon emails and LinkedIn messages that I received thanking me for writing it. It also led to *The Chronicle of Higher Education* requesting that I write a commentary on my thoughts about making endowed positions equitable. I wrote a piece I entitled "4 Steps Toward

Making Endowed Positions More Equal" (Hartlep, 2016). These scholarly pieces surely are important, and I think the book that you hold in your hands is special.

What's This Book About?

It could be said that this book is a festschrift for Asian/American endowed education professors. The professors who are included in this book are luminaries. According to the dictionary, a luminary is "a person who has attained eminence in his or her field or is an inspiration to others."[1] The endowed Asian/American professors in this book are inspiring, and the stories in this book are also. I wouldn't have been able to complete this book project without such dedicated, reflective, and ambitious contributors.

As I mentioned above, the idea for this book has been lurking in my mind for quite some time, even before arriving to Metropolitan State University (MSU). Before moving to MSU, I was an assistant professor of social foundations at Illinois State University (ISU), which like the Twin Cities of Minnesota, is located in Bloomington-Normal, another twin city. At ISU I received funding that allowed me to travel to conduct interviews with some endowed Asian/American professors of education. I traveled to Storrs, Connecticut to interview George Sugai. I traveled to Chicago, Illinois and visited with Asha K. Jitendra. In the end, the funding was not enough to interview all the professors I hoped to include in the book. Because I didn't want to let the book die, I changed methodology and decided to transition the book from being sole authored to co-edited. Dr. Ball and Dr. Kahlon were perfect for the job and accepted my invitation. Dr. Ball was a co-author of the original study, and I had previous writing experience with her. We collaborated and published *Asian/Americans, Education, and Crime: The Model Minority as Victim and Perpetrator* (Ball & Hartlep, 2017). Dr. Kahlon was a perfect addition to the editorial team because I had worked with her when she wrote the chapter, "Pleasing the 'Aunties': Navigating Community Expectations within the Model Minority both in the United States and in India," which was published in *Killing the Model Minority Stereotype: Asian American Counterstories and Complicity* (Hartlep & Porfilio, 2015).

SECOND EDITION[2]

Since our original study, "A National Analysis of Endowed Chairs and Distinguished Professors in the Field of Education," things have changed, which is why we have updated the analysis and provided it here for readers. This second edition introduction allows for a nice context for the chapters that appear in this volume.

I am appreciative of Kevin Wells who ran the statistical analysis. Dr. Wells is a prolific scholar in his own right, and a good friend. Thank you, Kevin!

While we attempted to include all Asian/American endowed professors of education in this edited book, we would like to point out those who met these criteria at the time of editing and writing, but who do not appear in the final volume.[3] Below we share an updated context (and analysis) of endowed chairs and how Asian/Americans fit within this context.

A NATIONAL ANALYSIS OF ENDOWED CHAIRS AND DISTINGUISHED PROFESSORS IN THE FIELD OF EDUCATION[4]

According to Kurtz (2014), "Compared to high school grads, workers with bachelor's degrees earn about $1 million more, and workers with associate's degrees earn about $325,000 more over a lifetime" (para 10) than do those without post-secondary degrees. However, college degrees are not created equally. Tsui (2003) writes that the selectivity or prestige of a college/university positively correlates with lifetime earnings. In the end, the more selective the college/university an individual attends, the higher the earnings he or she will make in his or her lifetime. But, does the high cost in tuition required by attending elite colleges/universities pay off? According to Eide, Brewer, and Ehrenberg's (1998) and Brewer, Eide, and Ehrenberg's (1999) research findings, it does. Attending an elite college or university translates to meaningful lifetime earnings and a plethora of other positive outcomes.

It is at this juncture that our analysis breaks new ground, by studying the demographics and backgrounds of those faculty holding endowed chairs and distinguished professor titles in the field of education (Urbancic, 2008). Specifically, we are interested in determining if there are discernible patterns within the composition of elite positions in the professoriate, denoted as endowed chairs/professorships and distinguished professorships. Because no existing studies specifically look at the demographics and composition of endowed and distinguished faculty members in the field of education, this research relies on social network theory (Borgatti, Mehra, Brass, & Labianca, 2009; Wasserman & Faust, 1994) to guide its collection and analysis of originally collected data. Social network theory argues that the composition of one's social circle has real and measurable impacts on one's life. Social network theory is interested in the extent and nature of interactions between group members, and how these interactions impact everything from socioeconomic status, to employment, to the racial makeup of friendship groups. In this introduction we focus our analysis on three networks: (a) race, (b) gender, and (c) graduate school prestige. After reviewing the existing literature on endowed chairs in education and non-education fields, we hypothesized that our national sample of endowed and distinguished faculty would be disproportionately White, male, and doctoral graduates of elite[5] colleges/universities.

We first offer a brief review of the literature, beginning with definitions of endowed and distinguished positions. Second, we outline our research questions and hypotheses—which were influenced by social network theory—as well as our data sampling strategy. Next, we share our analyses and study findings. We then discuss the implications for policy and practice that this research holds. Finally, we conclude by identifying the study's limitations and forecasting possibilities for future research.

REVIEW OF THE LITERATURE

Endowed chairs (ECs) and distinguished professorships (DPs) are typically awarded to full professors who have accomplished much in their respective field. Kamath, Meier, and Rao (2006) state the following:

> For nearly 150 years, outstanding professors at U.S. universities have been rewarded by receiving the designation of [endowed professor or] distinguished chair. . . . The primary purpose for establishing these named positions is to provide recognition to faculty members for their accomplishments by giving them additional compensation, funds for travel, and in some disciplines, equipment and labs, and assistance with their research and teaching. Recently, there has been tremendous growth in the number of named chairs in all academic areas, but especially in business disciplines where schools seek to attract and retain qualified faculty members, but university budgets may not provide sufficient resources to do so. (p. 17)

Because we could not locate existing studies specifically analyzing the demographics and composition of endowed and distinguished faculty members in the field of education, this research relied on social network theory (Wasserman & Faust, 1994) to guide our analysis. One possible explanation for this gap in the literature may be that the number of said academic positions in education is low compared to other programs and fields of study, such as the hard sciences, economics, mathematics, and engineering (STEM). This is a question worthy of future pursuit but outside the scope of this study, because no extant datasets contain exclusively EC and DP data in education. By comparison, such data do exist in other fields outside of education. For example, faculty directories exist for finance, marketing, economics, and management that list EC and DP faculty.[6]

Performing a review of the literature on ECs and DPs proved insightful. The majority of the previous research on endowed and distinguished professorships has been conducted in fields outside of education. For instance, research has been carried out in the fields of accounting (Meier & Kamath, 2005; Rezaee, Elmore,

& Spiceland, 2004, 2006; Tang, Forrest, & Leach, 1990), economics (Kamath, Meier, & Tousey, 2005), finance (Metwalli & Tang, 2001), gerontology and geriatrics (Bell, 1986), management (Metwalli & Tang, 2002), nursing (Fitzpatrick, 1985, 2000; Fitzpatrick, Fitzpatrick, & Dressler, 2005), real estate (Weeks, Finch, & Hardin, 2007), and law (Delgado & Bell, 1989).

In terms of race and gender, Stone collected data on African Americans holding endowed university chairs in 1993, 1997, and 2001 (Stone, 1993, 1997, 2001). Although Stone's publications contain lists of African American faculty holding endowed positions, none of these lists are field-of-study specific. By comparison, Hartlep and Theodosopoulos (2014) sampled endowed and distinguished faculty of education, finding nationally 42 African American endowed faculty, 20 of whom are women and 22 men, and nine African American distinguished faculty: eight men, one woman. Although Hartlep and Theodosopoulos' (2014) study is helpful in that it is field- (education), gender-, and race-specific (African Americans), it is nevertheless limited in that it does not make interracial comparisons.

Because Thompson, Bonner, and Lewis' (2016) *Reaching the Mountaintop of the Academy: Personal Narratives, Advice, and Strategies from Black Distinguished and Endowed Professors* highlights a sampling of distinguished and endowed professors who are African American, it doesn't allow researchers to test if there is a shortage or abundance of African American distinguished and endowed professors in the field of education relative to other races. Unasked is the question, "Are African Americans more or less likely to hold endowed/distinguished positions when compared to Whites in the field of education?" Hartlep and Theodosopoulos' (2014) and Thompson et al.'s (2016) research is unable to answer this question, a gap this research sought to fill.

Giroux (2009) has critiqued higher education for adopting corporate practices, for example allowing companies such as BMW to endow professorships. Giroux (2009, 2014) is concerned—as are others (see Food &Water Watch, 2012; Washburn, 2000)—that the funding of endowed positions by private corporations and companies may lead to diminished academic freedom and that the growing ties between universities and business may lead to an education that is less critical. This study sheds light on this important debate within the field of higher education, specifically in Colleges and Schools of Education, because it quantifies the funders of these specific ECs and DPs. For example, this study asks, "Are endowed or distinguished chairs in education more likely to be family-named, corporate-named, or university-sponsored?"

In terms of the prestige of one's alma mater, Kamath et al. (2005) examined distinguished professorships in the academic field of economics in the United States from the 1995/96 and 2001/02 academic years using data from the *Prentice Hall Guide to Economics Faculty*. They found that the typical distinguished professor in economics is most likely to be a man, a full professor, and employed by a private institution. They also found that graduates of U.S. public universities are less likely than graduates of private universities to occupy named professorships of economics at private universities with a Carnegie classification of R1.

PURPOSE OF THE RESEARCH

We were interested in examining, at a national level, professors of education holding an endowed or a distinguished chair/professorship. These prestigious positions (ECs and DPs) often constitute the highest honor colleges or universities can bestow upon a faculty member (Thompson et al., 2016).[7] As a result, EC and DP positions are generally reserved for scholars whose work substantially advances a discipline or field of study. When looking at the literature on ECs and DPs in the field of education, it is undeniable that this practice has been under-researched by scholars. Specifically, we were concerned that although EC and DP positions may be put into place to advance a given discipline, true advancement may not take place if such positions are not occupied by a diverse group of scholars. Today, the importance of diversity in higher education is widely recognized: We argue that this diversity must extend all the way to the top—to EC and DP positions—if higher education is to become truly diversified.

This study is a national-level study examining the status of EC and DP positions within colleges and schools of education using current and originally collected data to respond to nine research questions.[8] We now turn to articulating the nine research questions we sought to answer, and to explain the analytic approach we took in this Internet-based research (Jones, 1999).

RESEARCH QUESTIONS AND HYPOTHESES

We posed the following nine research questions (RQs), and made the following nine hypotheses (Hs):

RQ1: Are men or women more likely to hold endowed or distinguished chairs/professorships in education?

H1: Men will be more likely than women to hold endowed or distinguished chairs/professorships in education.

RQ2: Are certain races more likely to hold endowed or distinguished chairs/professorships in education?

H2: Whites will be more likely than other races to hold endowed or distinguished chairs/professorships in education.

RQ3: What is the mean time since receiving one's Ph.D. for attaining endowed or distinguished chairs/professorships in education?

H3: The mean time since receiving one's Ph.D. for attaining endowed or distinguished chairs/professorships will be 20 years.[9]

RQ4: Are professors who earned their doctorate from an elite college/university more likely to hold endowed or distinguished chairs/professorships in education than professors who earned their doctorate from a competitive or general college/university?[10]

H4: Elite college/university alumni will have a distinct advantage when it comes to the likelihood, they hold an endowed or distinguished chair/professorship in education.

RQ5: Are endowed or distinguished chairs/professorships in education evenly distributed across regions of the United States?

H5: No, the East coast will have a disproportionately higher number of endowed and distinguished positions.

RQ6: Which states have the most endowed chairs/professorships in education?

H6: Massachusetts, New York, and California will have the most endowed chairs/professorships.[11]

RQ7: Are endowed or distinguished chairs/professorships in education held more often by holders of Ph.D.s or Ed.D.s?

H7: Endowed chairs/professorships will be held more often by holders of Ph.D.s.

RQ8: Do patterns exist when examining recipients of endowed or distinguished chairs/professorships in education by decade?

H8: Yes, the 1980s, the 1990s, and the 2000s will be high points in the number of faculty receiving endowed or distinguished chairs/professorships.

RQ9: Are endowed or distinguished chairs in education more likely to be family-named, corporate-named, or university-sponsored?

H9: Endowed or distinguished chairs will be most likely family-named.

THEORETICAL FRAMEWORK

In this second analysis, we again used social network theory to guide our approach. Pescosolido (2006) distinguishes between three characteristics of social networks: their (a) structure, (b) content, and (c) function. Structure refers to the skeleton of social networks; for example, the size, density, and makeup of the network. Content refers to resources that flow within and across the social networks.

Function refers to the function the social network serves, including functions at the pragmatic level, emotional level, and so forth.

We contend that social network theory is a logical and useful theoretical framework for this research because social relationships can be an essential component of doctoral education and academe. As a result, social networks serve functions and result in material consequences for professors, students, and the colleges and universities that employ or serve them. Consequently, social network theory provides a context for higher education that we can use to (re)interpret this study's statistical findings.

Social network theory is associated with Simmel's (1955) *Conflict and the Web of Group Affiliations* and Durkheim's (1951) *Suicide*. Simmel's work is based on the following premise: "Society arises from the individual and the individual arises out of association" (p. 163). One's association to others is an essential element of one's being. According to Simmel (1955), the type of social ties one has is of utmost importance. Simmel distinguishes between "pre-modern" (p. 128) social ties (simple, close knit, intolerant of outsiders) and "modern" (p. 151) social ties (complex, interrelated, open to diversity) (Blau, 1993; Giddens, 1990; Pescosolido, 2006).

Meanwhile, Durkheim's (1951) classic work focuses on suicide rates across Europe, with an emphasis on the level of integration and regulation experienced by people given the structure of the society in which they live. Durkheim (1951) focuses on the types of social structures that arise out of differing levels of two types of social interaction: (a) integration (as opposed to isolation) and (b) regulation (as opposed to lack of regulation). Durkheim argues that rates of suicide will be highest among people who experience low levels of integration and regulation in society; suicide is more likely to occur in groups of people whose social ties are weaker and whose lives are less regulated by society at large.

A key facet of social network theory is the concept of homophily. The homophily principle states that "contact between similar people occurs at a higher rate than among dissimilar people" (McPherson et al., 2001, p. 416). This principle has been referred to by the adage "birds of a feather flock together" (McPherson et al., 2001). Although homophily may seem intuitive, its implications for the demographics and makeup of education's ECs and DPs are serious and complex. McPherson et al. (2001) note that one of the most salient effects of homophily is that "people's personal networks are homogeneous with regard to many sociodemographic, behavioral, and intrapersonal characteristics" (p. 415). This means educators' social worlds are limited. We have limited access to information and experiences, which in turn affects our attitudes, outlooks, and professional outcomes. Noteworthy for the purposes of the current study is how the functions of homophily—in terms of race/ethnicity, gender, and class—are responsible for creating the most sizeable gaps in our social networks (McPherson et al., 2001). For the purposes of this study, we consider *status homophily* with regard to race and ethnicity; sex and gender; and education, occupation, and social class.

Status Homophily

Status homophily encompasses ascribed characteristics (race/ethnicity, sex/gender, age) and acquired characteristics (education/occupation/social class, network positions, behaviors). As McPherson et al. (2001) theorize, the dimension of status homophily is inclusive of the characteristics most often associated with social stratification. Following McPherson et al., we expect status homophily in the world of higher education not simply to be present, but to effect significant consequences. We highlight some of these consequences in the implications for practice and policy section below.

Race and Ethnicity Homophily

According to McPherson et al. (2001), of all the characteristics of status homophily, race and ethnicity play the most significant roles when it comes to the divisions of social networks. Intersectionality can be understood as the intersection of statuses (such as the intersection of race and socioeconomic status); where statuses intersect, one's experiences may be further compounded by this intersection (see Crenshaw, 1989). The intersectionality (Cole, 2009; Crenshaw, 1989) of these characteristics can compound one's racial/ethnic status and cause further division:

> Race and ethnicity are clearly the biggest divide in social networks today in the United States, and they play a major part in structuring the networks in other ethnically diverse societies as well. In this domain, the baseline homophily created by groups of different sizes is combined with the differences in racial/ethnic groups' positions on other dimensions (e.g., education, occupation, income, religion) and the personal prejudices that often result from the latter to create a highly visible, oft studied network divide. (McPherson et al., 2001, p. 420)

Thus, given the apparent strength of status homophily, compounded by race homophily and the additional influence of intersectionality, we expect to find racial homophily present in the EC and DP population we sampled.

Sex and Gender Homophily

Although categories of race/ethnicity are numerous and diverse, the concept of gender tends to be understood traditionally in dichotomous terms: male and female. Although in society there are roughly the same number of men and women, research on gender and social networks indicates that segregation along gender lines is salient in specific environments. For example, McPherson et al. (2001) find that work environments tend to be highly segregated along gender lines (also see Bielby & Baron, 1986; Kalleberg et al., 1996).

Gender differentials in the workplace translate to imbalanced power relations, with the dominant gender—male—being the most powerful within work environments (McPherson et al., 2001). Considering past research findings in sex and gender social network literature, we expect gender homophily to be present in the EC and DP population we sampled.

Education, Occupation, and Social Class

McPherson et al. (2001) posit that "unlike age, race, and gender, education, occupation and social class are largely achieved, rather than ascribed, characteristics" (p. 426). Social class typically locates people in specific neighborhoods and schools, churches, and social organizations; education organizes people by age and achievement; occupation groups people along areas of specialization. Therefore, a great deal of homophily is aligned with these three achieved characteristics, along relatively firm if not ascribed lines (McPherson et al., 2001). Specifically, in terms of education, McPherson et al. (2001) argue the following:

> All educational groups show inbreeding tendencies, as well as a social distance effect: People are both more likely to confide in others who share their same educational level, and become less and less likely to form such a tie as their difference from others' achievement increases. . . . The edge categories of extremely high and low education show the biggest inbreeding tendency . . . with a socially significant divide between the college-educated and those without college experience and another major distinction between the white collar and blue collar occupations. (p. 427)

Evidence of homophily is regularly found in the multi-classed realm of education, and we anticipate education and occupational homophily to also be present in the EC and DP population we sampled.

Based on social network theory, we expect to find homophily among ECs and DPs of education in terms of race, gender, and graduate school prestige. We hypothesize that our research will confirm—at least partially—that birds of a feather really do flock together and that most ECs and DPs will be—to use another colloquial phrase—pale, male, and stale (White, male, and comparatively advanced in age). We anticipate that ECs and DPs in schools of education resemble those who preceded them (by the decade), and are followed by those who resemble them, along each of these characteristics. We discuss implications of homophily among ECs and DPs in our *implications for practice and policy* section.

METHODOLOGY

Data

The research team consists of three professors: An Education Studies scholar, a sociologist, and a statistician. The research team collected data by examining the faculty web pages of colleges and schools of education in the United States. The first author, with the assistance of an undergraduate research assistant, began by examining the top-100-ranked education graduate schools.[12] *U.S. News and World Report* was used, rather than the *Forbes* list, because the latter disregards public reputation, which causes some colleges to score lower than in other ranking formulas. Reputation is an important factor to consider in this research, given our reliance on social network theory. We collected the following data points: (a) name of the EC/DP, (b) gender and race of the EC/DP, (c) highest degree the EC/DP earned, (d) institution where the EC/DP earned it and when it was earned, (e) when the EC/DP received the EC/DP position, and (f) the current e-mail address of the EC/DP.

In addition to searching college/university websites, we also searched Amazon.com and Google Books. We used the search terms endowed chair, endowed professor, and distinguished professor on the presumption that ECs and DPs have strong publication records and have likely published books; we hoped to, therefore, be able to find their institutions, and/or the name of their endowed or distinguished position via this search in case they had not turned up via other means. Although we admit this searching strategy is rather haphazard, the team's purpose was to uncover ECs and DPs who do not teach at top-ranked colleges/universities and who may have been overlooked in the previous analysis. In addition to searching on the Internet for ECs and DPs, we also employed a snowball sampling technique (Brown, 2005), which proved quite helpful. Because we collected the e-mail addresses of ECs and DPs, we sent personalized e-mails three times to (a) confirm already-collected data and (b) inquire whether they knew ECs or DPs who met the study criteria, but who were not on our list. The initial data collection and verification process took researchers two years to complete (Fall 2013 through Fall 2015). The data and analyses were revised and updated in the fall of 2017 and the fall of 2019.

Study Participants

Inclusion criterion was as follows: an individual professor currently holding either a distinguished, named, or endowed faculty position (EC or DP) in the field of education. The analytic sample of our analysis was $n = 605$ professors. Missing data accounted for approximately 2.8% of the total data from this dataset. Because the statistics in this study were primarily descriptive or simple group comparisons, missing data was only eliminated from the specific comparisons or descriptions involving those missing items. In the following sections, statistical analysis is offered against each research question (RQ). To assess significance, goodness-of-fit chi-square tests were run assuming a proportional population to most adequately address the research questions. After responding to each of the nine RQs, we present implications, as well as limitations and future research possibilities.

FINDINGS

RQ1. Are Men or Women More Likely to Hold Endowed or Distinguished Chairs/Professorships in Education?

In their study of marketing named chairs, Kamath et al. (2006) found that most were held by men. Likewise, Hartlep, Ball, Theodosopoulos, Wells, and Morgan (2016) found that in education, men held significantly more endowed and distinguished positions than women. With our current data, however, we found that there was no statistically significant difference ($\chi2$ (1) = 2.45 p = .118, Cramer's V = .07) between the number of endowed positions held by men (n = 253, 53.6%) and those held by women (n = 219, 46.4%). Unlike the endowed professorships, we did find a significant difference ($\chi2$ (1) = 3.98 p = .046, Cramer's V = .17) between the number of distinguished professor positions held by men (n = 78, 58.6%) and those held by women (n = 55, 41.4%). Thus, our hypothesis, which supports the prediction of social network theory, was rejected in the case of endowed professors, but we failed to reject in the case of distinguished professors.

RQ2. Are Certain Races More Likely to Hold Endowed or Distinguished Chairs/Professorships in Education?

Previously, in the first edition, we had taken this question at face value. We looked only whether or not certain races were more likely to hold an endowed or distinguished professorship. Our results found race to be a significant predictor, $\chi2$ (4, n = 463) = 1075.9, p < .001, Cramer's V = .76, of whether an education professor held an endowed chair/professorship in this sample. White people (n = 373, 80.6%) held proportionately more endowed positions, compared to African Americans (n = 53, 11.4%), Asian Americans (n = 16, 3.5%), Latinx Americans (n = 17, 3.7%), and all other reported races (n = 5, 0.9%). We also found race to be a significant predictor, $\chi2$ (4, n = 133) = 362.68, p < .001, Cramer's V = .83, of distinguished positions in this sample. Proportionately, White people (n = 114, 85.7%) held the most distinguished positions, followed by African Americans

(n = 13, 9.8%), Asian Americans (n = 4, 3.0%), Latinx Americans (n = 2, 1.5%), with no one fitting into the "all other reported races" category (n = 0, 0.0%).

But in this second edition, a more nuanced approach would be to base this question on whether or not endowed and distinguished faculty were a proportional representation of the population of the United States as a whole. Based on data from the U.S. Census (U.S. Census, 2020), we compared endowed and distinguished racial proportions to those of the United States. In this case, we still found race to be a significant predictor of whether an education professor held an endowed chair/professorship, $\chi2$ (4, n = 463) = 96.658, p < .001, however the effect size was much smaller with Cramer's V = .23. In the U.S. population, White people make up 60.1% of the population, Latinx Americans 18.5%, African Americans 13.4%, Asian Americans 5.9%, and all other races 2.1% (compared to 80.6%, 3.7%, 11.4%, 3.5%, and 0.9% respectively among endowed professors). Like endowed professors, we also found race to be a significant predictor of whether an education professor held a distinguished position, $\chi2$ (4, n = 133) = 41.27, p < .001. As with endowed positions, the effect size for distinguished positions was much smaller with Cramer's V = .28.

Another way to quantify the racial diversity of endowed and distinguished professors is through the use of Simpson's diversity index (Simpson, 1949). Essentially, the diversity index is the probability of two randomly selected people belonging to the same racial category. When the number is higher, the sample is more diverse. For example, in our study we examine White, African American, Asian American, Latinx American, and all other races. If we assumed these racial groups were equal in proportion, the diversity index score of DI = 0.80. When using U.S. population proportions, the diversity index score of DI = 0.58. Within endowed faculty, it is 0.34 and among distinguished faculty it is even lower at DI = 0.25. Based on the evidence presented, our hypothesis was confirmed, further validating the tenets of social network theory.

RQ3. What is the Mean Time Since Receiving One's Ph.D. for Attaining Endowed or Distinguished Chairs/Professorships in Education?

In the case of the mean time between receiving one's Ph.D. to attaining endowed chairs/professorships, the highest mean time was for White people at 21.2 years, followed by Latinx Americans at 20.8 years, African Americans at 19.3 years, Asian Americans at 15.2 years, and all other reported races at 14.3 years. The mean time for women was 19.3 years and the mean time for men was 21.9 years. Scheffe's (1959) method of multiple pairwise comparisons indicates neither race nor gender alone were statistically significant. The only comparison that showed significant differences was between White men (M = 22.7, SD = 9.5) and White women (M = 19.3, SD = 8.3), t(334) = 3.51, p < .001, g = .39.

Table 1.1 Mean Time Between Ph.D. and Endowed or Distinguished Chairs/Professorships

Race	Gender	Endowed Positions			Distinguished Positions		
		n	Mean	SD	n	mean	SD
White	Female	150	19.25	8.34	43	25.84	9.19
	Male	186	22.73	9.45	60	28.17	9.00
	Total	336	21.17	9.17	103	27.19	9.11
African	Female	20	19.80	7.49	2	20.50	6.36
American	Male	24	18.79	10.22	10	14.50	8.29
	Total	44	19.25	9.00	12	15.50	8.08
Asian American	Female	4	15.50	7.42	1	3.00	-
	Male	11	15.09	8.46	3	20.67	10.41
	Total	15	15.20	7.93	4	16.25	12.26
Latinx	Female	9	21.33	8.83	-	-	-
Americans	Male	8	20.25	5.44	-	-	-
	Total	17	20.82	7.23	-	-	-
All other	Female	1	7.00	-	-	-	-
Reported Races	Male	2	18.00	12.73	-	-	-
	Total	3	14.33	11.02	-	-	-
Combined	Female	186	19.28	8.24	46	25.11	9.59
Races	Male	235	21.86	9.61	73	25.99	10.07
	Total	421	20.72	9.11	119	25.65	9.86

Note: SD = standard deviations

The highest mean time for distinguished positions was for White people at 27.2 years, followed by Asian Americans at 16.3 years, and African Americans at 15.5. The mean time for women was 25.1 years, whereas for men it was 26.0 years. For distinguished positions, Scheffe's method indicated there was one statistically significant difference between groups. Unlike endowed positions, there were several significant differences in mean time between receiving their terminal degree and appointment to a distinguished position. There were significant differences between White people (M = 27.2, SD = 9.11) and African Americans (M = 15.5, SD = 8.08), $t(113)$ = 4.25, $p < .001$, g = 1.30, as well as White people (M = 27.2, SD = 9.11) and Asian Americans (M = 16.3, SD = 12.26), $t(105)$ = 2.33, $p < .001$, g = 1.19. There were also significant differences between White men (M = 28.2, SD = 9.00) and African American men (M = 14.5, SD = 8.29), $t(68)$ = 4.49, $p < .001$, g = 1.54 as well as between White women (M = 25.8, SD = 9.19) and African American men (M = 14.5, SD = 8.29), $t(51)$ = 3.57, $p < .001$, g = 1.27. Mean times broken down by gender, race, and position type are shown in Table 1.1. Our original hypothesis was that the mean time between earning one's terminal degree and endowed or distinguished chairs/professorships would be 20 years. Overall, this was roughly the case (M = 20.7) for endowed positions, whereas for distinguished the mean was 25.7 years.

RQ4. Are Professors Who Earned Their Doctorate from an Elite College/University More Likely to Hold Endowed or Distinguished Chairs/Professorships in Education Than Professors Who Earned Their Doctorate from a Nonelite College/University?

Elite versus non-elite was determined by creating an index for institutional prestige. Although rankings of elite universities exist for the hard sciences, such as the Academic Ranking of World Universities (http://arwu.org), commonly referred to as the Shanghai Ranking, no such ranking exists for the field of education. Therefore, we examined two different metrics. First, we created our own index for institutional prestige by classifying the status of a doctoral degree into four categories: (a) elite, (b) competitive, (c) general, and (d) other. In our index, elite refers to colleges ranked 1–25 in the 2018 Best Education Schools in *U.S. News and World Report*.[13] Meanwhile, competitive refers to a rank of 26–50, general refers to a ranking of 51 and above or to unranked institutions, and other refers to institutions outside of the United States.[14] Second, we dichotomized data according to whether the degree granting institution was a member of the American Association of Universities (AAU). The AAU is an organization of 63 leading research universities in the United States and Canada.

Using our own index for institutional prestige, we found prestige to be a significant predictor of endowed chairs/professorships in this study, $\chi2$ (3) 78.8, $p < .001$, $n = 472$, Cramer's V = .24. Faculty members who had earned their doctoral degree at an elite institution of higher education held the highest proportion of endowed chairs/professorships ($n = 198$, 41.9%), followed by general ($n = 112$, 23.7%), other ($n = 89$, 18.9%), and competitive ($n = 73$, 15.5%). Prestige was also found to be a significant predictor of distinguished chairs in this study, $\chi2(3) = 25.0$, $p < .001$, $n = 133$, Cramer's V = .25. Unlike endowed faculty, distinguished faculty from general institutions held the highest proportion of positions ($n = 52$, 39.1%), followed by competitive ($n = 38$, 28.6%), elite ($n = 31$, 23.3%), and other ($n = 12$, 9.0%). When examining the AAU metric, faculty receiving their terminal degrees from AAU universities comprised 67.4% ($n = 308$) of endowed and 70.3% ($n = 90$) of distinguished positions. The evidence shows that for endowed professors/chairs, those who hold degrees from elite colleges/universities or AAU universities were significantly more likely to hold endowed positions. For distinguished positions, the evidence is mixed. While the highest

Figure 1.1. U.S. Census Regional Designations

percentage graduated from AAU universities, the largest percentage of positions were at institutions that were classified as general.

RQ5. Are Endowed or Distinguished Chairs/Professorships in Education Evenly Distributed Across Regions of the United States?

Figure 1.1 below shares the nine regions of the United States according to the U.S. Census. Table 1.2 illustrates how endowed chairs were distributed across U.S. regions. The top regions were West South Central (n = 94) and Pacific (n = 67), and for distinguished positions, the top regions were South Atlantic (n = 33) and East North Central (n = 27). For distinguished positions, there were none in the West South Central region and only two in New England. Contrary to our hypothesis, endowed positions were fairly evenly distributed across the nation with the east coast holding no advantage over other parts of the nation. Distinguished positions, however, were more concentrated on the eastern seaboard.

RQ6. Which States Have the Most Endowed or Distinguished Chairs/Professorships in Education?

Of the 37 states (including Washington, DC) with endowed chairs/professorships, we found that California (n = 54) was the state with the most, followed by Louisiana (n = 48) and Massachusetts (n = 33). The top three most diverse states based on Simpson's diversity index (Simpson, 1949) were Wisconsin (DI = .61), Oregon (DI = .56), and Texas (DI = .55). Also notable was that 10 states had diversity index scores of DI = 0 where all endowed faculty were White (AL, AR, DC, DE, MD, NH, NJ, SC, VA, and WY). Of the 28 states with distinguished chairs, North Carolina (n = 17) had the most, followed by Alabama (n = 11), California (n = 10), New York (n = 10), and Pennsylvania (n = 10). The top three most diverse states based on Simpson's diversity index scores were South Carolina (DI = .50), Wisconsin (DI = .48), and Missouri (DI = .44). There were a total of 19 states with diversity index scores of DI = 0, in 17 of those, the distinguished faculty were 100% White (AZ, CO, FL, GA, IA, KS, MA, MD, MI, MN, NE, NJ, NY, TN, UT, VA, and WA), in New Mexico, the single distinguished faculty member was Latinx American, and in Kentucky, the single distinguished faculty member was African American.

Our initial hypothesis was that MA, NY, and CA would have a higher number of endowed or distinguished positions due to the higher concentration of elite universities. This could have been the case for endowed faculty had it not been for the large number of endowed positions in Louisiana. This may be a byproduct of how public universities are funded there. The highest numbers of distinguished positions were found in NC, AL, CA, NY, and PA, also rejecting our initial hypothesis.

Table 1.2 Endowed or Distinguished Position by Nine Regions of the United States

Region of U.S.	Endowed Positions	Distinguished Positions
East North Central	59 (12.5)	27 (20.3)
East South Central	22 (4.7)	14 (10.5)
Mountain	27 (5.7)	9 (6.8)
New England	43 (9.1)	2 (1.5)
North Atlantic	50 (10.6)	23 (17.3)
Pacific	67 (14.2)	12 (9.0)
South Atlantic	51 (10.8)	33 (24.8)
West North Central	59 (12.5)	13 (9.8)
West South Central	94 (19.9)	-
Total:	472 (100)	133 (100)

Note: Numbers in parentheses are percentages

Table 1.3 *Endowed Position by Decade*

Groups	1960s	1970s	1980s	1990s	2000s	2010s	Total
White	1	1	4	40	153	147	346
African American	0	0	0	3	14	33	50
Asian American	0	0	0	0	3	12	15
Latinx American	0	0	0	1	6	10	17
All Other Races	0	0	0	0	1	2	3
Female	0	0	0	17	76	103	196
Male	1	1	4	27	103	105	241

RQ7. Are Endowed or Distinguished Chairs/Professorships in Education Held More Often by Holders of Ph.D.s or Ed.D.s?

We find that endowed faculty of education were more likely to hold a Ph.D. (or D.Phil) (n = 395, 83.6%), compared to an Ed.D. (n = 61, 12.9%). Distinguished faculty of education were also more likely to hold a Ph.D. (n = 112, 84.2%) compared to an Ed.D. (n = 17, 12.8%). This finding supports our hypothesis, which was logical, given that a Ph.D. is a research-based degree, and endowed/distinguished faculty typically receive their positions due to high volumes of published, peer-reviewed research.

RQ8. Do Patterns Exist When Examining Recipients of Endowed or Distinguished Chairs/Professorships in Education by Decade?

Clear patterns emerged from our data (see Table 1.3). However, it is important to note that our sample included only current positions held by endowed and distinguished professors; it did not include retired professors or those no longer holding an EC or DP for other reasons. White men held the earliest endowed positions in our study (1960s, 1970s, and 1980s). This was followed by an influx of White women in the 1990s as well increasing representation from African Americans, Asian Americans, Latinx Americans, and all other reported races and ethnicities. This has continued with each decade showing an increasing number of people of color in endowed positions. The largest proportion (n = 204) of endowed faculty received their endowed position in the 2010s, followed by the 2000s (n = 177), and the 1990s (n = 44).

A similar pattern emerged with those holding distinguished chairs as for those holding endowed positions (see Table 1.4). The earliest distinguished positions were held by White people from the 1970s and 1980s, followed by African Americans in the 1990s, and Asian Americans in the 2000s. The largest

Table 1.4 *Distinguished Position by Decade*

Groups	1970s	1980s	1990s	2000s	2010s	Total
White	2	2	10	53	40	107
African American	0	0	1	5	6	12
Asian American	0	0	0	1	3	4
Latinx American	0	0	0	0	0	0
All Other Races	0	0	0	0	0	0
Female	1	0	2	29	17	49
Male	1	2	9	30	32	74

proportion *(n* = 59) of distinguished faculty received their positions in the 2000s, followed by the 2010s (*n* = 49) and the 1990s (*n* = 11). Our initial hypothesis was that the 1980s, 1990s, and 2000s would be the decades with the highest number of endowed or distinguished positions. This was not the case. The decade with the highest number of endowed positions was the 2010s, followed by the 2000s, and the 1990s with only six positions remaining from the 1980s. For distinguished positions, it was the 2000s followed by the 2010s and the 1990s.

RQ9. Are Endowed or Distinguished Chairs in Education More Likely to be Family-Named, Corporate-Named, or University-Sponsored?

The path to answering this question was challenging. Endowed positions are funded in a variety of ways. We found no less than seven major sources of funding as well as a general category for things that could not be identified.[15] We found that family-named chairs comprised the highest proportion (62.4%) with state legislature sponsored chairs and group sponsored chairs tied with the smallest proportion (0.8%). In the case of distinguished positions, family-named chairs made up 49.5%, university sponsored chairs making up 43.0% of positions. All other positions combined accounted for 7.5% of distinguished positions (see Table 1.5). Overall, family-named endowed or distinguished position made up the majority of funding sources, which confirmed our hypothesis.

STUDY LIMITATIONS

This updated analysis was not without its limitations. First, as in the first edition of this book, our data was gathered via the worldwide web. Inherently, the Internet and college/university websites may not be current or completely accurate. We found that the list of ECs and DPs changes regularly, and, with retirements

Table 1.5 Source of Funding for Endowed or Distinguished Positions

Type of Position	Endowed Positions n (%)	Distinguished Positions n (%)
Family	249 (62.4)	53 (49.5)
University	38 (9.5)	46 (43.0)
Individual	37 (9.3)	1 (0.9)
Corporate	24 (6.0)	2 (1.9)
Foundation	24 (6.0)	4 (3.7)
Group	3 (0.8)	–
Legislature	3 (0.8)	–
Other	21 (5.3)	1 (0.9)
Total:	399 (100)	106 (100)

Note: Numbers in parentheses are percentages

and unforeseen deaths, data changes frequently. Although we did our best to safeguard against inaccurate data by contacting faculty members directly (three times), we cannot claim 100% currency for our data. We welcome updates to our EC/DP database.[16]

Second, we may have overlooked eligible faculty of education. Again, we took precautionary steps by asking faculty members to review our list and inform us of overlooked eligible faculty members. During our third verification process, we learned of three EC/DP positions that were not in the dataset. Notwithstanding, there remains a possibility that we have failed to include some eligible candidates.

An additional limitation was the possibility for error when coding the racial data. For instance, when we found an EC or DP on a website, we judged the race of the professor. If we were unable to visually or socially construct her or his race, we contacted the professor to ascertain how she or he self-identifies. For instance, originally, we identified Dr. Linda Darling-Hammond as White. After member checking (Cho & Trent, 2006), we recorded her race as African American. Thus, there exists the possibility that the racial data was inaccurate. Future researchers might consider surveying participants; however, a drawback of such a design would be a reduced sample size and increased estimation bias due to survey nonresponse (see Groves & Couper, 2012; Groves & Heeringa, 2006).

IMPLICATIONS FOR POLICY, PRACTICE, AND FUTURE RESEARCH

This study has considered the characteristics of ECs and DPs of education and has framed our understanding of such characteristics as part of a larger web of factors—that of a network—postulating that networks have real and tangible outcomes for the individuals who comprise and inhabit them. Although much social scientific research has explained individual outcomes by pointing to individual characteristics (i.e., individual race linked to individual outcome), social network theory allows us to understand a range of individual characteristics within one's social network (Borgatti et al., 2009). As noted earlier, this perspective allows for the acknowledgment of intersectionality—that characteristics in combination with one another both create and limit opportunities for those who hold them, depending on the characteristics and the environment in which they are held. Diversity in higher education is critically important. We cannot wait for ECs and DPs who are White to retire their prestigious positions because, as our data show, these very same individuals will have mentored and trained up the next generation of ECs and DPs in their own image: White, male, and from elite colleges/universities. Instead, a more pragmatic practice would be early intervention (see Hartlep, 2016). Our findings align with the basic tenet of social network theory: The social connections contained in one's social network have real and measurable outcomes for individuals. According to our data, this holds true in terms of race, gender, education, and socioeconomic status. And, according to our data, social networks help to reproduce the existing social structure.

Another implication of our findings can be understood from the perspective of the institution, lest we forget that institutions themselves can be said to have perspectives when it comes to ratings, reputation, endowments, and so forth. Fairness and equity regarding academic reward systems should matter to institutions—at levels both personal and productive: that is, morale, productivity, and overall work environment stand to be impacted by perceptions of equity involving academic reward systems (O'Meara, 2011). Academic reward systems send powerful messages to those outside the institution concerning what the institution stands for (O'Meara, 2011).

Suggestions for policy and practice include mentoring racially and institutionally diverse students earlier than graduate school. For instance, current ECs and DPs could very well mentor undergraduates, encouraging them to continue their studies in graduate school. This practice of early intervention may allow students who attend less prestigious colleges/universities to work with and be socialized by ECs and DPs who may work at a prestigious institution of higher learning and/or have an elite pedigree.[17] By socializing with ECs and DPs who may be alums of elite colleges and universities, students of diverse educational backgrounds can begin to acquire the mindsets, skills, attitudes, and abilities that will enable them to become eminent scholars in the field of education. EC and DP positions could (and should) be used as tools for diversifying institutions of higher education, especially within colleges and schools of education. We noticed that some EC positions in our dataset are held by faculty of education who are relatively early in their careers; for instance, Dr. Rebecca Penerosa is the Beverley Taylor Sorenson Assistant Professor of Arts Education at Westminster College. In our first edition we noted that Dr. Travis Bristol was a Peter Paul Assistant Professor, a university-wide endowed professorship, in English education, with an affiliation in educational leadership and policy studies, at Boston University. He is no longer at Boston University; he is at UCLA, where he does not hold an endowed position. The foreword author of this second edition, Jonathan Wai, is an Assistant Professor of Education Policy and Psychology but holds the 21st Century Endowed Chair in Education Policy.

FUTURE RESEARCH

Our updated findings support the notion from social network theory that birds of a feather flock together. Future research could be conducted that examines a range of factors that may influence the process described previously: What are the norms for participation in the selection committee of incoming education graduate students? How does the teaching-assistant/research-assistant assignment process work? Is there a formal mentoring process in place? If so, how is it structured? How does it work? If not, what informal processes have developed? Finally, what tracking mechanisms are in place to keep track of incoming and outgoing students in the graduate program? And, what does data from tracking systems reveal to us? This research would be compelling and important because it could be used to determine if, in fact, social networks exist in relation to doctoral training and advisement. For instance, it is quite possible that minority ECs and DPs may mentor and advise White doctoral students who later go on to become ECs or DPs themselves. As Niehaus and O'Meara (2014) caution, "While networks can enhance social capital for faculty members, not all networks are created equal" (p. 4).

Future research might also look at the question of who funds (or if funds are attached to) EC and DP positions. In our research, we find that some ECs and DPs were in name only, meaning some faculty of education held an EC or DP that had no funds associated with the position.[18] This prospective research is valuable, especially in the context of social network theory. Are ECs and DPs valuable because they have financial funding behind them, or is it their symbolic power that makes them beneficial both to an individual faculty member's career and to the institution of higher education? For instance: Dr. Hartlep's former Dean, Dr. René Antrop-González, was an endowed professor before coming to Metropolitan State University. While a faculty member at the University of Wisconsin at Milwaukee, he was mentored by many scholars, but chief among them was

Dr. Beverly Cross, who holds the Lillian and Morrie Moss Chair of Excellence in Urban Education at the University of Memphis.

Researchers who are interested may also consider conducting qualitative investigations of ECs and DPs in the field of education. This study relied on statistical quantification (descriptive as well as inferential non-parametric statistics). The present volume follows the lead of Thompson, Bonner, and Lewis (2016) and captures the first-person experiences of EC and DP faculty via qualitative research, to determine the impact of these positions on students, lines of inquiry, and the field.

THIS BOOK

It is important to understand how contributors were selected. Initially, Dr. Hartlep contacted all of the Asian/Americans in the dataset. He informed each Asian/American endowed professor how very few there were and that he would like to honor them and their work. He requested that they select a person or persons who could write about them. Dr. Hartlep suggested that they be former or current graduate students and/or mentees. Once contributors were identified, they were invited to share their voice in the telling of their luminary's story. We wanted their voice to be present so that the reader could understand their relationship to the luminary and thus their perspective on his/her story. The chapter contributors wrote individual pieces and were given free rein on how they wanted to structure their chapter. We did not dictate how chapter authors structured their chapter, as the story of each EC/DP featured in this collection is in many ways unique. Thus, by giving chapter authors flexibility, chapters reflect the diversity of members of this group. It also would be presumptuous of us, the book editors, to pre-ordain and pre-identify trends and topics. For this reason, we allowed chapter contributors to write stories that they wanted. Many times, the chapter contributors met with the endowed professor and discussed a variety of topics before, during, and after writing their chapter.

We are reminded by Pang (1996) about the power of silence. Some of the Asian/American professors who were eligible to be included in this book may not have felt comfortable providing stories or asking their advisees to write about them. This is more than merely being humble; it speaks to the power of letting their actions speak for them. *Asian/American Scholars of Education: 21st Century Pedagogies, Perspectives, and Experiences* shares the knowledge of Asian/American luminaries in the field of education. Because Asian/Americans are underrepresented in the field of education nationally at the K–12 level (Lor, 2010; Toldson, 2011), they necessarily are also underrepresented in academe. The "Education and Struggle" Peter Lang book series is an ideal home for *Asian/American Scholars of Education* because of the rich narrative accounts that the book shares. It also acknowledges the struggle that Asian/American education scholars have been waging when it comes to being seen as legitimate scholars deserving of endowed status.

Permissions Acknowledgment

This chapter is derived in part from an article published in *Educational Studies* on March 30, 2016, available online: http://www.tandfonline.com/doi/full/10.1080/00131946.2016.1142994

NOTES

1 https://www.dictionary.com/browse/luminary
2 The authors would like to thank Hannah M. Wilk, undergraduate research assistant, for her dedicated and excellent work on this project.
3 Bic Ngo, the Rodney S. Wallace Professor for Advancement of Teaching and Learning at the University of Minnesota; Kenji Hakuta, the Lee J. Jacks Professor of Education at Stanford University; Michelene Chi, the Dorothy Bray Endowed Professor of Science and Teaching at Arizona State University.
4 A version of this section was previously published as an article: Hartlep, N. D., Ball, D. B., Theodosopoulos, K., Wells, K. E., & Morgan, G. B. (2016). A national analysis of endowed chairs and distinguished professors in the field of education. *Educational Studies*, *52*(2), 119–138.
5 We define *elite* status in the findings section of this introduction.
6 http://www.jrhasselback.com/FacDir.html
7 Endowed positions come with many privileges, such as a dedicated office staff, a robust budget, large amounts of time to think, and minimum teaching responsibilities. See Sam Minner's (2002) self-reflection on holding an endowed professorship. His reflection on holding this position for three years is available here: http://www.aahea.org/articles/endowed.htm
8 It only examines EC and DP positions in North America. We appreciate the anonymous reviewer who pointed out that these positions sometimes have politicized histories at institutions of higher education. Keeping this in mind, we do not consider EC and DP of education in Canada and other countries, although future researchers may consider this fruitful.
9 Typically, EC and DP positions are given to Full Professors. Earning tenure as an Associate Professor and then obtaining Full Professor status takes time (or "generally takes a minimum of 12 years"), which leads to our hypothesis of 20 years.
10 The college/university classification of Elite, Competitive, and/or General is explained in the Findings section of the article.
11 These particular states have a substantial number of elite/prestigious colleges/universities who are known for excellence in research.
12 http://grad-schools.usnews.rankingsandreviews.com/best-graduate-schools/topeducation-schools/edu-rankings

13 https://www.usnews.com/best-graduate-schools/top-education-schools

14 Thirteen professors earned doctorates outside the United States: Erna Alant, D.Phil at University of Pretoria, South Africa; Wolfgang Althof, Ph.D. at University of Fribourh, Switzerland; Arthur N. Applebee (Died in 2015), Ph.D. at University of London, U.K.; Stephen Brookfield, Ph.D. at University of Leicester, U.K.; Eamonn Callan, Ph.D. at University of Alberta, Canada; Frank Farley, Ph.D. at University of London, U.K.; Andy Hargreaves, Ph.D. at University of Leeds, U.K.; Paul L. Harris, D. Phil at Oxford University, U.K.; Nonie K. Lesaux, Ph.D. at University of British Columbia, Canada; Peter L. McLaren, Ph.D. at University of Toronto, Canada; Jonathan Osborne, Ph.D. at King's College, University of London, U.K.; Marek Oziewicz, Ph.D. at University of Wroclaw, Poland; and Roy Pea, D.Phil at Oxford University, U.K.

15 We routinely found articles on the Internet that described the EC/DP and the specific benefactor/donor or partner.

16 See http://tinyurl.com/Endowed-Distinguished

17 Programs like this already exist, such as the American Educational Research Association's (AERA) Undergraduate Student Education Research Training Workshop. According to its website, this workshop is designed to build the talent pool of undergraduate students who plan to pursue doctoral degrees in education research or in disciplines and fields that examine education issues. Applicants are sought who have potential and interest in pursuing careers as education researchers, faculty members, or other professionals who contribute to the research field. Thus, by beginning the mentoring process earlier, and with diverse students who attend less selective institutions of higher education, the social network of academe may become more diverse than it currently is.

18 Personal Communication with Endowed Professor in California. We do not identify this scholar for confidentiality.

REFERENCES

Ball, D., & Hartlep, N. D. (Eds.). (2017). *Asian/Americans, education, and crime: The model minority as victim and perpetrator.* Lanham, MD: Lexington Books.

Bell, W. G. (1986). Endowed positions in gerontology *and geriatrics in higher education: Results from a preliminary survey. Educational Gerontology, 12*(6), 507–518. doi: https://doi.org/10.1080/0380127860120603

Bielby, W. T., & Baron, J. N. (1986). Men and women at work: Sex segregation and statistical discrimination. *American Journal of Sociology, 91*(4), 759–799.

Blau, J. (1993). *Social contracts and economic markets.* New York: Plenum.

Borgatti, S. P., Mehra, A., Brass, D. J., & Labianca, G. (2009).Network analysis in the social sciences. *Science, 323*(5916), 892–895. doi: https://doi.org/10.1126/science.1165821

Brewer, D. J., Eide, E. R., & Ehrenberg, R. G. (1999). Does it pay to attend an elite private college? Cross-cohort evidence on the effects of college type on earnings. *Journal of Human Resources, 34*(1), 104–123. doi: https://doi.org/10.2307/146304

Brown, K. (2005). Snowball sampling: Using social networks to research non-heterosexual women. *International Journal of Social Research Methodology, 8*(1), 47–60. doi: https://doi.org/10.1080/1364557032000081663

Cho, J., & Trent, A. (2006). Validity in qualitative research revisited. *Qualitative Research*, 6(3), 319–340. doi: https://doi.org/10.1177/1468794106065006

Cole, E. R. (2009). Intersectionality and research in Psychology. *American Psychologist*, 64(3), 170–180. doi: https://doi.org/10.1037/a0014564

Crenshaw, K. (1989). Demarginalizing the intersection of race and sex: A black feminist critique of antidiscrimination doctrine, feminist theory, and antiracist politics. *University of Chicago Legal Forum*, 140, 139–167. Retrieved from http://philpapers.org/archive/CREDTI.pdf

Delgado, R., & Bell, D. (1989). Minority law professors' lives: The Bell-Delgado survey. *Harvard Civil Rights-Civil Liberties Law Review*, 24, 349–392.

Durkheim, E. (1951). *Suicide*. New York: Free Press.

Eide, E., Brewer, D. J., & Ehrenberg, R. G. (1998). Does it pay to attend an elite private college? Evidence on the effects of undergraduate college quality on graduate school attendance. *Economics of Education Review*, 17(4), 371–376. doi: https://doi.org/10.1016/S0272-7757(97)00037-X

Food & Water Watch. (2012). *Public research, private gain: Corporate influence over university agricultural research*. Washington, DC: Author. Retrieved from http://documents.foodandwaterwatch.org/doc/PublicResearchPrivateGain.pdf

Fitzpatrick, J. J. (1985). Endowed chairs in nursing: State of the art. *Journal of Professional Nursing*, 1(3), 145–147. doi: https://doi.org/10.1016/S8755-7223(85)80141-1

Fitzpatrick, J. J. (2000). Endowed chairs and professorships in schools of nursing: A 1999 update. *Journal of Professional Nursing*, 16(1), 57–62. doi: https://doi.org/10.1016/S8755-7223(00)80012-5

Fitzpatrick, J. J., Fitzpatrick, M. L., & Dressler, M. B. (2005). Endowed chairs and professorships in schools of nursing: A 2004 update. *Journal of Professional Nursing*, 21(4), 244–252. doi: https://doi.org/10.1016/j.profnurs.2005.05.002

Giddens, A. (1990). *The consequences of modernity*. Stanford, CA: Stanford University Press.

Giroux, H. A. (2009). Neoliberalism, youth, and the leasing of higher education. In D. Hill & R. Kumar (Eds.), *Global neoliberalism and education and its consequences* (pp. 30–53). New York: Routledge.

Giroux, H. A. (2014). *Neoliberalism's war on higher education*. Chicago, IL: Haymarket Books.

Groves, R. M., & Couper, M. P. (2012). *Nonresponse in household interview surveys*. New York: John Wiley & Sons.

Groves, R. M., & Heeringa, S. G. (2006). Responsive design for household surveys: Tools for actively controlling survey errors and costs. *Journal of the Royal Statistical Society: Series A (Statistics in Society)*, 169(3), 439–457.

Hartlep, N. D. (2016, November 18). 4 steps toward making endowed positions more equal. *The Chronicle of Higher Education*. A12.

Hartlep, N. D., Ball, D., Theodosopoulos, K., Wells, K., & Morgan, G. B. (2016). A national analysis of endowed chairs and distinguished professors in the field of education. *Educational Studies*, 52(2), 119–138.

Hartlep, N. D., & Porfilio, B. J. (Eds.). (2015). *Killing the model minority stereotype: Asian American counterstories and complicity*. Charlotte, NC: Information Age Publishing.

Hartlep, N. D., & Theodosopoulos, K. (2014, October 9). African Americans who hold endowed and distinguished professorships in education. *The Journal of Blacks in Higher Education*. Retrieved from https://www.jbhe.com/2014/10/african-americans-who-hold-endowed-and-distinguished-professorships-in-education/

Jones, S. (Ed.). (1999). *Doing internet research: Critical issues and methods for examining the net.* Thousand Oaks, CA: Sage.

Kalleberg, A. L., Knoke, D., Marsden, P. V., & Spaeth, J. L. (1996). *Organizations in America: Analyzing their structures and human resource practices.* Thousand Oaks, CA: Sage.

Kamath, R. R., Meier, H. H., & Rao, S. R. (2006). Examining a decade of named marketing chairs in the United States. *Journal of Business & Economics Research, 4*(5), 17–28.

Kamath, R. R., Meier, H. H., & Tousey, S. L. (2005). An investigation of named professorships of economics in the United States. *Journal of Economics and Finance Education, 4*(2), 48–60.

Kurtz, A. (2014, August 5). Yes, a college degree is still worth it. CNN Money. Retrieved from http://money.cnn.com/2014/06/24/news/economy/college-worth-it/index.html

Lor, Pao. 2010. Hmong teachers: Life experiences and teaching perspectives. *Multicultural Education, 17*(3): 36–40.

McPherson, M., Smith-Lovin, L., & Cook, J. M. (2001). Birds of a feather: Homophily in social networks. *Annual Review of Sociology, 27*(1), 415–444. doi: https://doi.org/10.1146/annurev.soc.27.1.415

Meier, H. H., & Kamath, R. (2005). A multidimensional investigation of named professorships in accounting: 2002–2003. *Journal of Education for Business, 80*(5), 295–301.

Metwalli, A. M., & Tang, R. Y. W. (2001). Finance chair professorships in the United States. *Journal of Financial Education, 27*, 64–71.

Metwalli, A. M., & Tang, R. Y. W. (2002). Management chair professorships in the United States. *Journal of Education for Business, 77*(3), 131–136. doi: https://doi.org/10.1080/08832320209599061

Minner, S. (2002). The guilty pleasures of an endowed professor: My adventure at the very top of the academic food chain. *AAHE Bulletin, 54*(7), 7–9.

Niehaus, E., & O'Meara, K. (2014). Invisible but essential: The role of professional networks in promoting faculty agency in career advancement. *Innovations in Higher Education, 40*(2), 1–13. doi: https://doi.org/10.1007/s10755-014-9302-7

O'Meara, K. (2011). Inside the panopticon: Studying academic reward systems. In J. C. Smart & M. B. Paulsen (Eds.), *Higher education: Handbook of theory and research* (pp. 161–220). New York: Springer. doi: https://doi.org/10.1007/978-94-007-0702-3

Pang, V. O. (1996). Intentional silence and communication in a democratic society: The viewpoint of one Asian American. *The High School Journal, 79*(3), 183–190.

Pescosolido, B. A. (2006). Sociology of social networks. In C. D. Bryant & D. L. Peck (Eds.), *The handbook of 21st century sociology* (pp. 208–217). Thousand Oaks, CA: Sage.

Rezaee, Z., Elmore, R. C., & Spiceland, D. (2004). Endowed chairs in accounting worldwide. *Accounting Education: An International Journal, 13*(1), 29–50. doi: https://doi.org/10.1080/0963928042000174483

Rezaee, Z., Elmore, R. C., & Spiceland, D. (2006). An examination of the status and attributes of chair professorships in accounting. *Accounting Educators' Journal, 16*, 97–118.

Scheffe, H. (1959). *The analysis of variance.* New York: Wiley & Sons.

Simmel, G. (1955). *Conflict and the web of group affiliations* (K. H. Wolff & R. Bendix, trans.). New York: Free Press.

Simpson, E. H. (1949). Measurement of diversity. *Nature, 163*(4148), 688–688.

Stone, C. (1993). African Americans holding endowed university chairs. *Journal of Blacks in Higher Education, 2*, 127–130. http://www.jstor.org/stable/2962585

Stone, C. (1997). African Americans who hold endowed university chairs. *Journal of Blacks in Higher Education, 17*, 105–109. doi: https://doi.org/10.2307/2963248

Stone, C. (2001). A roster of African Americans who hold endowed university chairs. *Journal of Blacks in Higher Education, 33*, 121–125. doi: https://doi.org/10.2307/2678940

Tang, R. Y. W., Forrest. J. P., & Leach, D. (1990). Findings from a survey on accounting chair professorships. *Journal of Accounting Education, 8*(2), 241–251. doi: https://doi.org/10.1016/0748-5751(90)90005-R

Thompson, G. L., Bonner, F. A., & Lewis, C. W. (Eds.). (2016). *Reaching the mountaintop of the academy: Personal narratives, advice, and strategies from black distinguished and endowed professors.* Charlotte, NC: Information Age.

Toldson, I. (2011). Diversifying the United States' teaching force: Where are we now? Where do we need to go? How do we get there? *The Journal of Negro Education, 80*(3), 183–186.

Tsui, L. (2003). Reproducing social inequalities through higher education: Critical thinking as valued capital. *Journal of Negro Education, 72*(3), 318–332. doi: https://doi.org/10.2307/3211250

Urbancic, F. R. (2008). A multiattributes approach to for ranking Ph.D. programs. *Journal of Education for Business, 83*(6), 339–346. doi: https://doi.org/10.3200/JOEB.83.6.339-346

U.S. Census Bureau QuickFacts: United States. (n.d.). U.S. Census Bureau. Retrieved from https://www.census.gov/quickfacts/fact/table/US/PST045219

Washburn, J. (2000, March 1). The kept university. *Atlantic.* Retrieved from http://www.theatlantic.com/magazine/archive/2000/03/the-kept-university/306629/

Wasserman, S., & Faust, K. (1994). *Social network analysis: Methods and applications.* Cambridge, UK: Cambridge University Press.

Weeks, H. S., Finch, J. H., & Hardin, W. G. (2007). Endowed real estate positions and the faculty who hold them. *Journal of Real Estate Practice and Education, 10*(1), 61–79. doi: https://doi.org/10.5555/repe.10.1.37j222734745706m

CHAPTER ONE

A Critical Case for Making the Invisible Known

The Mentorship, Scholarship, and Leadership of Professor A. Lin Goodwin

CRYSTAL CHEN LEE

Professor A. Lin Goodwin is Dean of the Faculty of Education and Professor of Education at The University of Hong Kong. Previously, Dr. Goodwin was Vice Dean at Teachers College (TC), Columbia University, New York, where she continues to hold an endowed chair as the Evenden Professor of Education. She served as Vice President of the American Educational Research Association (AERA)—Division K: Teaching and Teacher Education from 2013 to 2016, and was co-director (and architect) of a joint MA in Educational Leadership and Change between Teachers College and the National Institute of Education (NIE) in Singapore. In 2014, she received a $7.5 million U.S. federal grant to support her second teaching residency program at Teachers College: TR@TC2. In 2015, she was honored as a Distinguished Researcher by AERA's Special Interest Group (SIG): Research on the Education of Asian and Pacific Americans (REAPA), and was named the inaugural Dr. Ruth Wong Professor of Teacher Education at NIE.

Dr. Goodwin's research focuses on teacher and teacher educator identities and development; their multicultural understandings and curriculum enactments; the particular issues facing Asian/American teachers and students in U.S. schools; and on international analyses/comparisons of teacher education practice and policy (see Goodwin & Chen, 2016; Goodwin, Low, & Darling-Hammond, 2017).

Her work appears in top education journals including the *Journal of Teacher Education* (see Goodwin et al., 2014), *Educational Studies* (see Goodwin, 2017),

Action in Teacher Education (see Roegman, Pratt, Goodwin, & Akin, 2017), *Teacher Development* (see Goodwin & Kosnik, 2013), *Education and Urban Society* (see Goodwin, 2002), *Teaching Education* (see Goodwin, 2010), and *Teachers College Record* (see Goodwin, 2010); her most recent book, published in 2017 (with Low & Darling-Hammond) is entitled *Empowered Educators in Singapore: How High-Performing Systems Shape Teaching Quality* (see Goodwin & Low, 2017; Goodwin, Low, & Darling- Hammond, 2017). In addition, Dr. Goodwin has served as a consultant to a wide variety of organizations including school districts, philanthropic foundations, higher education institutions, and professional educational organizations around issues of teacher education, diversity, educational equity, and assessment. Her work in teacher education and curriculum development has taken her to many different countries such as Poland, Thailand, Brazil, Jordan, Mongolia, Latvia, Singapore, China, France, and Bermuda among others, where she has collaborated with educators to bring about school, teaching, and curriculum change.

The critical case in academia oftentimes lies at the intersection of the (in)visible. Critical cases explore contextualized social and political landscapes to offer inquiry on the complexities of power dimensions, and the ways in which race, ethnicity, gender, and class lie among and between them. In such cases, there is often a powerful force behind not just the movement but also the endeavor and the long-standing commitment to social justice (Dyson & Genishi, 2005; Shor, 2012). The work of the scholar and the educator brings what is (un)seen into the light, naming the theoretical underpinnings, groundings, and reasons for what and why things are, and how educational practices should evolve and move forward. Oftentimes, it is someone who has been and knows what it means to be marginalized and invisible, and who intends to commit to the education and success of those who also are. After all, a fight for the marginalized is a fight for all.

This chapter is about one powerful force, Dean and Professor A. Lin Goodwin of The University of Hong Kong—a force of wisdom, a force of strength, and a force of integrity in what is now a very pressing time in teacher education. It is a time when misconceptions about the profession are made—a time when privatization overrules the public; and a time when test scores begin to replace the human. Teachers and their students are becoming invisible behind the numbers, and now is the time for the invisible to be pushed forward to the platform.

Thus, it is an opportune time to write this chapter on Professor A. Lin Goodwin honoring how she, a force of mentorship, scholarship, and leadership, has pursued these very acts of social justice in the field of teacher education, rendering the invisible visible, and bringing to light what is unseen to those who come after her.

Her story is one of significance, one of a unique critical case. The journey of Professor Goodwin's success was in many ways one about rendering the invisible minority, bringing to light the Asian/American experience particularly in academia. As her former doctoral research fellow and an Asian/American woman of color at Teachers College, Columbia University, Professor Goodwin's experiences have shed light on my own by allowing me to think about the ways in which I may work to see, as Professor Goodwin says, "what people are not saying." Professor Goodwin's own autobiographical experiences as an Asian/American can be characterized as a long journey: from being an immigrant to teacher, to teacher educator, to teacher of teacher educators. Although her work has centered around the work of teachers and teacher education both nationally and internationally, this chapter sheds light on Professor Goodwin's own journey and how her journey has informed her generous support and mentorship of me as one of her doctoral students, an Asian/American woman in academia.

BRINGING THE TEACHING PROFESSION TO LIGHT: THE WORK THAT SHE CHOSE TO DO

In 1981, Lin Goodwin arrived at Teachers College not knowing that nine years later she would become a professor at the same institution. As a first generation immigrant from Singapore, and the first member of her family to attend college, her aspirations were simple—get a college degree and get a job. Her mother had sacrificed to save enough to pay for the first year of university, but after that Lin was expected to support herself. She worked her way through college, graduating *cum laude* with dual certification in general and special education from Central Connecticut State College (now University). She began her career as a special education teacher of young adults aged 18–21, and then high school students, grades 9–12. After teaching for several years, she decided to resume her education and enrolled for graduate study at her alma mater given her positive experiences as an undergraduate. However, while the graduate course work was manageable, she found that she wanted more and looked to pursue a degree at a well-established institution. She was in search of "good experiences," ones that would take her beyond the development of skills for employment and stretch her thinking. She chose to go to Teachers College because having weighed the quality of the education vs. the expense of the school, she wanted to do her graduate degree at a "good place." So she sold her car and moved to New York City (NYC). When she arrived, she chose to pursue the Ed.M. because she thought, an "advanced master's must be better than the M.A." Although her choices were happenstance at the time without the benefit of advice, guidance, or family experience, they ended up being great ones that afforded her the mentorship, scholarship, and leadership to become the Vice Dean and an endowed professor at the very same "name school."

When she began as an Ed.M. student, she remained driven by the same goal she had in college—to look for opportunities in order to support herself. School was expensive; living in NYC was pricey; and she needed to pay her own bills. Yet, her persistence and work ethic led her into the very field where she is now a prolific and significant scholar: teacher education. While taking courses as a master's student, she also supervised teachers, tutored, babysat, worked as a staff developer, work study in financial aid, event planner, general gopher, and research assistant. She said, "If you had five cents to pay me to do something, I would do it." In her words, she meant when there was work to be done, she was there. She also was very engaged in department activities, sat in on preservice courses, and volunteered. As a consequence, faculty came to know her personally and she made strong connections with them.

Initially, she thought she would become a principal upon graduating because at the time, it was the only next step available to teachers who aspired to advance in the profession. While she had never planned to pursue a terminal degree, her involvement in teacher education fueled her interest and passion, which was further buoyed by the encouragement of the faculty in her master's program. But she knew she could only do it if she were awarded a scholarship. And she was. This doctoral journey would further prepare her entry into teacher education work. Due to her involvement in the preservice elementary program, she was encouraged to apply for a full-time instructor position with them. She applied not once, not twice, but three times. The first time she applied, she was told she was not hired because she was not yet a doctoral candidate. The second time she applied—with strong program faculty encouragement—she was told she was not hired because she *was* a doctoral candidate. On the third time, even though she was already frustrated with being "kicked to the curb," she was told that though she had the job, her position was contingent on the program attracting 40 students (instead of the previous year's 11 students). Forty students did commit and so she began as assistant director/instructor of the program. This work soon became what she *chose* to do; it was far more than a job she had to do. She credits this aspect of her doctoral experience as one that exposed her to numerous opportunities, and encouraged her to take on many different responsibilities and make connections in the field.

Lin Goodwin emphasizes that her only saving grace for being able to finish her doctoral degree while working full-time is that she is able to "churn it" when she needs to. In the same semester that she took (and passed) her qualifying exams, she also wrote and defended her dissertation proposal. The next year, as the spring term progressed, she took two weeks off from work to write from the early hours of the morning to the late hours of the night to finish the dissertation because she had made a promise to a good friend that they would walk across the graduation stage together that May. Indeed, she did it. Under the advisement of

Dr. Karen Zumwalt and Dr. Henry Passow, she received her doctorate in 1987. At the time, she was also directing a large grant from the Mellon Foundation to recruit talented liberal arts graduates to become secondary teachers. Because she had made a two-year commitment to the program, she remained with TC beyond graduation. In her role, she designed and managed all aspects of the program, including traveling across the country to multiple institutions to recruit college graduates into the teaching profession. She also served as the instructor for each cohort of students in a core urban education course, and supported them in the many TC teacher preparation programs in which they were enrolled. Her experience became extensive, and she started to become a force in sustaining and retaining teachers in the field.

In the second year of her two-year commitment, as she began searching for an academic position, a tenure-track faculty position opened up in the Department of Curriculum and Teaching at TC. At first, Lin was hesitant to apply but she decided that it was an opportunity to consider, just like the other positions she was exploring. Although there were many applicants, she was selected—nine years after entering the halls of Teachers College as a student. To this day, she calls Teachers College, "a basket full of riches."

THE CONVERSATION BETWEEN BLACKS, BROWNS, AND WHITES (BUT CERTAINLY NOT ASIANS)

Professor Lin Goodwin's tenure at Teachers College began in 1990, and at the time, her circle of mentors grew even sweeter and stronger with a new senior faculty hire: Professor Celia Genishi. The two of them, Lin and Celia, would become the greatest of friends; not only were they both passionate about teacher education, but also they were able to journey through an invisible conversation in the halls of academia: the micro-aggressions surrounding Asian/American (female) bodies. Although Professor Goodwin's tenure at Teachers College has made a far and wide impact in the field of teacher education and she has certainly contributed to the "basket full of riches," this portion of the chapter turns to an untold story of her own—one that must be heard in order to give further justice, especially justice for faculty of color. The conversation should no longer be invisible.

Lin's friendship with Celia grew because they were able to "check stories" with one another. While other colleagues might have dismissed an insensitive and marginalizing comment as a "joke," Lin knew she could confide in Celia. Celia would often respond to Lin indicating that the certain incident or comment, "happened to me too." Celia took Lin's experiences seriously; she knew the many ways people engaged in micro-aggressions (and outright racist acts), thereby failing to acknowledge Lin's full identity. Both of them could see how the Asian/American minority was invisible in the academy; the conversations surrounding race were focused on black, brown, and white bodies, but certainly not Asian ones. They were considered the pseudo-whites, the model minority—minorities that came with privilege. Asian/Americans were presumed to be silent and their silence was taken as passivity and acquiescence rather than as a result of being shut out of conversations. No attention was given to Lin or her Asian/American colleagues. Lin referenced the many ways in which participants at conferences, for example, would presume that she came from a place of privilege because of her race, and how this assumption is often placed on Asian/Americans without any regard for their history or context. In fact, she remembers being told by a white woman at the American Educational Research Association (AERA) Annual Meeting, who came to a Research on the Education of Asian and Pacific Americans (REAPA) Special Interest Group meeting, that she (Lin)/they had nothing to worry about because they were all "fine and doing well" (socio-economically, educationally, socially, etc.). Rather than remain silent, Lin challenged the woman on her racist comment—telling her about working from the time she was in high school, and about the many jobs she had including cleaning toilets—did that fit the stereotype of "doing well"? As seen from her own story, Lin is one who knew how to work in order to do what she had to do. But in doing what she had to do, she also made choices about what she wanted or needed to do—her decisions were never just about money; they were always about first "saying yes" to opportunities and then paying bills.

To highlight this notion of invisibility as an Asian/American (faculty) member, Lin presented a paper at a REAPA SIG session at the 2001 AERA Annual Meeting in which she named four ways Asian/Americans are perceived in U.S. society: (1) the child, (2) the servant, (3) the villain, and (4) the whore.

First, Lin described her own experience as a faculty member in which she was only treated like a *child*; colleagues would place their hands on her face and indicate how "young" and "cute" she was; they would comment, "Oh, you are too young to know that—that was before your time!" Their physical touch and attitude were never acknowledged as wrong in their eyes, and Lin emphasized that no one would be acting in this manner with other faculty members. Second, Lin identified the *servant* role, as "Give it to the Asian girl—she will do it; she'll clean up, do it well, and be quiet about it." She discussed how people often assume that the Asian/American woman will work hard and get the job done; this assumption is further highlighted by an anecdote where one term, she was assigned to serve as an external examiner on 17 different dissertations.

The last two roles, the *villain* and the *whore*, are especially portrayed in media, and also reflected in her own experiences: examples include the evil Fu Manchu or Suzie Wong, the sexualized girl toy. Lin emphasized that these media portrayals mirrored the experiences she has had, even in higher education. For example, her straight-forwardness and honesty have been villainized, and she has often been seen as dour or too tough because she was expected to be "nice and smiling" rather than being a focused, serious scholar. However, Lin believes that the experiences she's had, and the subsequent lessons she's learned, have allowed her to speak back and stand up for equal rights because the Asian/American experience should not be seen as inconsequential, and that those in higher education should work to dismantle and fight against such assumptions.

Despite these assumptions and misconceptions, the fight for faculty of color has not been absent at Teachers College. When Lin was hired as a new faculty member in 1990, there were also 13 other new hires at the same time, half of whom were faculty of color. They met regularly to discuss issues in higher education, but also to create community among themselves. In their discussions and subsequent projects with schools and communities, they were active in their work for social justice because they saw that a fight for faculty of color was a fight for everyone. It is with this stance that Lin Goodwin continues to advocate for not just the Asian/American voice, but also the voices of all students and educators so that those who have been invisible can be made known.

THE MENTORSHIP, SCHOLARSHIP, AND LEADERSHIP OF PROFESSOR A. LIN GOODWIN: A SHARED ASIAN/AMERICAN EXPERIENCE

Now, in 2017–2018, I have seen Lin Goodwin continue to lead and encourage many. Having had the privilege of working as her doctoral research fellow, Lin has certainly been one to bring what is invisible to light for me. Professor Goodwin champions that "mentoring is part of the giveback" in which the key to mentoring is grounded in the philosophy of generosity. I have been blessed and incredibly honored to receive her generous spirit. As Lin would say, we often have many different kinds of mentors—ones that shape us to take on different identities. I have also been fortunate to receive the kindness and generosity of many mentors at Teachers College such as my dissertation advisor, Professor Michelle G. Knight-Manuel, who has taught me how to be a researcher, and my teaching mentor, Professor Marjorie Siegel, who has taught me to advocate for students. I have been incredibly blessed to learn from my committee member, Professor Ernest Morrell, who has taught me to embrace the critical mind in my theoretical groundings. With these scholarly giants by my side, I particularly attribute Professor Goodwin's mentorship as invaluable for she has taught me to be a leader, an educator, and a scholar of color.

In my second year as a doctoral student in 2013, a mutual colleague asked me if I would be interested in applying for a research assistantship under Lin Goodwin's new residency program, Teaching Residents at Teachers College (TR@TC)—an urban teacher residency program funded by the U.S. Department of Education Teacher Quality Partnership. I was hesitant, not because I did not find the work intriguing, but because I was already a research assistant on another project focusing on literacy among immigrant students. Yet, like Lin, I was eager to grab the opportunities, "the basket full of riches," at Teachers College, and I applied for the position. It was from this one small step that I was introduced to Professor Goodwin.

As a new research assistant on a very large and well-seasoned team, I spoke very little at first, not because I was passive (an assumption that many had previously also assigned to me), but because I was choosing to listen in order to understand the research. I had only begun my second year, and words such as "multi-faceted mixed methods studies," and "coding for analysis," were new terms that I was learning in the discourse. From Fall 2013 to Spring 2014, I worked quietly, under the radar, trying to gain my bearings while coding and writing with team members I was getting to know. However, my first solo encounter with Lin Goodwin occurred at the 2014 American Association of Colleges of Teacher Education (AACTE) conference when on a quiet night during the conference, Lin and I had a rare dinner together alone. While other research team members had separate plans that night, Lin and I ended up meeting at the hotel restaurant, and opted to have dinner together. It was indeed a rare opportunity to have dinner with Professor Goodwin, a person whom I admired so deeply and who had a strong reputation in the field. Although I was one of her research assistants, I never had time alone with Lin. When I walked into the restaurant with her, I realized that in her kindness and generosity, she had chosen to spend the evening with me. The conversation began with my research interests and my percolating dissertation topic on literacy and immigrant girls. She listened intently, offering her own advice, but never in an intimidating way. In fact, she often asked questions, and when I asked her about her own story, she spoke of her journey into teacher education with clarity and passion.

However, what struck me most about our conversation was our mutual connection around the Asian/American experience. I had never shared about my own experience as a child of immigrant parents, and how such a childhood had informed my journey into education. My parents were well educated, and had emigrated from Taiwan to the United States for graduate school. Arriving to America from top Taiwanese universities, my father pursued a Ph.D. in computer science at University of California at Berkeley (UC-Berkeley), the top university for computer science in the 1980s, while my mother, who held an English degree, pursued a Master's in Information Science at a state school nearby. In 1987, I was born in

Oakland, California, and grew up as my parents' firstborn, living in UC-Berkeley family housing while my father finished his dissertation. In 1988, our family moved to New Jersey so that my father could work as a computer science researcher at the prestigious AT&T Bell Labs conducting innovative research that he had always loved to pursue. To this day, he is still loyal to the company as the Director of Inventive Science at AT&T. My mother settled into life as a homemaker, and we lived in the suburbs while speaking Mandarin Chinese and English as a family.

Life for my parents seemed quite idyllic at the time; they were pursuing their American dream when suddenly, life took an unexpected but blessed turn. In 1990, my brother, Jason, was born with Down syndrome. Having never had the experience of taking care of a disabled child, my parents sought out the help of others in a local church community. Their love and faith grew, and their perception of success and what it means to live a purposeful life became grounded in faith, hope, and love. Particularly so, they believed that education was key to the growth and development of not just me but specifically my brother. They advocated for disability rights in the school community, while they also pursued activities for me in gifted programs. They valued the individualized and differentiated education in public schools, and I grew up with a strong sense that the calling to be an educator was one of my own.

When I graduated high school, I chose to attend Rutgers—The State University of New Jersey—to pursue my B.A. in English and my M.Ed. in English Education. After graduation, I taught in a large Central Jersey suburban high school as an English teacher for three years from 2009 to 2012. Although I felt pedagogically prepared and trained to teach high school English, I was not prepared for the ways I was perceived as an Asian/American teacher. For one, I was the only minority in the entire English department of 31 English teachers and special education teachers. Among the 250 staff members, I was one of three Asian/American teachers, the other two being a Chinese language teacher and a biology teacher. Most staff members, even by year three, sometimes confused me with my two colleagues, and I was often asked if I was a math or science teacher because I was Asian/American. When I answered that I was in the English department, most responded with surprise. In addition, when peers and acquaintances inquired why I was a teacher, they often thought that I was a member of Teach for America, a corps of teachers who teach and lead in low-income schools after a few months of training. Most of my peers assumed that I would never want to actually *study* to be a teacher and had *formally learned* to become one—especially because I was Asian/American. Many of them assumed that because of my Asian/American upbringing, I only had three choices in life: to become a doctor, an engineer, or a lawyer. Being a teacher simply did not fit into the box of choices. To them, the visibility of a certified Asian/American teacher was a strange sight—one that is often missing from conversations around teacher education.

These conversations and my work as an education intern in a human rights agency led me to my doctoral studies in advocating for minorities in education and a pursuit of learning the complexities of teacher education. As an intern at International Justice Mission, an agency that works to rescue victims from violent oppression, I developed social justice curricula that focused on how students could be involved in the fight against human trafficking. This interest led me to think about not just writing standalone curriculum that works for social justice, but a theoretical framework through which teachers could be advocates for the oppressed. I left the suburban high school environment, one which I thought was still valuable and essential to my growth as a teacher, to study in NYC. As a doctoral student, I pursued my interests in literacy and immigration with community-based organizations, while at the same time pursuing research interests in teacher education through Professor Goodwin's federally-funded urban residency program.

THE SPIRIT OF GENEROSITY AND HOLISTIC MENTORING

I shared these experiences with Lin that night over dinner, and in many subsequent conversations. It was comforting to hear that I could situate myself as an Asian/American educator and embrace my own positionality while becoming a researcher, scholar, and an aspiring professor. A few months after our initial one-on-one conversation, Lin invited me to take on an extra role as an assistant to her for the AERA Division K—Teaching and Teacher Education planning meeting. The program planning committee was coming to Teachers College, and Lin needed someone to run logistics and order delicious food and goodies for their hard work. I found my research role expanding into many other realms, and I embraced them dearly, knowing that embodying the role of a research assistant requires attending to matters of teacher education holistically—even the smallest of things, the layout of food and the precision of program details, all contribute to the workings of teacher education. In her mentorship, Lin taught me that in order to become successful, one must be able to understand the whole picture and pay attention to the small details—the spirit of generosity and kindness is one that must be embraced as educators. Scholarship is secondary to the pursuit of attending to the humanity of teacher educators, teachers, and students.

This spirit of humanity extended into Lin's mentorship of me. Oftentimes, she would inquire about my life outside of research even though we may have had many research papers to discuss at the time. She paid attention to my self-care, making sure that I was healthy and well taken care of inside the academy and outside of it. We shared conversations around teacher education, current events, wonderful places to eat in NYC, fellowships to apply for, and professors to connect with. Nothing too great or too small was hidden from our conversation, and she made my presence known to others in conferences, official meetings, and informal greetings with other professors in the field. Most importantly, Lin made me visible in an academic world where sometimes the Asian/American voice is unheard. She gave me the confidence to speak up when I needed to, and to be silent when it was time to listen. She held no judgments in my learning process, but rather was generous in her mentorship, knowing that in order to educate teacher educators who embrace the full humanity of students, we must mentor teacher educators holistically first. In such a way, Lin attended to the physical, moral, intellectual, and even aesthetic endeavors in my life. Since I am a singer, Lin once even came to my voice recital to support my interests outside of academia. Because of such holistic mentoring, my love and respect for Lin grew in immeasurable ways, and she became a role model, advisor, and friend to me.

THE PURSUIT OF SCHOLARSHIP

One of the main reasons why I was able to grow in my scholarship at Teachers College is because Lin was extremely helpful in cultivating my strengths, identifying my weaknesses, expanding my horizons, and presenting opportunities to me. For example, Lin taught our research team to write up four new papers a year, submit them for conferences, and make sure we achieve publication a few months after the conference. In turn, every academic year, we were conducting new studies, while publishing others. Lin modeled the ethics, the precision, and the creativity in producing scholarly articles that were most essential and relevant to current research landscapes. We looked up to her for her immense scholarly work on the landscape of immigrant students, teacher education, and the education of teacher educators. Oftentimes, as collaborators on teams, we looked to Lin to examine how or why our research was necessary. We not only paid attention to our theoretical frameworks and our methodology, but more so, Lin taught us to be persistent in defining and refining our findings and discussion. Particularly, Lin generously supported any opportunities for us to present our research, and we often traveled to many places as a team. She was a key mentor who carefully framed and read our studies, while giving us the freedom and liberty to determine the studies' course under her overarching framework for the program. We learned to meet weekly and set deadlines in order to collaborate fully and deeply as a team. From Lin, I learned that the pursuit of scholarship takes practice; it takes key attention to how a team is structured, why research is produced, and the constant follow-up process of revising and submitting a manuscript. .

LEADERSHIP IN LOCAL, NATIONAL, AND INTERNATIONAL CONVERSATIONS

Lastly, through her generosity of spirit and pursuit of scholarship, Lin is an incredibly humble force of leadership. As the new Dean of the University of Hong Kong and the former Vice Dean of Teachers College, both top universities of education in the world, she is an incredible leader who is well respected by all. As former Vice Dean, one of her numerous responsibilities was to oversee the Office of Teacher Education (OTE), one which she had spearheaded for more than a decade. Under her leadership, the OTE helped students navigate and obtain teacher certification, sponsored innovative teacher preparation programs such as the Teaching Residents at Teachers College and the Peace Corps Fellows program, hosted international visitors, and helped manage the Teacher Education Policy Committee at Teachers College. In addition to her responsibilities at OTE, Lin was also a national leader as the past vice president of AERA's Division K, the largest division of AERA. She led new initiatives on teacher education, vastly expanding the field and making an urgent call for quality and excellence in teacher education. For three years, she organized the programs in AERA with great attention to the ways in which scholarly research is presented in every aspect of the division; she has also sponsored dialog sessions that allow for conversations among scholars on diversity, social justice, and policy in the field. In doing so, she has been a champion for studying the education of teacher educators, most recently working with colleagues to initiate a new interdisciplinary program at Teachers College in educating teacher educators.

Yet, perhaps Lin is still best known for her international leadership through the years. As mentioned in her biography, Lin has served as a consultant to a wide variety of organizations; her salient work has taken her to many different countries such as Brazil, Singapore, Thailand, Poland, and China among others, where she has collaborated with educators to bring about teacher education, curriculum, and school reform. She also has been the co-director and architect of a joint MA in Educational Leadership and Change between Teachers College and the National Institute of Education (NIE) in Singapore. I have seen firsthand Lin's multiple keynote addresses and her ability to be a champion of change in teacher education policy throughout the world. In her kindness, she even extended an invitation for me to participate on a project in Poland where the Consortium for Policy Research in Education (CPRE) of Teachers College partnered with Fundacja Dobrej Edukacji (Foundation for Quality Education) to start a Poland Graduate School of Education with Warsaw University. Her connections reach far and wide, and this in and of itself is a testament to her humility and strength in leadership. In rendering the most pressing issues of teacher education visible, she has chosen to remain (in) visible—out of the spotlight—with grace and poise. Her model of leadership has become one that I aspire to. She holds a sustained strength to carry on such endeavors, and her journey of mentorship, scholarship, and leadership is a critical case not just for Asian/American scholars but most importantly, for the education of all.

The powerful force and the humble strength of Dean and Professor A. Lin Goodwin is a critical case, a case that speaks back to the positions of power in the academy. In her case, she demonstrates how Asian/Americans can mentor, lead, and champion agendas in education policy, curriculum, and reform. In her long-standing commitment to social justice, I have had the immense honor and privilege to work, walk, and serve alongside her, knowing that the work of education is never easy, but it is one that must be brought to light.

Now, as we wrap up this book chapter, as Lin has transitioned to become Dean of the Faculty of Education at The University of Hong Kong (HKU), I graduated in May 2017 and started a new position as an assistant professor of literacy at North Carolina State University. We often still converse and collaborate on research projects and are thinking of new international global projects where we can further build teacher leaders in global contexts. Most importantly, as a professor, I will embody the spirit and mentorship of Lin—championing my students to be advocates for social justice and those that are often (in)visible. She has taught me what it means to fight for the marginalized, knowing that such a fight is a fight for all.

REFERENCES

Dyson, A. H., & Genishi, C. (2005). *On the case: Approaches to language and literacy research.* New York, NY: Teachers College Press.

Goodwin, A. L. (2002). Teacher preparation and the education of immigrant children. *Education and Urban Society, 34*(2), 156–172.

Goodwin, A. L. (2010a). Globalization and the preparation of quality teachers: Rethinking knowledge domains for teaching. *Teaching Education, 21*(1), 19–32.

Goodwin, A. L. (2010b). Curriculum as colonizer: (Asian) American education in the current context. *Teachers College Record, 112*(12), 3102–3138.

Goodwin, A. L. (2017). Who is in the classroom now? Teacher preparation and the education of immigrant children. *Educational Studies, 53*(5), 433–449.

Goodwin, A. L., & Chen, C. (2016). New knowledges for teacher educating? Perspectives from practicing teacher educators. In C. Kosnik, S. White, C. Beck, B. Marshall, A. L. Goodwin, & J. Murray (Eds.), *Building bridges: Rethinking literacy teacher education in a digital era* (pp. 149–162). Rotterdam: Sense Publishers.

Goodwin, A. L., & Kosnik, C. (2013). Quality teacher educators = quality teachers? Conceptualizing essential domains of knowledge for those who teach teachers. *Teacher Development, 17*(3), 334–346.

Goodwin, A. L., & Low, E. L. (2017). Educating all children in multicultural, multilingual Singapore: The quest for equity amidst diversity. In W. T. Pink & G. W. Noblit (Eds.), *Second international handbook of urban education* (pp. 213–234). New York, NY: Springer International Publishing.

Goodwin, A. L., Low, E. L., & Darling-Hammond, L. (2017). *Empowered educators in Singapore: How high-performing systems shape teaching quality.* San Francisco, CA: Jossey-Bass.

Goodwin, A. L., Smith, L., Souto-Manning, M., Cheruvu, R., Tan, M. Y., Reed, R., & Taveras, L. (2014). What should teacher educators know and be able to do? Perspectives from practicing teacher educators. *Journal of Teacher Education, 65*(4), 284–302.

Roegman, R., Pratt, S., Goodwin, A. L., & Akin, S. (2017). Curriculum, social justice, and inquiry in the field: Investigating retention in an urban teacher residency. *Action in Teacher Education, 39*(4), 432–452.

Shor, I. (2012). *Empowering education: Critical teaching for social change.* Chicago, IL: University Chicago Press.

CHAPTER TWO

Scholarship as Meditation

Lessons Calling Us to Theory and Action

TIMOTHY BOLIN, CHARLOTTE ACHIENG-EVENSEN
AND KEVIN STOCKBRIDGE

INTRODUCTION

As a tri-authored contribution, this chapter brings together, in reflexive consideration, the lived experiences gathered from our interactions with Dr. Suzanne SooHoo, the Jack H. and Paula A. Hassinger Chair in Education at Chapman University. As her current and former students, we draw together our collective stories of learning and co-learning. Throughout this text we will refer to Dr. SooHoo as Suzi, the name by which we have come to know her as our mentor. Our purpose is to explore the ways in which she has engaged authentically and dynamically in a systematic pattern of mentorship. As a mentor she intentionally facilitates learning which prepares her students to be both change agents and members of the academy.

We entered this task through many shared conversations about Suzi and her specific approaches to our individual academic journeys. Each of us had countless stories of the questions, ponderings, and challenges she had thrown our way. We knew that she practiced mentorship using methods that were uniquely tailored to the individual. Yet, we realized that there was a consistent, contemplative pattern to the ways in which Suzi posed questions, and challenged us to ponder. We began to reflect upon what this pattern was, each person keeping a journal. Finally, we came together in an elongated afternoon session where we thoroughly discussed each of our perspectives. We decided to voice and note key touchpoints in our socio-academic growth as influenced by Suzi by recording our conversation that afternoon. Following this session, we transcribed the recording and added it to the data of our collective journal notes. Next, we individually coded the transcripts and notes for emergent themes. We met again to find points of confluence. As a group, we then identified what we considered to be our shared areas of focus by means of finding those which consistently arose in our coding. We arrived at the following:

(1) humility, (2) strength and resilience, and (3) hope.

Our chapter conceptualizes Suzi's mentorship as a patterned, meditative practice in which she calls us to query, thought, and action. She poses "why" questions and encourages us to wrestle with the consequential answers. From these possibilities, she challenges us to identify and move towards action. This pattern is both generative and iterative. There is a meditative flow to it. Suzi engages us through questioning. We, in turn, interact with her by thinking together through the query. Our collective response then leads to purposeful action. The meditation of learning births its active practice. Our reflections below are the fruit of our scholarly meditation on the example of Suzi.

WHY A TRIALOGUE?

Trialogue, the method used to create this chapter, is inspired by a phrase that Suzi often asks at the beginning of her classes: What could we know together that could not be known alone? Choosing to write our chapter as a trialogue intentionally reflects the relational ethic we have learned from our mentor. A trialogue, in the most basic sense, is an interchange between three different people or groups for the sake of arriving at fuller understanding of a single topic (Postma, Lauche, & Stappers, 2009). It has been used as a technique in the fields of philosophy, religion, and politics (Ingram, 2011; Kardasheva, 2012; Numrich, 2011; Schell, 2000). It complicates singular discourses and definitions through engaging multiple perspectives.

Historically, trialogues have been employed in critical circles to facilitate the convergence of dissimilar ideas. As such, they have shown the potential to lead to change or transformation (Numrich, 2011; Schell, 2000). Ingram (2011) explains that the interchange of multiple perspectives has the power to reveal the limitations of any one particular ideology. He also explains that trialogues are able to foster the development of new ideas through the exploration of both the intersections and omissions of schools of thought. Consequently, the benefit of trialogue is its potential to expand the knowledge of all involved by challenging monologic thinking. For this reason, we used trialogue to gain a greater understanding of the internal growth that has been facilitated by our experiences under the tutelage of a dynamic teacher-mentor. While we all had experiences with Suzi as our mentor, a fuller understanding of her being in the world and academy could only come through a collective dialog.

Dialog is more than the sounding of many voices, it also includes engaged silence. In advancing an alternate perspective of trialogues, Schell (2000) recommends approaching dialog with a deep sense of empathy. Rather than simply trying to understand the *content* of what the other is saying, one should strive to understand the *context*. One should attend to the relationship between the self and other. It is in the silences of conversation that listening occurs and connections are made. Schell (2000) acknowledges the complexities of empathetic listening. In some cases silence of response may be better than engaging; this is especially true when our interlocutor has no intent to seek mutuality in dialog. At other times, silence can honor the wisdom of the other, opening space for understanding to develop.

We agree with Richardson, Parr, and Campbell (2008) that "learning is something that is experienced through reflective and collaborative practice—it is a journey rather than something that is acquired as a product or a destination" (p. 281). Thus in our conversations regarding Suzi as a mentor, the three of us worked to create a context for mutuality in understanding the nature of her work with us. This required that we institute a cadence for listening to each other, digesting what we heard, and responding in an appropriate manner. This pattern of listening, digesting, and relevant response was not new to us. Suzi, herself, continuously modeled this rhythm in our interactions with her. We sought to inhabit her example in our own conversations and writing. Using trialogue as a methodology aided our written articulation of her process.

As three voices collaborating in a mutual task, we wanted to maintain our singular voices while simultaneously presenting a cohesive and coherent perspective on the culturally responsive methodology that Suzi utilizes in her work with students. As such, we turned to trialogues as an inclusive mode of communication. In this text, we have incorporated reflections, memories, and quotes from each of us about our beloved mentor that came from our research conversation. We have cited them as such. While we acknowledge that the written word cannot capture the rich, meaning-filled rhythms, syncopated undertones, and weighty unexpressed subtexts of conversation, we do attempt to weave together our reflections along the same vein as the conversations we enact regarding Suzi.

Humility (*Kevin Stockbridge*)

Meditation: " *Where are you? Where is Kevin in this research?" (Suzi SooHoo after discussing original plans for scholarship)*

The process of mentoring might be likened to an extended conversation between two parties. Every academic mentor will approach such a conversation in a different way. For Suzi, mentorship is clearly practiced in the spirit of critical pedagogy. It is an ever-developing interpersonal dialog between her and the students in her care. She is intentional in the ways she facilitates the development of critical scholars. Often, we find that a simple conversation is transformed into rich dialog when Suzi invites us to question our worldview. She does so by posing unexpected questions like the ones which open this section. Suzi does not impose solutions. Rather, she invites others to share their wisdom with her in a thoughtful exchange. Her practice recalls Paulo Freire's (2000) insistence that:

Dialog cannot exist without humility. The naming of the world, through which people constantly re-create that world, cannot be an act of arrogance. Dialog, as the encounter of those addressed to the common task of learning and acting, is broken if the parties (or one of them) lack humility. (p. 90)

By honoring the *other* through resisting the foisting of her own ideas upon her students, Suzi's humility ensures that mentorship has the potential to be the kind of encounter Freire envisions.

Engaging in our reflective conversation about Suzi, we clearly identified humility as a core characteristic of both her personhood and her work. We see in her the same zeal voiced by Freire (1998) in the *Pedagogy of Freedom: Ethics, Democracy, and Civic Courage*, "How can I be an educator if I do not develop in myself a caring and loving attitude toward the student, which is indispensable on the part of one who is committed to teaching and the education process itself?" (p. 65). This student-centered attitude is a hallmark of her presence in the university. Tim's words brought light to this attribute of our mentor:

I think it is interesting that, though she is ridiculously productive, she's always available. I don't think I ever see her not take the time to sit with someone. When she's sitting with me, she's one hundred percent there with me. ... Maybe present would be one of the words connected to the idea of being productive. Humble was the first word that I thought of. Yeah. Humble. Present. (Bolin, research conversation, May 18, 2016).

Suzi's willing presence and availability to her students is itself a lesson for us. It models humility as an ethical priority in our future work as scholars and teachers.

As her mentees, we began to ask ourselves: *What is this humble presence which comes to mind when we think of Suzi and her work with us?* When describing the dialog of learning, Freire (1998) tells us that humility means "being open to the word of the other, to the gesture of the other, to the differences of the other" (p. 107). It is a virtue that counteracts the dominance of authoritarian approaches to life and work. It is receptive and equitable. Suzi writes that the temptation to take dominating positions in reaction to injustice "is antithetical to my Taoist upbringing. The *other* in me sees the *me* in others. The message of worthiness and a respect for the wide spectrum of humanity must be translated in respectful ways so I continually seek these translations between rage and respect" (SooHoo, 2015a, p. 227). Her dedication to the wisdom of her heritage resists the hegemony of the Western academy. In deconstructing stereotypes of the passive Asian woman in the academy, she intentionally works in ways that resist the erasure of cultural epistemology and ontology that comes through the adoption of oppressive Western patterns of domination. We have all watched her in meetings and conferences as she complicates conversations by insisting on a fuller understanding of the power and ethical rigor of humility. So too, in her pedagogy, she has made it a practice to engage and model this humble, other-centered approach in ways that draw her students into relationships of learning and possibility.

Sometimes she does this with words but, more often, she employs another tactic. Charlotte spoke to this:

> You know what's interesting? When you talk about humility, I think about the word "silence" and having early conversations with Suzi SooHoo about silence. The conversations revolved around privileging of silence so that silence wasn't a lack, nor silence a weakness, nor silence a vulnerability. But silence is a generative place. Silence is a place that is life giving. Silence is the birthplace of action. (Achieng-Evensen, research conversation, May 18, 2016)

One cannot understand the meaning of "humility" without understanding what it means to be silent and the profound power that this unvoiced language can have in the world. Speaking of her upbringing Suzi writes, "As a young child I learned to bridge the gap between my Chinese-speaking grandmother and me, her English-speaking grand-daughter. Through silence, I sent messages, knowing words did not tell it all, that meaning is deeper with silence" (SooHoo, 2015a, p. 226). From her youth, Suzi learned to translate the depth of lived experience through the powerful act of silence. It was a humble act of being in the world, valid and potent.

Freire (1998) says that, in the midst of conflict and oppression, silence may be one of the greatest actions we can take: "What humility asks of me when I cannot appropriately react to a given offense is to face it with dignity. The dignity of my silence, of my look. They will translate whatever protest is possible at the moment" (p. 109). Silence is an essential part of the language of humility. Silence is Suzi's invitation, not to fill the world with endless talk, but to actively engage with others by listening. Early in my graduate career, I had forgotten the importance of engaging with respect and stopped listening to the words of my mentor. It is then that I learned that silence is a humble way that Suzi indicates that she has been met with disrespect. Her loving silence did not come as punishment but as a profound invitation for me to embrace humility. Humble silence does not demand a self-focused response of "I'm sorry," as much as the acknowledgment of the dignity of the other before us.

Suzi has shown all of us how silence can be a humble remedy to the violence of dominating voices. "Humility means yielding and honoring other possible ways of knowing while honoring at the same time not knowing thus, giving way to streams of certainty, for waves of ambiguity" (SooHoo, 2013, p. 201). She has cultivated in her mentees this space of silence, which opens us to new ways of knowing and being welcoming to what is yet to be realized. I noted:

I believe that this virtue that Suzi has inherited from her own culture, and which has informed her scholarship in the academy, is going to continue through us as scholars. Because Suzi invites us to come with her, and in some way, we find attunement with this virtue ... I think what we are starting to discover is the nature of Suzi's humility, the nature of smallness. I dare say, we are moving into an understanding of the silence that speaks (Stockbridge, research conversation, May 18, 2016).

STRENGTH AND RESILIENCE (*CHARLOTTE ACHIENG-EVENSEN*)

Meditation: "I know who you were, but who are you now dear one?" (Suzi SooHoo, after I came back from the research field)

As a child, I grew up hearing the Swahili proverb, "jaribu, uone," *try and you will see* ("Ambition," n.d., 408). If I wanted to go outside and play in the equatorial rain, "jaribu uone." If I declared a new ambition for life, it was a given that those words would follow the cascade of advice that I may or may not have sought. Often, I wondered what my Uncles meant as they spoke these words to me. Were they declaring a preemptive challenge for my upcoming mal-intentioned actions? Or, were they encouraging me to frontier new circumstances and navigate new situations? Most likely, they intended to do both. There were times when I sought to assert myself against wise counsel and my Uncles were warning me of natural consequences. And then, the times when they were pushing me to overcome my limitations. More than an epithet or harbinger, *jaribu uone* became a reassuring call to action from these Uncles who were my first mentors. It became a way to position myself within the strength of past experiences and the resilience for future action.

Jaribu uone resurfaced as my call to sanity in the nebulous and isolating world of doctoral studies. As my scholarly mentor, Suzi modeled genuine and meaningful academic risk-taking. I watched her transparency as she tried to engage her community of scholars into social justice action. I followed her as she traveled over international waters to forge culturally responsive relationships with an indigenous community of learners in Aotearoa New Zealand. I sat beside her as she committed to both local and national action all the while compelling her students into their own social responsibilities. In these ways I discovered Suzi's strength, her will in purposefully forging forward toward a goal despite present and impending obstacles, to be evident in how she inhabits her relationships. As Kevin, Tim, and I reflected together in conversation, I observed:

It is important, the way that she [Suzi] builds a relational community. There are multiple aspects. There's definitely a "bringing together" to learn. And, she facilitates this learning in a very systematic way. She's got a way of allowing an individual to come to a place where she is learning. And she connects, at least for myself—us to other places where that authentic scholarship can be extended (Achieng-Evensen, research conversation, May 18, 2016).

Suzi's strength is worked out in her ability to create open spaces for learning, academic contribution and professional growth. Scholarship, for her, is embodied in her students and their success. Kevin, our third author notes, "It is that gentle work of teasing out, that's why it takes the kind of patience that I think, Suzi has … Sometimes she sees the right time to strike and she strikes when the iron is hot, and really pushes you, with certain moments. Other times, it's a gentle kind of teasing" (Stockbridge, research conversation, May 18, 2016).

As intentional as Suzi's work is, it does require a measure of openness and therefore, resilience. As a mentor who invites students into deep processes of thought and reflexivity, Suzi displays a great deal of vulnerability. Her mentorship is not curtailed by limiting fears—What if a student cannot hear or accept the layered questions she consistently asks? What if her intentions for one's academic growth is misunderstood? Instead of focusing her work of facilitation and guidance on the possibilities of pushback, Suzi tailors her mentorship to suit the individual. In this way, she seems to view mentoring as a practice of scholarship. For Suzi, *jaribu uone* is an ongoing mode of action. Our first author states, "I like observing how Suzi embodies a lot about what she talks about" (Bolin, research conversation, May 18, 2018). He recognized the integrated and fully embodied selfhood that Suzi brings to her work with us. Tim continues, "Looking back at her actions on a day-to-day basis, in the classroom, and how she interacts with students, and how she overcomes problems, she always seems to kind of apply that same kind of patience, the same kind of humility with her daily life as well" (Bolin, research conversation, May 18, 2016).

For Tim, Suzi's discourse and daily actions are in alignment. She enacts what she theorizes. This is strength and coupled with her years as an educator, administrator, and scholar, this is an active, lived example of resilience. Despite the impediments of life and the machinations of scholarship within the academy, Suzi, for me, has taken up the role of Eldership as laid down by my Uncles during my formative years. And, she remains a true scholar-practitioner devoted to mentoring engaged students. She observes both her strength and resilience when she states:

> As an Asian American woman, I continually search to locate myself between the lost and found spaces of socio-cultural identity. Who am I? Am I the quiet, subservient, dutiful daughter who never speaks or make waves? Or am I the industrious, androgynous worker—conscientious, efficient, and loyal? Perhaps I am the exotic seductress who charms those around her? Or maybe I am the cunning and powerful dragon lady? Or is it feasible that I might be the woman warrior, a crusader for social justice who combats oppressive power structures to liberate the oppressed? With unbound feet and social consciousness, she carves out a path for a new social order that brings voice to the people. (SooHoo, 2015a, p. 243)

Hope (*Timothy Bolin*)

Meditation: So What Are You Going to Do About It?

> *You told me to go out to the schoolyard and make friends*
> *Kids teased me about my glasses and locked me in the dark bathroom*
> *When they let me out, my face and my pants were wet.*
> *And my tormentors said, "So What Are You Going to Do About It?"*
> *You told me to be good, follow the rules and never speak unless called on*
> *I always raised my hand and waited my turn*
> *But it was the outspoken, articulate, risk-taking kid that became valedictorian.*
> *And the teacher said, "So What Are You Going to Do About It?"*
> *You said work hard and go to every practice*
> *I dribbled that ball until my fingers were numb*
> *But you recruited a new player, someone taller and faster.*
> *And the coach said, "So What Are You Going to Do About It?"*
> *They said they wanted me to attend their college*
> *They needed diversity on their campus*
> *But they didn't tell me I would be lonely and have no homeboys to kick it with.*
> *And college admissions said, "So What Are You Going to Do About It?"*
> *Find a girl, get married, have a baby*
> *It happened so fast*
> *Never got a chance to figure out if life would be better with Joe.*
> *And my parents said, "So What Are You Going to Do About It?"*
> *Make money, live in the suburbs, away from those "others"*
> *I don't know who I am anymore or where I came from.*
> *And society said, "So What Are You Going to Do About It?" (SooHoo, 2004)*

Suzi's poem inspires hope by reminding us that if we act together we can change the world. The theme of hope was a central aspect of our collective discussion and is an essential characteristic of Suzi's mentorship. She uses hope to highlight the possibility of change by facilitating mentor/mentee relationships that blossom into second-generation mentor relationships. I understand second-generation mentorship to be defined by relationships with my peers that represent extensions of Suzi's ethical, caring mentorship style.

Paulo Freire's (1998) philosophy regarding hope mirrors aspects of her mentorship style. Charlotte Sexton described hope as central to Freirean philosophy, "Hope is an ontological need ... Hopelessness is but hope that has lost its bearings, and become a distortion of that ontological need" (Freire 2004 as cited in Sexton, 2015, p. 319). As John Elias (1976) explained, Freire derived hope from the human relationship where a person derives purpose and meaning from collaboration with others. This is similar to Martin Buber's (1970) discussion of *being*, where humanity is defined in a deeply respectful relationship with the *other*.

Suzi's other-centered mentorship style generates a space for equitable relationships. As Moacir Gadotti (1994) explains, the ideal relationship should be "horizontal ... fed by love, humility, hope, faith, and confidence" (p. xv). While traditional mentorship relationships may preserve the institutional, administrative, or experiential power of the mentor over the mentee, Suzi's radically democratic power-sharing mentorship model opens the space for the mentee to grow. As Charlotte observed in our trilogue of Suzi's mentorship style, "There's definitely a coming together to learn ... she's got this stealth way of allowing an individual to come to a place where she is learning." Further, this allows for the development of second-generation mentorships to flourish, something I experienced with my colleagues Charlotte and Kevin who have been counselors, advisors, and cheerleaders as they have helped me through the ups and downs of navigating academia.

Suzi's mentorship is an extension of generating hope. She shows us the possibility of seeing things anew, of imagining new futures in all that we do as academics, activists, and community workers. Hope is integrally related to change and newness because it is relationally created between people. Therefore it is an ongoing process. As Lankshear (1993) explains, humans are "necessarily uncompleted beings since their humanity consists not in a finite finished state, but in (ongoing) engagement" (Lankshear, 1993, p. 97). In this vein, Kevin described Suzi's mentorship approach as preserving *unfinishedness*:

> That's how relationships can be, instead of just being good or broken, they are these unfinished things with unfinished people. In our movements of unfinishedness, we go through seasons of closeness and farness. As difficult as that may be, she's able to see things in that way ... I believe because she is really given to this idea of unfinishedness

and there being possibility, so she's able to mentor us in this way. (Stockbridge, research conversation, May 18, 2016)

In unfinishedness, we realize that we were different in the past and "may become different in the future" (Lankshear, 1993, p. 97).

Hope is the realization of agency by means of uncovering the human capacity to act upon the present in communion with the other. Suzi's mentorship style inspires her former mentees to extend hope and equitable mentorship to a new generation. She has the ability to pass on this sense of living hope. As I observed:

I think Suzi really radiates a level of hope. Hope-inspiring maybe, for myself, in the sense that sitting with her, even whether we're talking research or just talking in general, I'm left with this little bit of levity, a little bit lighter, because there's this hope

… I think maybe a part of who Suzi is. (Bolin, research conversation, May 18, 2016)

In collaboration with my fellow mentees I endeavor to propel the possibility of a new future with an intentional focus on ethical relationships with my colleagues, friends, and family.

CLOSING

Drawing this conversation to a close, we question what we have learned and what we have offered to you, our reader. We shared with you this meditation on the work of a scholar who has invited us to embrace the fruitfulness of ambiguity. Tim's words reveal the ways in which she has taught us lessons about holding the third space between stillness and action. He says that such an epistemology is about:

Reflecting and being patient, letting knowledge come to you, letting the relationships that need to be there come to you, rather than trying to push things to happen. But in the same sense, not being overly passive. You are actively engaging in where you need to be, what needs to happen, who should be present, while not being too quick to press yourself into a situation (Bolin, research conversation, May 18, 2016).

In the spirit of our mentor, we tried to remain in this third space of ambiguity. While we can share the knowledge that has come to us in this process, we do so *certain* that this process of discovery and revelation is partial and unfinished.

As we completed the construction and writing of this chapter, our beloved Dr. Suzanne SooHoo was traveling and teaching in China where she was named Honorary Director of the Center for Critical Pedagogy Research at Northeast Normal University in Changchun. We knew that, across the globe in the land of her ancestors, Suzi was sharing the lessons of a life dedicated to a more equitable world. We also knew that our mentor was on a trip that would challenge and enlighten her in ways that she has done for us. In a reflection on her experiences in China, Suzi sent a text stating: "To move from known to unknown is always a revolutionary, rather than merely cognitive, function" (SooHoo, personal communication, June 22, 2016). Such is the wisdom of a woman who encourages us to push beyond the assumptions of the Western academy into revolutionary, unknown possibilities. In this journey, we are her companions. As she reminds us: "Our consciousness of our unfinishedness and our vulnerability as human beings move us toward one another, breeding co-learning and co-creation" (SooHoo, 2015b, p. 253). So we walk together into the murky waters of the unknown, acknowledging that in taking a stance of humility, we enter into authentic strength enlivened by hope with this wonderful scholar, Dr. Suzanne SooHoo.

REFERENCES

Ambition. (n.d.). *Swahili Proverbs: Methali za Kiswahili*. Retrieved from http://swahiliproverbs.afrst.illinois.edu/ambition.html

Buber, M. (1970). *I and thou*. New York, NY: Charles Scribner's Sons.

Elias, J. L. (1976). *Conscientization and deschooling: Freire's and Illich's proposals for reshaping society*. Philadelphia, PA: Westminster Press.

Freire, P. (1998). *Pedagogy of freedom: Ethics, democracy, and civic courage*. Lanham, MD: Rowman & Littlefield Publishers.

Freire, P. (2000). *Pedagogy of the oppressed*. New York, NY: Continuum.

Gadotti, M. (1994). *Reading Paulo Freire: His life and work*. Albany, NY: State University of New York Press.

Ingram, P. O. (2011). Buddhist-Christian-science dialogue at the boundaries. *Buddhist- Christian Studies, 31*, 165–174.

Kardasheva, R. (2012). Trialogues in the EU legislature (D. o. E. a. I. Studies, Trans.). London: King's College.

Lankshear, C. (1993). Functional literacy from a freirean point of view. In P. McLaren & P. Leonard (Eds.), *Paulo Freire: A critical encounter* (pp. 90–118). New York, NY: Routledge.

Numrich, P. D. (2011). From epistemology to ethics. *Buddhist-Christian Studies, 31*, 161–163.

Postma, C., Lauche, K., & Stappers, P. J. (2009). *Trialogues: A framework for bridging the gap between people research and design*. Paper presented at the Proceedings of the 4th International Conference on Designing Pleasurable Products and Interfaces, Compiegne.

Richardson, C., Parr, M., & Campbell, T. (2008). Solitary dissonance and collaborative consonance: Trialogue as a reflective practice that resonates. *Reflective Practice, 9*(3), 281–291.

Schell, E. E. (2000). Tight spaces in and out of the parlor: Negotiation and the politics of difference. *JAC, 20*(4), 919–931.

Sexton, C. (2015). On the streets with Paulo Freire and Simone Weil, talking with Gamilaraay students about Helio Oiticica. In M. A. Peters & T. Besley (Eds.), *Paulo Freire: The global legacy* (pp. 319–333). New York, NY: Peter Lang.

SooHoo, S. (2004). We change the world by doing nothing. *Teacher Education Quarterly*, *31*(1), 199–211.

SooHoo, S. (2013). Humility within culturally responsive methodologies. In M. Berryman, S. SooHoo, & A. Nevin (Eds.), *Culturally responsive methodologies* (pp. 199–220). Bingly: Emerald.

SooHoo, S. (2015a). Humility within critical pedagogy. In B. J. Porfilio & D. R. Ford (Eds.), *Leaders in critical pedagogy* (pp. 225–234). Rotterdam: Sense Publishers.

SooHoo, S. (2015b). School as a place of becoming and belonging: Starting with one child to whole school reform. In M. Berryman, A. Nevin, S. SooHoo, & T. Ford. (Eds.), *Relational and responsive inclusion: Contexts for becoming and belonging* (pp. 243–258). New York, NY: Peter Lang.

CHAPTER THREE

Kioh Kim

No Failure Is Too Great to Overcome

BRIAN C. KIM

My father, Dr. Kioh Kim, never imagined that he would become an endowed professor of Instructional Technology in the United States. He grew up in a small village in South Korea shortly after it had been ravaged and devastated by the Korean War, where the idea of living in America or pursing higher education was not even a remote possibility. He did not learn the value of education as both his parents and his four older siblings never advanced past high school. As a child, his family of seven lived in a small one-bedroom hut with no electricity until he was five years old. From such humble beginnings, my father forged a successful career in education. However, his life was not always straightforward, and his accomplishments are the result of his failures. To develop the drive and the charisma that have enabled his achievements, he first needed to sink to a point where all hope seemed to be lost. His educational philosophies and pedagogical approaches have developed from these difficult experiences in his early life. His background has informed his firm belief that any student, regardless of background or circumstance, has the ability and capacity to learn if given the right opportunities.

Born on March 13, 1966 to a mailman and a housewife, my father was the fifth of six children. Raised in the countryside far from any major city, he compensated for a childhood lacking in material entertainment by finding his fun in nature. In the winter, he would skate on wood slats on frozen ponds, and when the weather improved, he would rummage through the forest and make slingshots out of wood to use against his friends. He was an innocent, kind, and curious boy who was fascinated by the world and its technological advancements. In fact, one of his favorite activities as a child was chasing the occasional bus that passed through town and catching a ride on the back for miles and relishing the smell of exhaust. However, nothing compared to my father's love of sports. He was the best athlete in his town. No one in his town, Shindoan, could outrun him or strike a soccer ball quite like him. His dream was to become a professional soccer player and one day represent his country in the World Cup. He played soccer with his friends for hours on end, frequently well into the night, by only the light of the moon.

My father's town was limited to an elementary and middle school, so when it came time for him to attend high school, a decision had to be made. The closest high school was located approximately two hours away by bus, in Daejeon, a large city in central South Korea. Only two of his older sisters had attended high school, but because my father was the sole son in the family, his parents decided that he should have the opportunity to do so. South Korea has a traditional, androgenic culture, and especially in the late 20th century, parents went to great lengths to ensure a promising future for their sons. Since the commute was long, my father left home and moved into the city to stay in a *hasukjib*, a boarding house where students can rent a room and receive prepared meals. His parents, financially strained from a single paycheck, sacrificed a great deal so that my father could attend high school. He was one of a handful of students from his village to pursue further education in the city. His entire family had high hopes that he would do well and possibly go on to graduate from college, an accomplishment never achieved in his family. With optimism and a sense of confidence, my father believed that he could be successful, but nothing from his experiences in a small village could have prepared him for what came next.

Sitting on the bus, waving to his parents and the rest of the town as their silhouettes narrowed to emptiness, my father came face-to-face with reality: he was all alone. It was his first time leaving his family as he made his way into the city. In a small village, everyone was his neighbor, family, or friend. He always personally knew the people with whom he interacted, and at the end of day, he always returned to the safety of his home. However, as the bus moved further away from everything he had ever known, my father could not help but feel scared. In fact, he describes his first night in the *hasukjib* as his most frightening memory. Lying in bed by himself, he had never felt such isolation, as he had always slept in the same bedroom with the rest of his family. He reached out his hand in the complete darkness, trying to feel for his parents or siblings, but only air slipped through his fingers. Memories of his home flooded his thoughts, and he suddenly started to cry. The urge to see his family was so strong that first night, that in the middle of the night, he ran all the way to the bus station, tears streaming down his face, to catch the last bus to his village. He arrived at his house around 3 AM as his family was sleeping, but nothing stopped him from running into his mother's arms as sleep finally consumed him.

My father has very few regrets in life, but his biggest stems from his high school years. He had always been an excellent student, capable of mastering the information taught by his teachers. He was smart and therefore the coursework in his new high school was not a problem. However, he was immediately considered an outsider by his peers, as they were all friends who had grown up together in the city. My father was the only student in his grade to transfer from a village, and had to endure stereotypes of being inferior, poor, and irrelevant. Naturally, he had no friends, and became the target of bullying from day one. He had to tolerate constantly getting punched, slapped, and verbally abused in school. As was common in those times, kids would bully him in the classroom in front of the teacher, who would turn a blind eye or make an inconsequential remark in response to the abuse. My father never hit anyone back for fear of the ramifications and because he had never hit anyone before. There were many times when he wanted to give up and return to his village, but the thought of disappointing his family by not finishing high school motivated him to continue.

There was a group of about ten boys who were especially mean to my father. They would track him down outside of school and make his life miserable, almost to the point where he was afraid to leave his *hasukjib*. One day, during the weekend, my father was riding the bus by himself to another part of town, when the group of boys boarded. They immediately spotted him and made their way slowly to the back of the bus where he was sitting. My father tried to keep to himself and stare out the window, but suddenly, a huge right fist smashed into his face. Before he knew it, the boys threw my father into the aisle and began pummeling him with punches and kicks. None of the other passengers did anything, but the bus driver, noticing the ruckus, stopped the bus and made his way to the back. Much to the dismay of my father, the driver yelled at them to take the fight outside. The bus had stopped near the side of a large forested hill, so the group of ten boys forced my father out and told him to walk up the slope, away from pedestrians. He could have easily outrun all of them, and the thought of escape crossed his mind, but fear trickled throughout his body, freezing his muscles. At the top of the hill, the boys gathered in a circle around my father, and one member stepped out and told him to never mess with them again and to leave them alone. Suddenly, out of nowhere, a football sized rock smashed into my father's head, leaving him immediately unconscious.

When he regained consciousness, it was completely dark, and he could feel a huge laceration on his head that was covered with dry blood. He began to cry and longed for the safety of his mother's arms. However, gradually, the tears subsided, and thoughts of vengeance entered his conscience. He decided on that hill, painted in his own blood, that he would never allow himself to experience such humiliation ever again. No longer was he going to portray weakness and cower in the presence of bullies. Instead, he was going to take the fight directly to them.

From that point on, my father became a completely different person. In retrospect, even he cannot believe the transformation that occurred. In order to protect himself, he became obsessed with learning martial arts. He started to skip school in order to attend taekwondo classes, and instead of textbooks, he began carrying martial arts books in his backpack. My father also knew that he could not challenge a group of ten high school boys by himself, so in what feels almost like a movie plot, he began to recruit his own mischievous gang. He would assert his dominance over other boys by fighting them, and winning, and gradually his group began to grow. As a group, my father and his new friends began to drink excessively and smoke cigarettes.

During this dark time in my father's life, he lost completely the sense of who he was as a person, a son, and a student. Whereas previously, he would visit his family in his village once or twice a month, he stopped going altogether. Furthermore, because my father had missed so many classes, he was expelled from his high school. Although his life was spiraling downward in a hurry, none of this mattered to my father. He continued to fight others constantly, and as he now describes, nothing scared him. He would blindly walk across interstates and highways because he was not afraid of getting hit by a car. He would taunt and insult police officers right to their face because he was not afraid of law enforcement.

I believe all people have a defining moment in their lives that changes everything. It becomes the foundation for their future endeavors and dreams, and serves as a source of inspiration for their actions. It is something that is never forgotten. For some, it may be meeting their hero or traveling to a foreign country, but for my father, it was enduring a near death experience, not of himself, but of someone he loved.

On a rare occasion, my father had been visiting his family during the holidays for several days. When it came time to return to the city, his mother planned to go with him. She wanted to buy him food, and help him settle down before school started again; little did she know that my father had already been expelled by that point. My father had no intentions of going into the city with his mother, and instead, had plans to meet his friends later that night. So, without hesitation, my father went into the city by himself, assuming his mother would come later if so inclined.

After a night of shenanigans, drinking, and fighting, my father rolled out of a taxi heavily intoxicated onto the front door of his *hasukjib*. He was stumbling into his room when the host found him and told him to quickly go to the nearby hospital for something terrible had happened to his mother. My father was dazed and disoriented, but somehow made his way over to the hospital. It was there that he learned his mother had been hit by a large truck as she was crossing an intersection in the city by herself. He made his way into the hospital room where his father was sitting by his mother's side, but as soon as he entered, he passed out at the foot of the bed as the alcohol had finally consumed his body.

When my father woke up the next day, he saw something that he would remember for the rest of his life; the look on his father's face. Without saying a word, his father walked out of the room, and my father was left alone with the unconscious body of his mother. Kneeling beside her bed, he broke down in tears because he knew the accident was completely his fault. If only he had waited and traveled into the city together with his mother, then she never would have gotten into the accident. My father did not know if his mother was going to survive or die, it was completely out of his control. In that moment, his façade of a careless and naïve teenager washed away, and he became the sensitive, loving son who rushed back home in the middle of the night because he missed his family. Much like the revelation that occurred at the top of a hill, my father realized that he could no longer live his life on the current track: it could only lead to tragedy and death. He had originally thought his actions could only affect himself, but staring at his comatose mother proved otherwise. I believe this is where my father's educational philosophy has its origins. He decided he could no longer continue his previous lifestyle, and instead, turned to the one investment that could improve his life: education. He had always been a good student when determined to do well, but after a long time away from formal education, he knew the path would be difficult. Nevertheless, he started to believe that he, a high school drop-out who had never accomplished anything but drinking and fighting, could learn. This is a tenet that my father has embodied during his educational training, and one that he instills in his students and his children.

Under law, my father could not return to high school after being expelled, so he decided to take the General Education Development (GED) exam. This test is extremely difficult in South Korea and it is offered only twice a year. In addition, his score on the test was the sole determinant of whether he could attend college. My father decided to take six months and enroll in an institute that specifically tutored students for the GED exam. When he told his family of his plans, however, no one believed him, and frankly, they were right not to. Who would believe that such a kid as him could attend college? It was silly, so instead, his family tried to persuade him to enroll in a technical institute and learn a skilled trade. It was a reasonable suggestion, but my father absolutely resented the idea. He believed in himself, and that was sufficient. For six months, my father studied from sunrise to well beyond 2 AM for the GED exam. He had to commute two hours, round-trip, by bus from his home to attend the institute—time which he spent memorizing thousands of English vocabulary words. He describes it as one of the toughest years of his life, and there were many moments when his concentration and determination started to fade. However, through unrelenting determination, he received an excellent score on the exam and was admitted to Chungnam National University, a prestigious university located in Daejeon, South Korea. In addition, his mother recovered from her coma during this time.

Before entering college, my father served in the Korean military for six months, a mandatory duty for all Korean males. In college, my father majored in English Literature and met my mother in his freshman year. It was a rewarding time for him as he was able to shed his high school experiences and create a new identity for himself. Without his past exposed to shadow him, he was able to comfortably pursue his passions and interests. My father ultimately graduated with a Bachelor of Arts (B.A.) in English Language and Literature in 1992 becoming the first in his family to achieve this distinction.

My father initially had no plans to pursue a doctorate in the United States. After college, he got a job teaching English to K–12 students at a private academy in Daejeon for two years. It was this experience that prompted his interest in education, as he found himself deeply invested in and excited for his students. In order to become a more effective teacher, he returned to Chungnam National University and obtained his Master of Arts (M.A.) degree in English Education in 1996. Then, upon the recommendation of the English Department and his major professors, he got a job as the coordinator of the Office of International Programs at Chungnam National University. In this role, he was responsible for managing and developing sister relationships between Chungnam National University and universities in foreign countries including Australia, China, Japan, Taiwan, Thailand, and the United States. He had the opportunity to meet several individuals associated with these foreign universities and learn about their culture and educational theories. Unknown to him at the time, these contacts would form the foundation of his decision to ultimately leave South Korea and pursue a professional career in the United States.

In addition to his position at Chungnam National University, my father continued to explore his passion for teaching as an adjunct instructor at Daedok College, a junior college also located in Daejeon. Many of his students had performed poorly in high school and on the college entrance exam, requiring them to attend a two-year university rather than the traditional four-year track. However, my father loved this opportunity because he saw his reflection in many of his students. They had little interest in listening to the teacher or staying motivated, which my father could relate to as his time had been consumed thinking about martial arts during class and skipping school during his high school days. He believed he could connect with his students, and in return, they would respect and listen to him. During this time, my father experimented with several different educational styles and instructional strategies in order to maximize engagement and ensure that no student fell behind. He found that group activities were very effective, and instead of giving constant oral lectures, he emphasized the need for students to teach one another. These are teaching styles he continues to use in his classroom today, more than 20 years later.

In 2000, my father was 34 years old and had two kids: a five-year-old son and a three-year-old daughter. He had a stable job, and his career was promising as international programs within Chungnam National University were growing at a rapid rate. In addition, he was honoring his Korean cultural duties as the eldest and only son in the family by providing for and taking care of his parents, who were living with him and his family at the time. As both my father and my mother had working careers, it was my grandparents who raised my sister and me. In all senses of the word, my father was happy, but he could not shake this nagging idea that had lingered in his head for several years: the opportunity to study in the United States.

None of my father's current success would have been possible without Professor Harriet Swedlund. As the coordinator of international programs, my father was constantly exposed to opportunities abroad, and he could not help but imagine how his life might change if he enrolled in a program. However, he believed he would be neglecting his duties as a son if he left his parents, a reality that he could not accept. At the time, Chungnam National University had a strong relationship with South Dakota State University, in which Professor Swedlund, the director of international programs, was heavily involved. My father knew her well, and every year, when she came to visit South Korea, she urged my father to consider studying in the United States. She saw potential and drive in my father, and realized he had the capability to be successful in America. For several years, my father politely declined, but she never gave up trying to persuade him otherwise. Finally, in 2000, my father made the difficult decision to move to the United States. However, he promised his parents that this was not permanent and once he finished his doctorate degree, he would return to South Korea. So, at an age when most of his peers were reaching the peak of their careers, my father uprooted his family of four and moved to Brookings, South Dakota.

At South Dakota State University, my father graduated with a Master of Education (M.Ed.) in Curriculum and Instruction with a concentration in English as a Second Language in 2001. We then moved to Laramie, Wyoming, home of the University of Wyoming, where my father ultimately earned his Ph.D. in Instructional Technology in 2005.

Those five years when my father was a graduate student at South Dakota State University and the University of Wyoming were incredibly difficult as he had to overcome many obstacles. Because my father had immigrated at such a late age, and English was not his first language, the language barrier was extremely stressful. In fact, his first foray into learning English was when he attended the GED institute in his late teens. While he used basic and conversational English in Korea to communicate with foreign colleagues, my father had to suddenly take classes and write papers all in English. Compared to his other doctoral classmates, he was spending significantly more time finishing assignments. I clearly remember my father going into the office for several hours after dinner every day because he had to preview tomorrow's information or else he would struggle to follow along in class. It was exhausting, but necessary, and gradually my father's English improved and he found it easier to be a student. In addition, because we always lived in small towns where a Korean community was almost non-existent, my father had to quickly learn English in order to survive outside of the classroom.

My father also experienced a financial barrier as he tried to provide for his family on a graduate student stipend. Because my mother could not work due to her visa status, our family of four had to survive on roughly $20,000 a year before taxes. For most of the time, we lived in a one-bedroom graduate apartment and slept in the same room. When my sister and I got bigger, my father started to sleep on the couch in the living room. We would frequently resort to eating ramen noodles and Hamburger Helper meals; this was an unfortunate source of stress for my father as he felt remorse for me and my sister that he could not feed us more fruits and vegetables at a time when we needed nutrients to grow. We were never able to take vacations during this time, and traveling back to South Korea to see our family was inconceivable. In order to make extra money, my father and mother sold their wedding rings and other pieces of jewelry and presents they were given for their wedding. As I put these financial pressures into context, I can understand the amount of stress that my father had to endure while studying for his graduate degrees. Graduate school is already hard enough when trying to take care of oneself, but to add a whole family with two young kids, the challenge becomes almost impossible. However, my father not only succeeded in his career, but he also managed to raise two intelligent, caring, and healthy children—an accomplishment of which he is most proud.

My father's greatest support during his graduate studies was my mother. While my father was consumed by his studies, my mother focused on building a new life for our family in South Dakota and Wyoming, a far cry from the Korean countryside of her childhood. Although she had studied English Literature in college, her conversational skills were elementary, forcing her to quickly learn the language. She would watch hours of cartoons, like *Arthur*, with me and my sister and take us to the library every day and listen as librarians read children's books. She managed our finances, spoke to my teachers, and learned about the systems governing America like banking and taxes (on these subjects my father's knowledge is still to this day rudimentary at best). More importantly, she kept our family stable and healthy so that my father had no distractions. For him, our home and family were his reprieve from the stress of school. When he would come home early, I played baseball and soccer with him, and spent countless hours improving my tennis skills. In the winter, my father enjoyed snow activities with me and my sister as we went sledding and built snowmen. Ultimately, he found strength and comfort in being a parent and cultivating his young family, even as his journey carried him painfully far away from his own parents.

After completing his Ph.D. in 2005, my father had to make another decision that would once again change the trajectory of his entire life. He had promised his parents and family that he would return to South Korea once he had finished his Ph.D., and he was fully prepared to do so if not for my sister and me. At that time, I was 10 years old and my sister was eight, and we had fully assimilated into American culture and society. Effectively, English was our first language as we had completely lost our ability to speak and write in Korean. We had made friends, participated in several extracurricular activities, and become accustomed to American traditions and practices. My father decided that he could not force my sister and me to abandon the life we had and move to another country. It was too much to ask and he knew that we would have better opportunities in the United States. So, my father remained at the University of Wyoming as a visiting assistant professor for one year. In 2006, he became a tenure-track assistant professor at the College of Education at Northwestern State University in Natchitoches, Louisiana.

In 2011, he became an assistant professor at the University of Louisiana at Monroe (ULM) in Monroe, Louisiana. He was promoted to Associate Professor and granted tenure in 2014.

Today, my father is the Kitty DeGree Endowed Professor of Education and Director of the Doctor of Education program in Curriculum and Instruction at ULM. His endowed position was named after Dorothey Phillis Hall DeGree (July 29, 1922–October 25, 2012). Dorothey, or Kitty, for short, was a real estate developer, and late in her life was the largest single donor to ULM. During his time in higher education, my father has demonstrated a vigorous passion for teaching and research: writing several books and book chapters, publishing over 40 research papers in both respected journals and conference proceedings, and presenting at more than 70 regional, national, and international conferences.

First and foremost an educator, my father teaches a diverse range of courses for students and faculty including Applications of Technology in the Classroom, and English as a Second Language Workshops. While he is currently immersed in various university responsibilities, he has produced nine doctorate students as a major professor and has been a committee member for an additional 20 students. In addition, under his leadership, the Ed.D. program at ULM has continued to flourish, and in 2016 was ranked seventh in Best Online Doctorate in Education by GoGrad. In 2017, the program was nationally ranked ninth in Best Value Colleges for an Online Doctor of Education by College Values Online.

Recently, in 2018, the program was nationally ranked eighth in Best Online Doctorate in Curriculum and Instruction Programs by The Best Schools. In fact, the Ed.D. program at ULM is currently the largest in the state of Louisiana.

In addition to his commitment to students, my father continues to maintain an ambitious research agenda. His research interests include pre/in-service teachers' technology integration into their classrooms, pre/in-service teachers' computer-based technology skills and values, and various aspects of English as a Second Language student life. The latter has become especially important to my father as it directly relates to his personal life. My father has also worked collaboratively with several faculty members and his doctoral students.

Translation has emerged as an important part of my father's academic legacy and interests. Considering his possible role as an educator who can bridge cultural and educational gaps between South Korea and the United States, my father has become very interested in this field. Recently in 2013, my father published an English-to-Korean translation of the best-selling book *The First Days of School: How to Be an Effective Teacher* by acclaimed writer and teacher Harry Wong. This book provides Korean teachers and students with firsthand narratives of American classroom environments and experiences and outlines the classroom management practices that American teachers and students formulate, learn, and apply in their classroom activities. Additionally, my father invited Harry Wong to ULM in 2015 to deliver a special lecture.

My father realizes that his current success could not have been possible without the guidance of his mentors, like Professor Swedlund, and the establishment of unique opportunities that allowed him to emigrate. He understands that many students in foreign countries still hope to study in the United States, but finding affordable and worthwhile programs can be challenging. Therefore, in order to give what was once given to him, my father has made it his mission to use his position at ULM as a platform to create sister relationships with several foreign universities. In fact, he was awarded the ULM Foundation Award for Excellence in Service in 2016, which acknowledged his service and role in establishing and maintaining strong academic international programs at ULM that positively affect the students, the university, the surrounding community, and the participating global regions. Shortly after assuming his position at ULM, he started a program with several universities in South Korea and Japan that involved sending American student teachers to foreign K–12 classrooms while reciprocally receiving international students to American K–12 classrooms. Another program he has initiated employed federally funded grants, worth at least $150,000 per year, from Korean universities to pay for short-term (one or two semesters) visiting students to intern at local businesses in Monroe, Louisiana while taking courses at ULM. Some of these businesses include local engineering firms and the headquarters of CenturyLink, a telecommunications company with an annual revenue of $18 billion. In addition, my father has created programs for Korean students to pursue a master's degree at ULM for one or two years, and many of these students have continued their academic journey at other universities to pursue doctorate degrees. However, my father is not satisfied, and envisions several more exchange programs with other countries.

Currently, on most days you can find my parents splitting their time between educating new generations of college students and enjoying Louisiana weather on the golf course. For the most part, he has moved past his failures and forgiven himself. However, there will always be one decision that will forever burden him, a sacrifice by which he defines himself: the choice to stay in America after obtaining his Ph.D. He had promised his parents that he would return with his family after finishing his education, but after graduating he realized that through his and my mother's hard work, my sister and I had become completely assimilated to American life. He had to reconcile two competing forces of wanting to remain true to the earlier generation of his family in Korea and wanting to give the new generation of his family that he had created every opportunity to lead successful and meaningful lives. Ultimately, my father chose to stay in America because he could not ask my sister and me to completely uproot our childhoods and start again in South Korea.

His parents respected and understood his decision, but his mother, especially, had difficulty adjusting to this new reality and became severely depressed and physically ill. From the moment he made his decision, my father believed he was neglecting his role as a Korean son to provide for his parents. Gradually, his mother's health improved as they adjusted, and although both his parents have passed away, they lived every moment proud of what their son, a high-school dropout turned esteemed educator, had accomplished. My father has not fully reconciled this decision, and he never will. It continuously burdens him, but it also serves as his personal motivation to succeed. I believe that people perform best when they are trying to prove themselves, and my father works hard every day to justify his decision. He may live far from his family and his roots but he teaches their lessons of sacrifice and perseverance to his children and students every day. He constantly strives toward higher levels of achievement in the name of his family, both the oldest and newest generations.

I am proud of what my father has accomplished, including his endowed professorship and successful exchange programs, but I am most proud of the fact that he is willing to share his story. It is not an easy one to share, and I can understand if he were to conceal it from others and be ashamed. However, he has embraced his past and allowed it to serve as the foundation of his educational philosophies and demeanor in life. He truly epitomizes the value of learning from one's mistakes and helping others avoid such pitfalls. There were many times during his educational journey when he wanted to quit and the stress of financial burden and responsibility for a family of four felt overwhelming. However, with determination to never return to a life of meaninglessness, and the image of his mother in a coma with an uncertain future, my father was able to succeed. Failure is inevitable in life, but if there is one thing my father has taught me, it is that no failure is too great to overcome.

CHAPTER FOUR

"Then and Now"

Chasing Academic Goals and Living American Dreams, the Dual Narrative of an Asian/American Endowed Professor

DAVID WESLEY LAUSCH

INTRODUCTION

The fabled foothills of the Himalayan Mountains look north toward "the forehead of the sky," Mt. Everest, and south toward the lush fertile plains teeming with rivers and valleys of India and beyond. It was there, nestled in a small, frigid Nepalese village with fewer than 3,000 inhabitants,[1] without electricity or access to transportation, where the story of Krishna Bista began.

What is Dr. Krishna Bista's story? Is Dr. Bista's narrative bounded within his accomplishments as an Asian/American endowed professor of education at an American university, or is Dr. Bista's narrative complex, both personally and professionally, and ongoing? Employing narrative inquiry methods to qualitatively explore his story, through in-depth interviews, both formal and informal, conducted within borderland spaces he and I occupied, this chapter explores Dr. Bista's experiences, both personal and professional (Connelly & Clandinin, 2006). Found within the umbrella of qualitative methodology, a narrative inquiry method requires this approach. Clandinin and Connelly (2000) state that "collaboration [takes place] between researcher and participants, over time, in a place or series of places, and in social interaction with milieus" (p. 20).

As Dr. Bista and I view reality as socially constructed and understood through specific and social perspectives (Crotty, 1998), we sought to explore Dr. Bista's experiences using a social constructionist lens, which allows us to uncover parallel dimensions of his narrative within multiple experiences over time. In this chapter, I seek to creatively express the intertwined tension between Bista's "then" and "now" stories framed within Frank's (2012) model for Dialogic Narrative Analysis (DNA). Creatively analyzing and synthesizing threads of experiences over time to create a story or stories, without an end, DNA's guiding questions include the following:

First, what multiple voices can be heard in any single speaker's voice; how do these voices merge, and when do they contest each other? Second, what makes stories distinct from other forms of narration; what counts as a story, and what does not? Third, why is someone choosing to tell a story, among other expressive possibilities? What particular stories does the storyteller seek to utilize? Fourth, what stakes does the storyteller have riding on telling this story, at this time, to these listeners? (Frank, 2012, p. 33).

For Krishna Bista's story to emerge, I sought to explore threads within his lived experiences that in some way meaningfully overlapped. However, recognizing a dual story that was emerging of "then" and "now," within the context of academic pursuit and excellence, I wished to keep his story space intact as it represented the narrative of Dr. Krishna Bista's life (Riessman, 2008). The division of every page into block stories with independent themes was framed within Frank's (2012) model for DNA—creatively analyzing and synthesizing threads of experience over time to create a story or stories, without an end.

Thus, once I had co-created Dr. Bista's stories with him from his experiences, I member-checked with Dr. Bista to ensure his lived experiences were accurately told in the story form I had produced (Merriam, 2009). Finally, leading up to the culminating experience of his life, having successfully navigated personal challenges and becoming a professor and endowed chair at the University of Louisana Monroe, Bista's narrative is told in parallel format transitioning between stories that are personal and professional, an unconventional non-Western narrative approach, which is most appropriate when recounting an Asian/American's experience (Christian & Kauffman, 1989; Ho, 2009) This format reflects the nature in which Dr. Bista recounted his experiences throughout our interviews and attempts to provide the reader with some understanding of his complex and continuous "then" and "now" dual narrative.

THEN

The Dream Begins

A large family of 17, made up of sisters and brothers, uncles and aunts, grandparents and more all living under one roof, sharing the same dining table and kitchen for many years, the Bistas were farmers and, according to their caste,[2] allowed to raise goats, cows, and water buffalo. Considered to be well-off by local standards, Bista, his siblings, and cousins helped their elderly family members tend to their family's cattle and vegetables. Yet Krishna was set apart from the others—his gift was his intelligence and as he did well in school, he had less to do with the family's herd and agriculture. "I was the only kid to go to school in my family. My other siblings did not complete high school in four years, it took them forever," reflects Krishna. While helping with his chores on weekends, weekdays belonged to Krishna. Insistent on pursuing academic excellence, following in the footsteps of another boy in their village whom he idolized, as well as a relative who was a teacher, Krishna studied hard and did well, very well. Six days a week, seven hours a day, Krishna attended school. Elementary school required a two-hour round-trip journey by foot, and while high school[3] was a bit closer to his home, neither school provided students with lunch.

Gender and Education

Krishna was fortunate. He was a boy and as such, given preferential treatment by his family and the community. Krishna recalls, "The societal expectation is that whichever kid is doing better academically in the family, they will allow him to study. It is a family's judgment and it happens even today, they give preference to males over females. In my society, boys have more opportunities to go to the city, to get money and receive support from their families."[4] So, Krishna used his male gender status to his benefit, by attending public school regularly.

In Krishna's village, and throughout Nepal, annual exams were crucial for all students to do well on in order to advance to the next level; most importantly, in high school, strong exam scores were essential for those wishing to attend university. The national exam in high school required seven days to take. Three hours per day, at least, all high school seniors were provided the exact same questions at the exact same time throughout Nepal, from 7:00 AM to 10:00 AM. Proctored by a board of examination, students were given first or second group status based on the percentage they received on their exams. Krishna remembers,

Each exam is worth 100 points, so 700 points in total. The competition is extremely fierce. For those who receive the highest score, your name is announced nationwide and you receive a monetary award, as well as other awards. Most importantly, for those in the top ten rank nationally, college is free. They go by district, and there are 75 districts in the country. I was from the eastern part of the country and I was ranked first in my entire village as well as in the district. I was able to go to the capital and college after I got the award.

NOW

Trajectory of Teaching

Pursuing higher education in the United States, Dr. Bista[5] was initially educated and trained at Troy University in Alabama (2007–2009). He then went on to study at Arkansas State University in Jonesboro (2010–2013), where he completed a master's degree in Postsecondary Education/English and a doctoral degree in Educational Leadership/Higher Education. Dr. Bista has taught several years in K–12 schools and colleges, both in Nepal and the United States. As a scholar in the field of International and Comparative Education, and through extensive educational experiences in Nepal and the United States, Dr. Bista brings a multicultural background and a wide range of professional experiences into current academic discourse. He has published several research articles, edited books, and written book chapters and book reviews. His academic presentations and publications focus on the college experiences of students, primarily related to the issues and concerns of international students in teaching and learning, international faculty experiences, and internationalization of higher education.

Dr. Bista has been the primary advisor on doctoral dissertations and master's theses. He is an innovative and respected researcher in the field of International Education. He is one of a handful of researchers who examine the international student experience using a critical perspective. His outstanding commitment and leadership to the field is evidenced through his early initiative to establish the *Journal of International Students*, a quarterly peer-reviewed publication on international education. Dr. Bista is an active participant and member at the Comparative and International Education Society (CIES) and other academic associations including the American Educational Research Association (AERA).

THEN

Teaching During War

Finishing high school and scoring first on his national board examination, Krishna initially attended university in Nepal's capital, Kathmandu, where he majored in humanities with minors in mathematics, English and economics. Acknowledging hardships, Krishna says, "My primary years did not go well. I was really lonely and missed my family. I barely survived." But Krishna's third and fourth years were very different. "The second two years changed my entire life. I was traveling back to my village, which required a two-day bus ride and then one-day walk to home from the bus station. While returning to the capital city, right after the national holiday break, I met a military officer on the same public bus." The civil war was raging at that time between the Maoists and Nepalese government.[6] Impressed with Krishna's care for his co-passengers, a woman and her infant on the bus ride, the military officer invited Krishna to stay with his family and continue his studies at the university while tutoring his children. It was a great opportunity for Krishna, but association with the military officer "meant I couldn't travel outside of the city anymore. I was given a false identity to keep my family safe, but they still had to go to different parts of the country to live with relatives." For him, staying with another family in the city also provided a sense of belonging and security while the civil war raged around him.

The Nepalese Civil War was an armed conflict between the Communist Party of Nepal (Maoist) and the government of Nepal, fought from 1996 to 2006. During the conflict, more than 19,000 people (including both civilians and armed forces) were killed and an estimated 100,000–150,000 people were internally displaced as a result of this conflict. Although the war ended with the Comprehensive Peace Accord signed on November 21, 2006, the post-war period did not bring hope to the lives of Nepalese youth. The trend of outbound mobility increased for both students like Krishna and other scholars. Many of Krishna's professors left the country to pursue employment in the United States, some in Canada and Australia. This conflict disrupted the majority of social, cultural, and educational activities throughout the country.

There were some negative consequences in Krishna's family as well as a result of the conflict. His entire family (including parents, grandparents, uncles, aunts, and relatives) had to leave the village (Krishna's birthplace) because it was not safe to stay there. His uncle, who was serving on the Nepal Police Force was killed in a counterattack. His great aunt was murdered in broad daylight, and her gold jewelry stolen while she was out taking care of her goats. In that era, people who called themselves Maoist were underground. They used to enslave locals to collect their food or to strengthen their force. Villagers were scared to get out of their houses and do local chores—working on the farm, taking kids to school, etc.

Continuing with his studies in college in Kathmandu, Krishna spent two years attending classes, tutoring the officer's children, and teaching in local elementary schools. There, he met with the principal of a local elementary school. Willing to do anything to become a teacher, Krishna told the principal, "I will work free of cost for a month." Impressed with Krishna's willingness to be professionally tested without pay, the principal offered him his first real salary, $5 per month to teach elementary students. But, the school did not have computers or libraries; it only had chalk and blackboards. Krishna recalls, "I didn't know what to do. It was tough to teach the first couple of months. You just get a couple of books and lecture elementary students." So, Krishna played and danced and laughed with the kids. Though dubious at first, the principal soon realized

Krishna's methods of interaction were creating a positive learning environment for the students. Krishna was promoted to teach in the middle school. After learning a great deal and promoting his brand of teaching, moving to many different schools, he finally landed a teaching job at a school with computers and libraries (unusual in much of Nepal) making $40 per month. Krishna recalls, "It gave me a good scope of what teaching looked like in the capital versus the village."

NOW

Research Contributions to the Field of Education

Over the years, Dr. Bista has contributed to three major areas of research: (1) international education, (2) social media in teaching, and (3) college student experiences. His research focuses on college access and academic success of minority and international students. His research and his research association/network in the *Journal of International Students* provides a platform for scholars interested in international education. Dr. Bista's journal is a peer-reviewed publication that publishes theoretical and empirically-based research articles, narrative essays on study-abroad experiences, book reviews, and reflective writing about transnational education. His audiences include scholars and researchers of international education, academic professionals working with international students in a variety of programs, and others who are interested in international students attending college and university. His book publications have included notable works such as:

- *Campus Support Services, Programs, and Policies for International Students* (2016a), which explores the role of university administration in successful implementation, regulation, and support of study abroad experiences highlighting topics relating to legal issues, safety concerns, curriculum development, and intercultural communication;
- *Exploring the Social and Academic Experiences of International Students in Higher Education Institutions* (2016b), a reference source for the latest research on the issues surrounding study abroad students in culturally diverse educational environments; and
- *Global Perspectives and Local Challenges Surrounding International Student Mobility* (2016c), a book that investigates comparative research regarding the implementation of effective strategies needed when working with native and non-native individuals in educational settings.

Dr. Bista is currently working on *Global Perspectives on International Student Experiences in Higher Education: Tensions and Issues* (2018b), which examines a wide range of international student experiences, including student life, engagement in degree courses and extracurricular activities, experiences of teaching and learning, use of technology, experiences of feedback and assessment, and other areas of student involvement; and *International Student Mobility and Opportunities for Growth in the Global Marketplace* (2018c) which focuses on the recent trends in global student mobility in Australia, Asia, North America, Latin America, the Middle East, and Europe where the emerging educational trends and practices are prominent.

THEN

Transitions and American Interactions[7]

While pursuing his university degree in education, the intensity of Nepal's civil war grew. Schools and colleges were closed for months, buildings were destroyed, large groups of students joined the rebel groups, or formed protests to ban the movement. These acts further exacerbated tensions between students. Krishna remembers, "Everything and everyone was affected. Many of my family members were kidnapped. After paying ransoms, they promptly left our village and the country. Many teachers were also kidnapped and released after having paid ransoms." He was told by his professors to go and live elsewhere. So, he started applying to universities in Canada, the United States, and the United Kingdom.

He decided to study in the United States, but he didn't know much about traveling, where to buy an airplane ticket, what a layover was, or how to navigate airports. He recalls the details of his first international trip: "In Thailand, I had to stay overnight, a 10-hour layover. I had no hotel. They spoke English, but different English. I had to write on a piece of paper to communicate with them."

After a flight through Japan, Dr. Bista arrived in Seattle where he encountered an American for the first time. "The first thing was the entry point. We waited in a long line. I saw a big, giant officer. I was shivering; I didn't know what to say. When the first guy exited, I approached the officer. He scolded me harshly for stepping up to the counter instead of waiting to be called. I couldn't believe it." On to Tennessee and finally Alabama, his journey was made a bit easier with the kind words of a co-passenger, a woman in her 60s, Susan. Bista recalls,

Susan asked me some questions; I told her my journey took 32 hours. She gave me her number to stay in touch. We exchanged emails. She sent books and DVDs related to education and American culture. Since she was an educator and writer, she encouraged me to read and write more professionally.

Years later, when he was set to graduate in the United States, he invited Susan to his ceremony. She had become part of his motivation to succeed. She drove two hours to attend his graduation.

Krishna's Nepalese mentors working in the United States, as well as cheap tuition for U.S. universities, became the impetus for Krishna to consider the United States as his destination of choice. However, "Traveling to the United States caused me culture shock. Every single thing surprised me. I didn't know where to go in the buildings and there was a campus town, but I always got lost." The system was different. "I went to visit an elementary school and a teacher invited me to go to a cafeteria with others. We had to pay up front. I was looking at the list price and thought it said $49. I took out all of the money in my pocket and gave it to her. It was roughly $35 or $40. I told her, I'm sorry. I don't have enough money. Can I buy half of the ticket? She was shocked. I didn't understand the sign ... it said 49 cents ..."

NOW

Research Articles

With 16 research papers published in peer-reviewed academic journals, Dr. Bista's scholarly contributions are impressive (Bista, 2011a, 2011b, 2012a, 2012b, 2014, 2015a, 2015b, 2015c, 2015d, 2015e, 2018a; Bista & Cox, 2014; Bista & Dagley, 2015; Bista & Foster, 2011, 2014; Bista & Saleh, 2014; Saleh & Bista, 2015). Notable amongst them is his co-authored article "Higher Education Preparation and Decision Making Trends Among International Students" (Bista & Dagley, 2015) published in *College & University*. Using qualitative techniques such as interviews, Bista examines how international students acquired college information when they were still in their home countries. His article "Silence in Teaching and Learning: Perspectives of a Nepalese Graduate Student" (Bista, 2012b) published in *College Teaching* explores the concept of silence among international students by examining the existing body of literature relating to cultural norms. Bista (2012b) cites Lao Tzu by noting the following,

The nature of silence is complex in any classroom with international or domestic students. Instructors sometimes fail to recognize that the classroom silence of foreign students is unlike their native counterparts. With an insider perspective, this article explores the concept of silence among international students by examining the existing body of literature relating to cultural norms. It also suggests a number of ways of dealing with silent students in a diverse classroom setting (p. 76).

Meanwhile, in his article "Is Twitter an Effective Pedagogical Tool in Higher Education? Perspectives of Education Graduate Students" (Bista, 2015c), published in the *Journal of the Scholarship of Teaching and Learning*, Bista presented the perspectives of education graduate students who used Twitter as a pedagogical tool for 15 weeks as a required social media activity in class. His findings indicated participants in each course responded positively to Twitter as a pedagogical tool.

THEN

U.S. University and Personal Finances

Krishna received his U.S. visa in 2007. Many Nepalese were heading to the United States at that time to study or work; they were trying to advance themselves in any way they could. Studying for a master's degree in adult/postsecondary education at Troy University in Alabama, a program that had two components—education and teaching English—Krishna also took English classes on the side.[8] But, it was a hard time for Krishna, especially financially. "In Alabama, I didn't have a scholarship. I didn't have a support system to pay the tuition." It was the first time Krishna considered dropping out of college, to work in order to pay his educational fees. "When I decided to come to the United States my family was all dispersed because of the war in Nepal between the government and the Maoists, so I didn't have the same support here that I had had for schooling in Nepal." He started looking into departmental support. "I told a professor my story. He offered me a job. He was interested in assisting and studying foreign students like me struggling in the United States."

Krishna loved American literature, especially poetry. It gave him an outlet to express his feelings, including feelings about leaving his family, trying to forget the war and his grandmother dying. As a result, when he first started graduate school, he wasn't able to focus. He sought solace in research, "I looked at the life of those international students who brought into their U.S. classrooms different cultures and I noticed a pattern, teaching styles differed based on ethnicities." Wanting to know and do more, Krishna looked beyond the education department, and into the international program at Troy, asking if he could teach a couple of classes for them. They agreed. Teaching and interacting with international students inspired Krishna to write his first research articles.

NOW

Teaching Contributions

Including his teaching assignments in Nepal and the United States, Dr. Bista has taught for 16 years in a range of educational settings, including six years in middle and high schools, and over a decade at various universities. Regardless of their educational level, over the years, Dr. Bista's students have responded with praise about his style of teaching, the content taught, and his personal care for them. Comments from students include the following:

Educational Statistics Student (Doctoral Course):

> This class has opened my eyes to the world of statistics. I had a narrow view of statistics, but now I am aware of all of the things that can be accomplished, both quantitatively and qualitatively. I felt as though an expert in the field was guiding me through the process.

Decision Making for School Improvement Student (Doctoral Course):

> I was able to take away information about students' experiences and expectations in high schools. I plan on using this information in my future teaching, as I now have a better idea of what students are experiencing.

Foundations of Educational Research Student (Master's Course):

> He was readily available, answered any questions that I needed to be addressed in a timely manner, and graded fairly. He kept in touch with the students regularly by checking in by email, making sure that we understood the topics for the week.

> Dr. Bista is an outstanding educator with exemplary knowledge, vision, and teaching skills. Dr. Bista was a great instructor. His prompt answer to every question as well as his clear directions was very helpful for me because this was my first semester in the program.

THEN

Chasing Academic Goals and Living "American Dreams"

After earning a master's degree at Troy University, Krishna moved to Denver, Colorado. He started teaching at a local community college for a while. But, he was motivated to go beyond a master's degree. In his own words,

When I finished my degree in Alabama and started phone interviews for community colleges, only one offered me a position. I started calling them back asking what am I missing. I had a ton of experience teaching. Some of the schools responded saying if I had a doctoral degree, I would be more competitive, so that motivated me.

Krishna taught in a General Education Development (GED) degree program part-time and worked part-time on campus in a restaurant to make ends meet. But, it wasn't fulfilling to him. He constantly compared the lifestyle he was living with what he wanted to do. "I didn't enjoy working outside of teaching. Many of my restaurant customers would talk about the books they were reading with me as I served food. Every single thing in academia was a part of my conversation." Working in the restaurant motivated Krishna to go back to school. So while he worked in his part-time jobs, he applied for Ph.D. programs. "I did have a couple of good people writing me letters. I applied to Seattle, Oregon, Maryland, El Paso, the District of Columbia, and others and I received offer letters. I compared the courses, and the assistantships." He decided on attending university in Arkansas since this was the college recommend by his mentors from his previous university. It was there he received a full scholarship to purse his doctorate.

Krishna received a doctorate in educational leadership/higher education, and a specialist education degree focused on community college teaching and administration. Taking three courses every semester, two towards the main requirements for his doctoral program and one towards his specialization in community college, he knew would give him a leg up. Between 2010 and 2013, he earned 99 credit hours including research hours that fulfilled both his doctoral program requirements and his community college specialization. During his study he taught several graduate courses and participated in research projects with his mentors. His mentors encouraged him to pursue all of his education interests. Looking back, Krishna thinks, "I needed that teaching and research experience if I was to be a college professor like them. But, I also traveled the country heading to academic conferences which help me build a professional network among scholars."

NOW

Culminating Appointment, the Endowed Professorship

Currently, Dr. Krishna Bista is the Chase Endowed Professor in Teacher Education in the School of Education at the University of Louisiana Monore. The university committee that oversees endowed professorships nominated Dr. Bista based on his merit as a prolific scholar and effective teacher. All tenure-track professors are eligible for the professorships at this university. According to Hartlep, Ball, Theodosopoulos, Wells, and Morgan (2016), "Endowed chairs (ECs) and distinguished professorships (DPs) are typically awarded to full professors who have accomplished much in their respective field" (p. 120). "Established by the Louisiana Board of Regents in 1990–91 […] [t]he program [was] designed to broaden opportunities for faculty enhancement on diverse types of campuses" (Letlow, 2015, para. 1). The program helps recruit and retain faculty whose research, teaching, and/or public service have "uniquely contributed to the missions of their departments and institutions" (Letlow, 2015, para. 2).

THEN AND NOW

Engaging Others

Dr. Bista's personal and professional achievements cannot be overstated, especially in light of the ongoing difficulties Asian/Americans face when working and studying in the United States and academia including discrimination, lack of representation, cultural biases and more (Ho, 2009; Roy, 2013; Tanimura, Tran, & Wong, 2012). Perhaps an understudied, but increasingly numerous subset of Asian/Americans, Nepalese students and faculty (Number of Nepali Students, 2016) also face various hardships in U.S. academia, which need to be addressed (Thapaliya, 2017). While some individuals and institutions are attempting to tackle Nepalese students' needs (Wood, 1990), few have assisted Nepalese attempting to enter U.S. academia as faculty members. Lessons from Dr. Bista's personal and professional stories may provide other Asian/Americans, particularly Nepalese, with a model for success.

Analyzing Dr. Bista's stories, one of the lessons most germane to his U.S. academic success was his desire to enter into other individuals' stories. Regardless of his academic or perceived social status, Dr. Bista constantly engaged with those around him. He listened to others' stories first, and then engaged in dialog directly with them. These interactions enabled him to grow a social network that served his needs. In Nepal, after engaging with a soldier on a bus, he was provided a room and food in the city, which then allowed him to continue his studies. As a student in the U.S., his social networking with various Americans enabled him to find employment in the university to offset his personal and educational costs. Perhaps more importantly, conversations with Americans provided him with awareness and knowledge of classroom and professorial norms and expectations that enabled him to navigate U.S. universities as a student. Later, American faculty offered him advice regarding academia's norms and expectations. Following the advice helped him to transition from student to professor as Dr. Bista used this social network to seek employment as an adjunct professor from one of his professors, while still pursuing his doctoral degree. Later, with colleagues, he utilized the same social network to create research teams which met their professional needs.

Often, international students and professors are afraid to engage beyond their racial, national, or social group. Asian/Americans in particular are beset by minority stereotypes in U.S. academia (Wingfield, 2016). Consequently, many may not seek to engage with other Americans, but rather depend on a social network situated in ethnicity (Estrada, 2006; Sun & Bian, 2012), or engage in academic networking via online platforms (Bhardwaj, 2017) to avoid in-person dialog. Dr. Bista's story is important to consider. His development and utilization of a social network (Goel & Grimpe, 2013) directly impacted his ability to follow his academic dream and meet his goal of becoming an American professor. Social networking provided Dr. Bista with ongoing support. The ability to utilize a network for support (Le, 2016) has been shown to directly lead to Asian/Americans' success in academia. Thus, to succeed as an international student and professor, Dr. Bista's story exposes the importance of developing a supportive social network. To do so requires entering into the stories of others while maintaining one's identity. Dr. Bista entered into many different stories over his lifetime and as a result, benefited immensely from doing so.

Narrative Interactions

My first interaction with Dr. Bista was a phone conversation regarding the experiences of international students in the state of Wyoming, as well as sending one of my manuscripts to his *Journal of International Students*. Having had positive and negative experiences while studying abroad and teaching, I empathized with international students in higher education institutions struggling with language and culture in the United States. Thus, upon my return to academia, I decided to focus my research on international student experiences, specifically students from Middle East and Asian backgrounds. Having read numerous research articles authored by Dr. Bista, as well as articles published in his academic journal, I decided to reach out to him to see if he'd like to partner on a research project.

Since then, we have been in contact sharing ideas for research, his journal, academic speaking engagement opportunities, and more. When the opportunity was presented to me to write a chapter on Dr. Bista's academic accomplishments as an Asian/American professor in the United States, I was honored to have the opportunity. But, after considerable reflection, I realized that Dr. Bista's life was much more than a series of academic accomplishments culminating in his position as a professor and endowed chair. The common thread throughout Krishna's story is academics; whether in Nepal or in the United States, the pursuit of knowledge has played a central role in his life. Thus, his life can be witnessed and situated through parallel veins of history, as a child academic in Nepal and as an adult academic in the United States.

I have been a part of Dr. Bista's academic story for two years. Humble, kind, and exceedingly intelligent, he has a tenacity to excel in all things academic. Inviting me to preside over a presentation session at the 2016 Mid-South Educational Research Association's (MSERA) annual conference, what was most apparent to me in our interactions both at the conference and beyond is his ability to wear several hats. Both personal and professional, a devoted father and husband, and a dedicated academic, Dr. Bista never skips a beat discussing possible research with a colleague, answering texts and emails, conversing with students, holding spontaneous meetings, and much, much more. Perhaps, most notably, his selfless giving of his time and attention has always impressed me the most. I am unsure if it was his humble beginnings, incredible journey through civil war, support from fellow Nepalese and Americans, or his humanist beliefs and practices that have made Dr. Krishna Bista the person he is today. Whatever the case, there is little doubt that he leads an exemplary life that is worthy of recognition, as a role model for the Asian/American community. He has hosted multiple workshops; spoken with many students in the U.S. and outside; has participated in community activities; and given talks in colleges and schools in Nepal including the American Center, a US-Embassy based educational center in Kathmandu, Nepal. At the University of Louisiana Monroe, he has developed Memorandum of Understanding (MOU) agreements with sister universities in Nepal, which has led to the successful recruitment of 200 Nepalese students for the university.

Reflexive Attention and Limitations

Attending to the researcher's subjectivity is crucial when conducting qualitative research (Ratner, 2002). As such, knowing and interacting with Dr. Bista over the past two years, I had to be exceedingly attentive to my own biases, values, and personal background, prior to, during, and after interviewing Dr. Bista for this chapter (Creswell, 2013). Acting as both an insider and outsider within Dr. Bista's story, due to our professional and personal interactions, I sought to understand and struggle with my positionality as a privileged white American male interviewing an academic professor from Nepal for the purpose of writing a book chapter (Sands, Bourjolly, & Roer-Strier, 2007). What was and is important to me, I thought, may not be as consequential to him, and what was and is important to him, he thought, may not be to me (Henwood, Pidgeon, Parkhill, & Simmons, 2011). Hence, central to our interviews, formal and informal, prior to and during the writing of this chapter, was our mutual awareness of the need to be critically reflexive respecting one another's identity, situation, space, and lived experiences (Emirbayer & Desmond, 2012), both as researcher and participant.

NOTES

1 27,474,000 people live in Nepal and there were 630 households in Chyangre village where he grew up according to the National Population and Housing Census, 2011.
2 125 different ethnic groups and castes comprise Nepal.
3 In 1951, Nepal had 10,000 students in just 300 schools. By 2010, the number of schools increased to 49,000.

4 Poverty, social exclusion of women, lower caste discrimination, and indigenous biases are now-adays the primary constraints to equitable access to education (Parajuli & Das, 2013).

5 There are about 300 professors of Nepalese origin teaching at colleges and universities in the United States. They represent all types of institutions from world-class universities such as Harvard University, Massachusetts Institute of Technology, University of Florida, and University of Chicago to small community colleges in all disciplines. The majority of Nepalese professors in the U.S. are in medicine, STEM, liberal arts, business and communication. Less than half a dozen of them are in teacher education programs (IIE, 2013).

6 According to Krishna, "Maoists used to go villages and harass the villagers for room and board. They constantly traveled across the country. No one was safe. Since my family had animals and some land, they used to come to our home at night requiring food and lodging to hide from the government forces. All of my family supported the government, but during the day, the government would arrive killing villagers for not supporting them. The government misunderstood who was and was not supporting them. Many people were killed, on both sides."

7 Due to several factors, the migration of Nepalis to the United States of America has escalated over the last decade. These factors include: a lack of educational and career opportunities, increased migrant networks, and political instability. However, many of the migrants tend to be highly skilled (Bohra-Mishra, 2011, p. 1527).

8 Despite linguistic, economic, academic, and visa barriers to studying in the United States (Thapaliya, 2017), over 8,000 students from Nepal study in the United States yearly. It is the 19th place of foreign origin for university students coming to the United States and contributes $260 million to the U.S. economy (Chow & Chambers, 2015).

REFERENCES

Bhardwaj, R. K. (2017). Academic social networking sites: Comparative analysis of ResearchGate, academia.edu, mendeley and zotero. *Information and Learning Science, 118*(5/6), 298.

Bista, K. (2011a). Academic dishonesty among international students in higher education. In J. Miller & J. Groccia (Eds.), *To improve the academy: Vol. 30. Resources for faculty, instructional, and organizational development* (pp. 159–172). San Francisco, CA: Jossey-Bass.

Bista, K. (2011b). Issues of international student retention in American higher education. *The International Journal of Research and Review, 7*(2), 1–10.

Bista, K. (2011c). Why are foreign students silent in the U.S. classroom? *Faculty Focus*. Magna Publications.

Bista, K. (2012a). Learning-centered community colleges and ESL program. *The Southeast Asian Journal of English Language Studies, 17*(1), 113–121.

Bista, K. (2012b). Multicultural literature for children and young adults. *The Educational Forum, 76*(3), 145–155. https://doi.org/10.1080/00131725.2012.682203

Bista, K. (2012c). Silence in teaching and learning: Perspectives of a Nepalese graduate student. *College Teaching, 60*(2), 76–82.

Bista, K. (2014). Internationalizing curriculum and pedagogy in higher education. *Multicultural Perspectives, 16*(3), 185–189.

Bista, K. (2015a). Asian international students' college experiences: Relationship between perceived quality of personal contact and self-reported gains in learning. *Journal of International and Global Education, 6*(2), 38–54.

Bista, K. (2015b). Higher education preparation and decision making trends among international students. *College & University, 90*(3), 2–11.

Bista, K. (2015c). Is Twitter a pedagogical tool in higher education? Perspectives of education graduate students. *Journal of the Scholarship of Teaching and Leaning, 15*(2), 83–102.

Bista, K. (2015d). Roles of international student advisors: Literature and practice in American higher education. *International Education, 44*(1), 89–103.

Bista, K. (2015e). The influence of country of origin and academic level on Asian students' gain of learning. *Journal of International Students, 5*(3), 300–305.

Bista, K. (2018a). Do academic and social experiences predict sense of belonging? Comparison among American and international undergraduate students. In A. W. Abe, L. Tran, & I. Liyanage (Eds.), *Reciprocal adaptability between international students and stakeholders: Responsibility, values and challenges* (pp. 1–11). New York, NY: Routledge.

Bista, K. (2018b). *Global perspectives on international student experiences in higher education: Tensions and issues.* New York, NY: Routledge.

Bista, K. (Ed.). (2018c). *International student mobility and opportunities for growth in the global market.* Hershey, PA: IGI Global.

Bista, K., & Cox, D. W. (2014). Cohort-based doctoral programs: What we have learned over the last 18 years? *International Journal of Doctoral Studies, 9*, 1–20.

Bista, K., & Dagley, A. (2015). Higher education preparation and decision making trends among international students. *College & University, 90*(3), 2–11.

Bista, K. & Foster, C. (2011). Issues of international student retention in American higher education. *The International Journal of Research and Review, 7*(2), 1–10.

Bista, K., & Foster, C. (2014). Internationalizing curriculum and pedagogy in higher education. *Multicultural Perspectives, 16*(3), 185–189. http://doi.org/10.1080/15210960.2014.926753

Bista, K., & Foster, C. (Eds.). (2016a). *Campus support services, programs, and policies for international students.* Hershey, PA: IGI Global. https://doi.org/10.4018/978-1-4666-9752-2

Bista, K., & Foster, C. (Eds.). (2016b). *Exploring the social and academic experiences of international students in higher education institutions.* Hershey, PA: IGI Global.

Bista, K., & Foster, C. (Eds.). (2016c). *Global perspectives and local challenges surrounding international student mobility.* Hershey, PA: IGI Global.

Bista, K., & Saleh, A. (2014). Assessing the need for global education program in post secondary education in the United States. *Journal of International & Global Studies, 5*(2), 19–39.

Bohra-Mishra, P. (2011). Nepalese migrants in the United States of America: Perspectives on their exodus, assimilation pattern and commitment to Nepal. *Journal of Ethnic and Migration Studies, 37*(9), 1527–1537. https://doi.org/10.1080/1369183X.2011.623626

Chow, P., & Chambers, J. (2015). International enrollments in the united states: 60 years of 'open doors' data. *International Higher Education, 59*, 17–18. https://doi.org/10.6017/ihe.2010.59.8483

Christian, B., & Kauffman, L. (1989). *Gender and theory: Dialogues on feminist criticism.* Oxford, UK: Basil Blackwell Ltd.

Clandinin, D. J., & Connelly, F. M. (2000). *Narrative inquiry: Experience and story in qualitative research.* San Francisco, CA: Jossey-Bass.

Connelly, F. M., & Clandinin, D. J. (2006). Narrative inquiry. In J. Green, G. Camilli, & P. Elmore (Eds.), *Handbook of complementary methods in education research* (pp. 375–385). Mahwah, NJ: Lawrence Erlbaum.

Creswell, J. W. (2013). *Qualitative inquiry & research design: Choosing among five approaches* (3rd ed.). Thousand Oaks, CA: Sage Publications.

Crotty, M. (1998). *The foundations of social research: Meaning and perspective in the research process.* Thousand Oaks, CA: Sage Publications.

Emirbayer, M., & Desmond, M. (2012). Race and reflexivity. *Ethnic and Racial Studies, 35*(4), 574–642. https://doi.org/10.1080/01419870.2011.606910

Estrada, A. (2006, December 11). Research shows Asian Americans less likely to seek social support. *The UCSB current.* Retrieved from http://www.news.ucsb.edu/2006/012195/research-shows-asian-americans-less-likely-seek-social-support

Frank, A. W. (2012). Practicing dialogical narrative analysis. In J. A. Holstein & J. F. Gubrium (Eds.), *Varieties of narrative analysis* (pp. 33–52). Thousand Oaks, CA: Sage Publications. Retrieved from https://in.sagepub.com/sites/default/files/upm-binaries/41823_2.pdf

Goel, R. K., & Grimpe, C. (2013). Active versus passive academic networking: Evidence from micro-level data. *The Journal of Technology Transfer, 38*(2), 116–134. https://doi.org/10.1007/s10961-011-9236-5

Hartlep, N. D., Ball, D., Theodosopoulos, K., Wells, K., & Morgan, G. B. (2016). A national analysis of endowed chairs and distinguished professors in the field of education. *Educational Studies, 52*(2), 119–138.

Henwood, K., Pidgeon, N., Parkhill, K., & Simmons, P. (2011). Researching risk: Narrative, biography, subjectivity. *Historical Social Research/Historische Sozialforschung, 36*(4), 251–272.

Ho, J. (2009). Letter from an american professor: An Asian American education in the south. *The Global South, 3*(2), 14–31. https://doi.org/10.2979/GSO.2009.3.2.14

Institute of International Education. (2013). Nepalese professors in the US colleges and universities. *Open Doors Report on International Educational Exchange.* Retrieved from http://www.iie.org/opendoors

Le, B. P. (2016). Choosing to lead: Success characteristics of Asian American academic library leaders. *Library Management, 37*(1–2), 81–90. https://doi.org/10.1108/LM-05-2015-0029

Letlow, J. (2015, September 23). Progressive bank establishes ULM endowed professorship. Retrieved from http://www.ulm.edu/news/2015/0923-progressive-bank-establishes-endowed-professorship.html

Merriam, S. B. (2009). *Qualitative research: A guide to design and implementation.* San Francisco, CA: Jossey-Bass.

National Population and Housing Census. (2011). Government of Nepal. Retrieved from http://cbs.gov.np/image/data/Population/VDC-Municipality%20in%20detail/VDC_Municipality.pdf

Number of nepali students in US jumps by 18.4 per cent. (2016, November 14). *Himalayan Times.* Retrieved from https://thehimalayantimes.com/nepal/number-nepali-students-us-jumps-18-4-per-cent/

Parajuli, D. R., & Das, T. (2013). Performance of community schools in Nepal: A macro level analysis. *International Journal of Scientific and Technology Research, 2*(7), 148–154.

Ratner, C. (2002). Subjectivity and objectivity in qualitative methodology. *Forum: Qualitative Social Research, 3*(3), 1–8. Retrieved from http://www.qualitative-research.net/index.php/fqs/article/view/829

Riessman, C. K. (2008). *Narrative methods for the human sciences.* Thousand Oaks, CA: Sage Publications.

Roy, S. R. (2013). Educating Chinese, Japanese, and Korean international students: Recommendations to American professors. *Journal of International Students, 3*(1), 10.

Saleh, A., & Bista, K. (2015). Assessing faculty perceptions of campus climate at a mid-southern university. *Review of Higher Education and Self-Learning, 7*(25), 1–14.

Sands, R. G., Bourjolly, J., & Roer-Strier, D. (2007). Crossing cultural barriers in research interviewing. *Qualitative Social Work, 6*(3), 353–372.

Sun, X., & Bian, Y. (2012). Ethnic networking in the transnational engagement of Chinese American scientists. *Asian Perspective, 36*(3), 435–461.

Tanimura, J., Tran, H., & Wong, A. (2012). The case for an Asian American law professor: An epistolary among three Asian American student activists at the University of Southern California Gould School of Law. *Southern California Review of Law and Social Justice, 21*(3), 469.

Thapaliya, R. (2017). Nepalese student's struggle & difficulties in the USA. Retrieved from https://www.huffingtonpost.com/rajan-thapaliya/nepalese-students-struggl_b_9590662.html

Weng, S. (2016). Moving towards normalcy for Asian Americans: The development of an informal support network. *Making Connections, 16*(2), 65–85.

Wingfield, A. H. (2016, June 6). The professional burdens of being a 'model minority'. Retrieved from https://www.theatlantic.com/business/archive/2016/06/professional-burdens-model-minority-asian-americans/485492/

Wood, H. B. (1990). Suggestions to nepalese students who wish to study in the U.S. *Himalayan Research Bulletin, 10*(1), 12.

CHAPTER FIVE

George Sugai

The Shaping of Success

LAURA KERN, KATE DOOLEY, BRANDI SIMONSEN,
JENNIFER FREEMAN AND ED KAME'ENUI

To laugh often and much; to win the respect of intelligent people and the affection of children; to earn the appreciation of honest critics and endure the betrayal of false friends; to appreciate beauty; to find the best in others; to leave the world a bit better whether by a healthy child, a garden path, or a redeemed social condition; to know even one life has breathed easier because you have lived. This is to have succeeded.

—Ralph Waldo Emerson (1803–1882; Willoughby, 2015, p. 99)

Professor George Sugai holds the Carole J. Neag Endowed Chair in Behavior Disorders at the University of Connecticut (UCONN) Neag School of Education. As the founding director of the Center for Behavioral Education and Research (CBER) at UCONN, George established and has propelled CBER forward over the last 10 years through his leadership. His curriculum vitae (CV) consists of over 130 peer-reviewed articles and research studies focused on diverse groups of students, practitioners, and policy makers. Despite publishing research on various topics, a common theme across his work is the improvement in outcomes for all students. In addition to his rich cadre of publications, he has been awarded more than $60.5 million in grant funding. He presently co-directs two prestigious federally funded centers: (a) Office of Special Education Programs' (OSEP) National Technical Assistance Center on Positive Behavioral Interventions and Supports (PBIS) and (b) OSEP's Early Childhood Personnel Center. George has mentored

future leaders in the field of Special Education through his instruction of graduate level courses in applied behavior analysis, emotional or behavioral disorders,
behavioral consultation, social skills instruction, and classroom/behavior management. He has also served as an advisor to the U.S. Department of Education
(DOE), U.S. Department of Justice (DOJ), and the U.S. Department of Health
and Human Services (HHS). George describes his primary interests as positive
behavior support (PBS), systems change, personnel preparation, behavioral disorders, social skills instruction, behavioral consultation, behavioral assessment
procedures, applied behavior analysis (ABA), and strategies for effective school-
wide, classroom, and individual behavior management.

Given the significant achievements detailed on his CV, it is clear George is
an accomplished academic. But as we contemplate his full accomplishments for
this chapter, we want to go beyond what is on his CV to describe an individual
who has made not just ripples, but great waves of change in education. Building
on the early work of behavioral scientists, George has taught us that any behavior is not a solitary event in time, but rather is influenced by the environmental
context, especially the events that occur before and after each behavior. As these
experiences accumulate over time, an individual develops a unique learning history that affects how s/he behaves and engages with the environment. Taking a
lead from this approach, we will thoroughly explore how George came to be a
leader in our field by delving into his learning history and the shaping of his life
experiences and accomplishments. George has also taught us that if we want to
effectuate system-wide social change, we must look at how people learn and meet
the needs of the individual and the society. To that end, we will share some of his
undertakings at multiple levels: his theoretical orientation, his early learning history and cultural background, his work with students with behavioral challenges,
his development and funding of key federal educational centers, and his efforts to
ultimately shape the future. It is with great pleasure that we, as George's past students, colleagues, and friends, share the journey of a man who exemplifies what
we wish leaders in the field of special education can emulate and what shaped him
into the leader he is today.

A "DAMN BEHAVIORIST"

George is a true behaviorist at heart. The theories of B.F. Skinner have clearly
influenced both his ideology and informed his applied professional undertakings.
As he puts it, "I'm just a damn behaviorist," with a smirk. He has taken the fundamental components of applied behavior analysis and an emphasis on positive
reinforcement, to change the lives of millions of students in schools across the
United States and the world. George's emphasis on positive behavior support has

focused on what can be done to prevent behaviors that interfere with students' progress and increase behaviors that will lead to better outcomes for students through proactive strategies and positive reinforcement. George has not stopped at the individual student level; he has also applied this theory to schools to effectuate systems-level change. As one of the most influential leaders in School-Wide PBIS (SWPBIS), George has contributed to scaling up the use of positive behavior support in schools, districts, states/provinces, and countries.

Thus, we would be remiss in talking about George if we did not take an opportunity to explain his beloved behavior analysis framework in a few short sentences. This is admittedly a very brief overview, as George and others have written books on this subject. For an applied behavior analyst, behavior occurs in context and is occasioned by what happens before (antecedent; i.e., a teacher tells her students to take out a book and read silently) and after (consequences; i.e., the teacher says to the class, "great job following directions") the behavior. The consequence either increases (reinforces), decreases (punishes), or has no discernable effect (neutral) on the likelihood the behavior will occur in the future. An individual's experiences as a member of a particular family, community, culture, and so forth also influence her/his behavior, as these groups tend to occasion and respond similarly to behavior. When we look at patterns of behavior in context, the events surrounding the behavior, and the individual's experiences, we can determine why someone engages in a behavior or, as a behaviorist calls it, identify the function of behavior. We use this information to predict the future occurrence of a behavior and to help individuals engage in socially appropriate behaviors (Cooper, Heron, & Heward, 2007).

The theory of behaviorism weaves its way through George's (and everyone's) life, impacting his behaviors and his success. As former students, colleagues, and friends of George, we have experienced this firsthand. For this chapter, we first describe George's early learning history and cultural experiences. Then we provide a theory of change based on the principles of ABA and PBIS that we think captures George's initial focus for supporting individual students with behavioral disorders, as well as his expanded focus on schools, districts, states/provinces, and countries in systems-level change. We explore a key part of this theory of change as we try to unravel a bit more of the behavioral shaping of Dr. George Sugai, the damn behaviorist.

GEORGE'S EARLY LEARNING HISTORY AND CULTURAL BACKGROUND

As we think about how George's behaviors evolved, we want to start with his learning history (personal experiences) and cultural background—the experiences in his early years that helped to make him the person he is today. George was born in Santa Cruz, California in 1951 as a third-generation Japanese-American. George's grandfathers came from Japan to the United States for farming work, and they settled in the Pinto Lake region of the Salinas Valley. His grandmothers were "mail-order" brides, pre-arranged by their respective families and sent by boat to California. During World War II (WWII), his mother and her family were jailed in internment camps for 2.5 years in Poston, Arizona. His mother graduated from Poston Camp High School. George's father moved with his family to Utah, where they were able to live freely with support from the local Salt Lake City community. After WWII, George's parents returned to Watsonville (in California) to restart their lives, and once re-settled, they married. The Japanese-American community represented a strong and resilient social and cultural foundation in rural California. With a high school diploma, George's father worked in various capacities as a farmer, landscaper, public school groundskeeper, and eventually as a city parks supervisor. While still maintaining a traditional homemaker role, his mother completed community college and worked as a bookkeeper.

Although his grandparents' and parents' direct connections to Japan and Japanese culture were strong, what George took most from his parents was a love and commitment to family. Many decisions made by his parents about family and children were directly influenced by their war and post-war experiences. At home, his parents spoke little Japanese and more English because they wanted George and his sister to be exposed to an Americanized way of living. Although they ate simple farm-style Japanese food, they also adopted more Western-style meals. His parents focused on the importance of family and supporting George and his sister to achieve more than their own generation. When George's father was offered a better job, they moved from Santa Cruz to Los Gatos, California in 1962. Part of that move was also seen as an opportunity to improve the children's education. Unlike Santa Cruz, where the Japanese-American community was well- established, in Los Gatos George and his sister were the only Japanese-Americans in their schools. Most of the students were white.

George's early experiences clearly shaped who he is and what he does. For example, George recalls that his parents were open to others with differences. One of the daughters of a close family friend was a girl with severe disabilities who was a little older than George, and he remembers playing with her just as he would with any other childhood friend. In another example, George warmly describes a number of summers spent with his grandmother and grandfather on their boysenberry and orange farm in the central valley of California. Although he was too young to pick berries, he has fond memories of playing with the children of migrant workers, trading baloney sandwiches for homemade bean-filled tortillas, and riding on his uncle's tractor.

His parents firmly believed that a Japanese/American could be successful with an education, as this would increase options for work and life in the United States; thus, they made every effort to move George and his sister in the direction of higher education. When George was accepted at the University of California at Santa Barbara (UCSB) in 1969, he became one of the first persons in his family to attend a four-year college. At UCSB, George studied Botany, which seemed to follow his experiences on the farms and his father's interest in landscaping, native plants, and forestry. He was also influenced by the environmental movement at the time, and thought that being a park ranger would be a great career. As part of his undergraduate training, George learned about the scientific method and its application to the understanding and study of nature. When George graduated with a degree in Biological Sciences, specifically in Botany, in 1973, he was fulfilling his parents' educational dream, extending his interests in environment and nature, and expressing his place within the social change movements of his generation.

While at UCSB, George worked at Camp Harmon, an Easter Seals summer camp for students with disabilities. He was excited about the job because it was among the redwood trees in the Santa Cruz mountains, triggered by his interest in Botany. Although he had no background in working with individuals with disabilities, George was made counselor of a unit that included campers ages 16–52 with a variety of physical disabilities (e.g., cerebral palsy, muscular dystrophy, Down syndrome, polio). He worked as a camp counselor in 1971 and Unit Director of the boys' counselors in 1972. This experience represented a major shaping event in his career path, directly shifting his focus from Botany to children with disabilities.

With this new experience and enthusiasm in working with people with disabilities, George returned to school and earned a teaching certificate and a Master of Science degree in Special Education in Behavior Disorders from the University of Washington (UW) in 1974. His master's program emphasized precision teaching and applied behavior analysis, and initiated his grounding in behaviorism. This shaping was not unexpected given his biological training in the scientific method.

While in his master's program, one of his major mentors, Rick Neel, suggested that he enroll in a practicum at the SAGE program for students with severe behavior disorders in Edmonds, Washington, an alternative education school for students identified with behavioral disorders. Through this experience, he became fascinated by the challenge of educating students who also presented significant norm-violating behavior and were ostracized from traditional public school classrooms. Thus, he narrowed his work in special education to students with severe behavior disorders (BD) and challenges.

Given the impetus from the "new special education law," PL 94–142, George was hired to develop one of the first special education resource rooms at the middle school level in the Aurora Public Schools in Colorado. He and his colleagues wrote some of the first Individualized Education Programs (IEPs), developed some of the first behavior intervention plans (BIP), and later went on to establish one of the first cross-district programs for students with behavior disorders. Although few "evidence-based practices" had been documented and few "good" models of IEPs and BIP were available, George and his colleagues were pioneers of the implementation of what is now known as the Individuals with Disabilities Education Act or "IDEA."

During subsequent summers, George continued his camp counseling work. In Colorado, he helped set up and run a summer day program for students with disabilities. During another summer he was head counselor for students with significant emotional and behavioral disorders at Camp Timbertop in Ridge, New Hampshire. Although the camp was psychoanalytically grounded, George maintained a more behavioral approach in his unit, and he proudly describes how his students earned "most improved" and "best unit" awards at the end of the summer.

Finding that he needed to learn more about educating students with disabilities, especially behavioral disorders, in 1978, George returned to UW to pursue his doctorate. Although his initial interest was development of alternative programs for students with disabilities, he found his focus shifting to behavioral sciences, applied research, and personnel preparation, and his program plan was directed toward a new career in higher education. He acknowledges that his cohort was important in shaping his doctoral experience, and fondly describes the support and relationships that were initiated and still exist with special education researchers and leaders, such as Don Bailey, Mark Wolery, John Emerson, and Susan Harris. During that time, he developed much greater fluency with behavior analysis, single subject research, and precision teaching, in large part because of this strong peer cohort. In 1980, he graduated with a Ph.D. in Special Education and Behavior Disorders from UW.

During his doctoral years at UW, George met his wife and fellow special educator, Betsy Fernandez, while doing observations in an alternative school for students with behavior disorders. Betsy was completing a practicum for her master's degree. United by their interest in education (and other mutual interests), George and Betsy ultimately married.

THEORY OF CHANGE: EFFECTING CHANGE FOR INDIVIDUAL STUDENTS TO SYSTEMS

For those of us who have had the pleasure of working with George or hearing him present at conferences, we know that George likes to use a clear theory of change to support his ideas. Those who have worked with George have likely been asked, "What is the mechanism of change?" or "How would you explain any change that you might see?" For George, a theory of change provides the framework to clearly (a) understand a problem or phenomenon, (b) propose an action to address the problem, (c) explain the results of that action, and (d) propose future actions. Thus, we believe it is important to describe George's work using a clear theory of change.

Our theory of change for Dr. Sugai begins with his learning history, which continues to accumulate across time. After exploring key aspects of George's learning history and cultural background, the next part of his theory of change focuses on what happens before the behavior (antecedent). Once we explore antecedents, we will complete the theory of change with consequences (i.e., what happens after a behavior has occurred). Because we are describing patterns of antecedents, behaviors, and consequences that span George's career, we have taken liberty to describe themes within each category. For consequences, for example, we choose to highlight the area of publication and grants. Overall, George has published over 130 peer-reviewed articles, numerous monographs, and five college textbooks. In Table 5.1, we highlight key components of George's theory of change that lead to products and his continued professional contributions to the field.

George's Initial Focus: Improving the Outcomes of Students with Behavioral Disorders Learning History

Before going to the University of Kentucky in 1979, where he began his academic career as Assistant Professor in Special Education, George was shaped by teaching and learning experiences at UW with Rick Neel (behavior disorders), David Ryckman (disabilities), Owen White (precision teaching), Norrie Haring (emotional disturbance, precision teaching), Felix Billingsley (developmental disabilities), Ellis Evans (educational psychology), Gene Edgar (precision teaching, behavior disorders), and Tom Lovitt (learning disabilities).

His major mentors at the University of Kentucky (UK) included Mike Nelson (behavior disorders), Ed Blackhurst (competency-based special education), Bill Berdine (mental retardation), Susan Dollar (talented and gifted, direct instruction), Carol Sue Englert (learning disabilities), David Gast (single subject research), Don Cross (educational assessment), Kay Stevens (behavior disorders), and Mark Wolery (applied behavior analysis, early childhood special education). At this point, his primary focus was applications of behavior analysis to support students with challenging behaviors.

In 1983, George left academia briefly to serve as Treatment Director at the Spaulding Youth Center in Tilton, New Hampshire, in order to gain additional applied experience and bring applied behavior analysis and precision teaching to the center. However, shortly after arriving, he discovered a major shift in personnel and a move away from behaviorism. Although he enjoyed working with staff to develop effective programming for children and youth with behavior disorders and autism, he found that this position was less than ideal and he moved on to pursue other career options.

In 1984, he accepted a grant-funded faculty position at the University of Oregon (UO) working on a grant led by Ruth Waugh. George shared this position with Gerald (Jerry) Tindal, who had been mentored by Stan Deno and Jim Ysseldyke. After successfully securing external funding, Ruth asked the College of Education to split her tenure-track position between George and Jerry. As such, George was promoted to Associate Professor with tenure in Special Education at UO in 1989. In 1991, George was awarded a sabbatical and served as a Visiting Research Fellow in Special Needs Education studies at Edith Cowan University in Mount Lawley, Western Australia. In 1997, he was promoted to Full Professor at UO.

George speaks fondly of his UO mentors and colleagues, who include Ed Kame'enui, Rob Horner, Jerry Tindal, Deb Simmons, Anne Todd, and Geoff Colvin. Equally influential were his doctoral students who have established their own successful careers in higher education (e.g., Tary Tobin, Tim Lewis, Randy DePry, Terry Scott, Teri Lewis, Shanna Hagan-Burke, Mack Burke, Brandi Simonsen, Diane Myers) and in the schools (e.g., Kimberly Ingram, Sarah Fairbanks, Jane Carter, Betsy Ramsey, Annemieke Golly, Larry Soberman, Kimberly Thier).

Antecedents. From 1984 to 2005, George's main focus was improving outcomes for students with behavioral disorders, which stemmed directly from his early learning history. In addition, George's ongoing applied and research experiences and his desire to address the dire outcomes for students with behavioral disorders in the absence of appropriate support, continued to direct his scholarship, teaching, and related behaviors toward improving outcomes for students with BD. With his colleague, Dr. Gerald Tindal, he established the Behavior Research and Training (BRT) group, and he was very happy with (or, as George might say, positively reinforced by) his work and collaborations at the University of Oregon.

Behaviors. As evidenced by his prior work and training, George had a natural affinity toward students with behavior challenges. Through his writing about best practices or instructional approaches, George has demonstrated his ongoing commitment to this at-risk population. He has contributed to developing effective assessments for this population, emphasizing the importance of addressing cultural diversity using an applied behavior lens and using screening data to identify students needing support early. He has also contributed directly to the development and use of social skills instruction and curricula for students to increase

Desired outcome	Learning history and cultural background	Antecedents	Behaviors	Consequences
Improved outcomes for students with behavioral disorders	Early personal, family, cultural, social experiences	Enhancing fluency with behavioral and prevention sciences	Applying behavioral sciences to applied problems and questions	Improved outcomes for all students, including those with behavioral difficulties and their families
Increased number and use of evidence-based practices	Early applied work experiences (e.g., camp, schools)	Educating students with behavioral difficulties who experience poorer outcomes than almost any other group of students	Conducting systematic research to applied problems	Research disseminated to a variety of audiences (researchers, practitioners, politicians and policy makers) through publications and presentations
Enhanced environments (classrooms and schools) for practice implementation	Advanced academic training and experiences (M.A., Ph.D.)	Working with families of students with behavior disorders	Publishing—Writing articles for peer refereed journals	
		Working in schools and districts that have been unsuccessful in meeting their education expectations and outcomes	Procuring funding—Writing grant applications for peer reviewed competitions	Grants awarded to study identified problems
Increased number of educators, school leaders, and researchers who have behavioral expertise	Research and research to practice experiences		Teaching—Communicating science-based behaviors to students enrolled in a course or program of study	External awards and other recognitions given to recognize achievement
	Dissemination experiences	Collaborating with general and special educators, school psychologists and counselors, social workers, administrators, etc.		
Enhanced policies and procedures that reflect evidenced-based practices and systems		Working with researchers, personnel preparers, policy makers, education leaders	Mentoring—Providing guidance and support to students and colleagues	Students and advisees become productive leaders in the field

Source: Authors.

Table 5.1: Key Components of George's Theory of Change

appropriate student behavior. Through it all, George used his applied behavior analytic lens to address behavior, focusing on why a behavior occurs repeatedly (function-based support), including his direct work with students, writing about function-based behavior support plans, and working with teachers and other professionals such as school psychologists, counselors, and administrators. Over his career, George has written extensively about students with behavioral challenges from an applied perspective, arguing that these students should receive evidence-based interventions. He has also integrated this work into his teaching and advising, mentoring some of the key leaders in our field.

Consequences. George has been awarded several federal grants to develop interventions that directly benefit students and teachers. These grant awards from the Office of Special Education Programs (OSEP) have focused on a range of topics, including, for example, behavior management (e.g., social skills), teacher preparation (e.g., on behavior management), and self-management (e.g., self-observation and self-recording). He also has worked on grants that address the function of behavior from an ABA perspective, including a functional examination of problem behavior and literacy difficulties in your children and comprehensive functional assessments for schools. Again, these grants addressed the needs of students with behavioral difficulties and those professionals that support them in schools. Through these grants and related scholarly accomplishments, George demonstrated improved outcomes for individual students with BD, which is the most meaningful "reinforcer" for his work. Despite these successes, George began to observe that improving outcomes for students with BD on a larger scale would require shifting his focus from the individual to systems-level interventions.

Shaping of School Systems to Promote Positive Outcomes for All Students Learning History

While engaging in work to support individual students with behavioral disorders, George began his work with key individuals who would help him to effectuate change in schools at a systems-wide level. Working with like-minded colleagues such as Geoff Colvin and Ed Kame'enui at the University of Oregon (UO), George began to expand the focus of behavior supports from individual students to schools through an OSEP funded project called Project PREPARE in 1991. This project developed the Effective Behavior Support (EBS) approach to promoting the use of teaching to improve the behaviors of students. Importantly, this project permitted the systematic development of an intervention model in which the intersection of behavior and the architecture of direct instruction were primary foci. Specifically, EBS emphasized the antecedents of managing or "teaching" new behavior to students. The emphasis of the project was on ensuring that students had been adequately "taught" the new behavior based on the design of instruction principles, including, for example, a clear and explicit model of the unknown behavior, adequate teaching examples of positive and negative instances of the behavior, proper sequencing of the modeled examples, adequate feedback, and scaffolding of support to ensure the behavior was adequately practiced and executed.

In addition, Hill Walker and his colleagues at the UO introduced George to the public health model of prevention and intervention that was first established in the field of psychiatry and public health (Caplan & Grunebaum, 1967). This prevention approach examined the need of the individual and matched that need with the appropriate level of prevention—primary, secondary and tertiary. At the same time, George began his work with Rob Horner and his colleagues at the Specialized Training Program (STP). Rob had been working with families and communities in the use of positive behavior support, primarily with individuals with developmental disabilities.

Through their collective work and prior piloted projects, George and Rob linked forces in 1995 to apply for a grant to support a federal center for Positive Behavior Interventions and Support (PBIS). This center was funded and introduced the application of applied behavior analysis and positive behavior support to the population of all children in schools, meeting their needs with a prevention-focused tiered system of delivery. Positive Behavioral Interventions and Supports has become a widely adopted framework and approach within the United States and internationally. As the center was re-funded for subsequent five-year cycles, one of George's former students, Tim Lewis, was recruited as a third co-director of the center. George, Rob, and Tim now co-direct one of the longest running, federally-funded centers in the field of special education.

In the early 2000s, George was approached by the University of Connecticut (UCONN) to consider accepting an endowed chair position in behavior disorders. This incredible opportunity would allow George to expand his efforts and pursue areas of study that would not otherwise be possible. His wife Betsy had family in the Boston area, and they were excited about opportunities for their two children on the east coast. The UCONN endowment also gave him financial support to start a research center and the opportunity to gather research faculty who shared a similar vision and theory of change. Thus, in 2005, George accepted the Carole J. Neag Endowed Chair Professor with tenure in Special Education at the Neag School of Education at the University of Connecticut.

As part of the endowed chair position, George was given the opportunity to recruit an assistant professor, and he recruited Brandi Simonsen (third author), whom he had met at the University of Oregon and was working as Director of an alternative program for students with BD in California. George worked with existing UCONN faculty members—Michael Coyne and Sandy Chafouleas—to establish the Center for Behavioral Education and Research

(CBER) within the Neag School of Education at the University of Connecticut. CBER was formally approved by the UCONN Board of Trustees in 2006, and George served as CBER Director. In 2016, George transitioned his role from director to Senior Research Scientist within CBER, where he continues to collaborate with current CBER co-directors, Michael Coyne and Brandi Simonsen.

Over the last 10 years, George has developed and shaped CBER into a highly respected, productive, and recognized working group by maintaining clearly defined goals, objectives, and working approach (theory of change). Words that characterize CBER include empirical, applied, experimental, and outcome-oriented. CBER research scientists have national and international visibility: Michael Coyne (early literacy, learning disabilities), Brandi Simonsen (PBIS, classroom and behavior management, behavior disorders), Sandy Chafouleas (behavioral assessment, behavioral health, school psychology), Lisa Sanetti (implementation integrity, school psychology), Natalie Olinghouse (writing, learning disabilities), Devin Kearns (reading instruction, learning disabilities), Allison Lombardi (college and career readiness, transition), Jen Freeman (PBIS, supporting high schools, behavior disorders), and Tamika LaSalle (school climate and culture, school psychology). Under George's directorship, CBER has become a highly respected working group among the many UCONN centers and institutes. CBER research scientists are involved in a wide range of professional national and international efforts, and are involved in shaping the national agenda for research, personnel preparation, technical assistance, and professional development.

Antecedents

For George, educating and supporting students with BD was more about changing and improving the adults' systems of support than changing student behavior. To effect lasting change, *adults* needed to adjust their behaviors too. That is, improvements were needed in the systems in place that supported the implementers of evidence-based practices. By investing in systems-change efforts within a prevention framework, George and colleagues worked to redesign the overall school or "host" environment to become more preventive. All students needed formalized supports to prevent the development of problem behavior (incidence prevention), and some students needed more intensive supports to prevent the worsening (frequency, intensity, duration, force) of existing problem behaviors (prevalence prevention).

Thus, to achieve meaningful improvements at the student and classroom level, George and colleagues have focused on systems change, prevention, and implementation considerations at the school, district, state, and federal levels.

Behaviors

George's second primary focus area is the examination and integration of a multitiered level of systems support (MTSS) approach for all students in school settings, which is foundational to PBIS and is prominent in his publications and grants. Although PBIS is widely associated with behavior support systems, George has encouraged schools to look at their academic and behavior systems as complementary. To that end, he has published articles on the applied and conceptual basis for PBIS and the importance of focusing on implementation integrity, integration, sustainability, and capacity development on those support systems. Although he is often associated with special education, he has encouraged the integration of special and regular education, mental health, juvenile justice, and other related school disciplines. Over the last 10 years, George and his colleagues have emphasized the application of prevention and behavioral sciences to a range of cross-discipline topics, including culture, decision-based data systems, academic-behavior influences, school climate, state and national policy, and systems change at the district and state levels. His behavior analytic theory of change is prominent across these efforts.

Consequences

George and his colleagues have been awarded multiple grants and contracts examining school-wide PBIS practices and systems implementation. As mentioned previously, in 1995, George and his colleagues were awarded a grant by the federal government (OSEP) to explore the use of school-wide PBIS at a national level by establishing a national technical assistance center on PBIS. Currently in its fourth round of funding, the PBIS Center has been introduced to more than 24,000 schools across the United States and has shown positive results in improving student behavior on a large-scale level. Other grants have included literacy initiatives across the state and federal levels and across multiple levels of schools (e.g., elementary, middle, high school). George has also worked with Mary Beth Bruder as co-director of an early childhood center that prepares leaders to work in early childhood special education.

As a result of the importance of his efforts and those of his colleagues, George is invited to present on the work of the PBIS Center and CBER at a variety of levels. He has presented in Washington, D.C. before a variety of congressional education and health committees and to staff within governmental departments (e.g., education, health). George is regularly invited to provide keynote and major presentations at national and international events (e.g., Association of Positive Behavior Supports, Council for Children with Behavior Disorders, School Mental Health Associations, Australia Special Education Administrators, Asian

Pacific Positive Behavior Supports) and a variety of state and regional events. In addition, George and his colleagues receive regular invitations to contribute to special journal issues, edited books, and topical research and practitioner briefs.

CONCLUSION: SHAPING THE FUTURE

As we have seen from George's learning history, George lives the life he encourages. He suggests that we arrange our work/life environments so that at least 80% of what we do is positively reinforcing. He exemplifies this approach in his emphasis of "family first," whereby a family situation takes precedent over other obligations. He surrounds himself with colleagues who promote preventive and positive approaches in school settings, and he makes every effort to model what he promotes (e.g., active supervision, more positives than negatives, pre-correction). In essence, George provides a model for all who have the privilege of working with him to be the positive change we promote.

As we conclude this chapter, we find ourselves applying another aspect of George's theoretical framework. In one of his foundational publications, Gresham, Sugai, and Horner (2001) explore the literature on social skills instruction. Applying an ABA perspective, they write that there are four phases of learning: acquisition (i.e., learning a task for the first time), fluency (i.e., practicing a task until it becomes automatic), maintenance (i.e., being able to perform the task again after time has passed), and generalization (i.e., being able to perform the task in different settings, with different people; Cooper et al., 2007). Generalization is the ultimate goal of teaching, as this final phase of learning allows individuals to become successful at applying their skills independently across contexts. George has promoted generalization and scaled his work from supports for individual students and educators to schools, districts, states/provinces and federal agencies in the United States and other countries. He has presented and provided professional development in Jamaica, Cayman Islands, Canada, New Zealand, Netherlands, Australia, Spain, Canada, Japan, England, and Denmark. George has worked to develop systems to support implementation of PBIS internationally and adapted practices for diverse cultures to ensure yet again that *all* students have access to education that will lead to successful outcomes. George's work approach reflects his generalized ability to organize environments for success; that is, self-managed behaviors that manipulate antecedents and consequences to promote desired behaviors.

We opened our chapter with a quote by Ralph Waldo Emerson that reflects what we have experienced with George. He has made us laugh and has earned our respect. He is literally a positive reinforcer for his students and colleagues. He has weathered and outlasted critics of a behavioral approach in schools. And, he has applied his function-based and behavior analytic theory of action to arrange his environments for success. Overall, George has taught us that we must look at the behavior of the individual and the influence of the system and focus on promoting the behavior that is socially and educationally important. He has helped to shape the world into a better place for all children and adolescents through his work with students, teachers, schools, and communities. We firmly believe that if we were to define success, George Sugai and the work that he has done with us would be our operational definition. George has dramatically influenced the personal experiences of his students, teachers, and those he has mentored and the field of special education. To that end, we share in his learning and cultural experiences, because what has shaped the success of George, has shaped us all.

REFERENCES

Caplan, G., & Grunebaum, H. (1967). Perspectives on primary prevention: A review. *Archives of General Psychiatry, 17,* 331–346.

Cooper, J. O., Heron, T. E., & Heward, W. L. (2007). *Applied behavior analysis* (2nd ed.). Upper Saddle River, NJ: Pearson, Merrill Prentice Hall.

Emerson, R. W. (2015). On success. In R. W. Willoughby (Ed.), *The quotable Emerson. Life Lessons from the words of Ralph Waldo Emerson.* Middletown, DE: CreateSpace Independent Publishing Platform.

Gresham, F. M., Sugai, G., & Horner, R. (2001). Interpreting outcomes of social skills training for students with high-incidence disabilities. *Exceptional Children, 67,* 331–344.

CHAPTER SIX

Rice Paddy Resiliency

The Transformation of a Chinese American, Scholar, and Endowed Professor for Global Leadership Studies[1]

RITA POIMBEAUF

INTRODUCTION

As the shadows began to fall, a frail girl stood barefoot in the flooded rice fields transplanting the fragile shoots. It was early spring in Qian Jin, China, a village in the northeast, and the water from melted snow was icy cold. The girl could no longer feel her feet, and her fingers were just as numb. Besides being hungry and weak, the young girl was terrified of the leeches that attached themselves to her legs and sucked her blood. To survive, she knew that she must plant the rice shoots that were allocated to her for that day before she could return to her meager tent for shelter. She, along with the others, worked 14 hours each day and this misery would be repeated the next day with no relief in sight.

Her head became light from the pain and her fright at the sight of the leeches on her legs, causing her to fall into the waters. The commune leader who watched over the planting came over to reprimand her for stopping work. She begged him to kill her, having lost her will to live and believing that there was no hope for her future. With no running water or electricity and with hardly enough to eat, the girl faced brutal living conditions. Her name was Yali Zou.

---

1 Information in this chapter is based on personal and telephone interviews conducted by the author with Yali Zou. Zou, Y. (2017, May–July). Personal interview and telephone conversations.

As a consequence of the Cultural Revolution (1966–1976), Yali was sent to the countryside to gain an understanding of the value of work and be re-educated by the peasants (接受贫下中农再教育). According to the calling of Chairman Mao, then the leader of the Chinese communist party, "Educated youth must go to countryside." In 1966, the calls began, "Climb the mountain. Go to the field" (上山下乡). During this period, the categorization of people into different ranks became a common practice fueled by the prevalent social ideology. The workers, peasants and soldiers were highly regarded, whereas the intellectuals were the less favorable category, known as the "stinking old ninth rank" (臭老九). Yali Zou was placed in that ninth rank. Mao believed educated youth could revolt against his government and he wanted them out of the cities. From her home in Jilin Province in northeast China, Yali reluctantly became one of the millions of students who were sent to remote and unfamiliar poor villages to receive re-education from the peasants. Re-education involved keeping the youth exhausted and isolated thereby rendering them unfit to cause trouble. Yali was separated from her siblings who were also dispersed to different remote areas leaving each one of them alone and unable to comfort one another.

Nonetheless, Yali survived her dire circumstances owing to the village leader's vision and especially his pity for Yali. Further, in Yali, he saw hope for his village. He always dreamed that someday his village's children could read and write. He asked Yali if she could teach the children to read and write. In the whole village, not a single person was literate. Yali used her temporary tent as a classroom and began teaching the children. Besides teaching them how to read, Yali found that she had to teach the children basic hygiene such as washing their faces and washing their clothes. She cut their hair to combat their lice problem. More importantly, she taught them to write their names and to sing songs. As a result, the village children became happy and enjoyed learning. The village parents were grateful for the care given by Yali when they heard about the school from their children. A sweet potato during that time was considered a luxury and Yali's students brought her sweet potatoes as gifts. Yet, Yali did not have enough food to eat and had to sometimes supplement with wild mountain vegetables and tree leaves. Gradually, the villagers started to trust her as they shared their family problems with her enabling her to help them even further.

When she visited the students' families, she learned that many, especially the women, suffered from arthritis due to long years of physical labor. Even worse, some of them had such compromised bodies and health that they lost their physical ability to work. Yali stepped in to help the people suffering from debilitating pain. Since no doctors were available in the countryside, she carried acupuncture needles with her to reduce her migraine pain and cope with any other health problems. Yali offered this acupuncture treatment to the villagers. As a result, many started to recover from their pain and were able to resume work. The news traveled that Yali could treat people and villagers from far away sought her help. People called her "barefoot doctor" (a doctor without a certificate). The country-side experience helped Yali recognize that education could transform the poor peasants' lives. Yali saved herself through teaching and her service to the villagers. The countryside leader, although an unlikely source, could be considered her first mentor. He recognized the importance of education and planted the thought in Yali of working in education.

EARLY WORK

In 1970, two years after Yali started working in the countryside, China enacted a new policy that allowed selected youth to return to urban areas for work in the factories. The fact that Yali changed the villagers' lives made her the first to be chosen. Yali returned to the city and worked in a factory producing steel and iron. In 1972, quite unexpectedly, an opportunity presented itself that changed Yali's life even more. The universities were reopened and everyone could take an entrance exam. Yali Zou did well on her exam—she was ranked number one in her city.

After her exam results were verified, Yali almost immediately enrolled at Shanghai Foreign Institute where she studied the Albanian language. China had few friends at the time and Albania was their chief ally. Yali was chosen to learn Albanian to help her country which was in need of translators. By 1974, she became an interpreter for the government. This led to a job as a translator for the prestigious Changchun Film Studio, where she translated movies including *Early Spring*, *The Last Winter*, *Cut Off Devil's Claw*, and *Oil Explosion*. Yali's trans-lations into Mandarin Chinese meant that Albanian films could be enjoyed in China. The young girl from the rice fields had now blossomed into a remarkably talented young lady. Yali was earning a good salary and making contacts within the government. She benefitted from a cadre of prominent Albanian mentors and influential film people. It was noted that Yali Zou was intelligent, hard-working and a fast learner who performed as an excellent interpreter.

HEARTBREAK

Being an official government interpreter, Yali Zou was enjoying enormous privi-leges. She wanted to remain in this much-respected position forever. Yet, this was not to ensue. Quite unexpectedly, Yali Zou was told she had a life-threatening tumor in the front part of her neck and was referred to the Shanghai Hospital. There, she was given information that shook her to her very core: she was told that she would have to undergo immediate surgery to remove her tumor. Such surgery would cause her to lose her voice; losing her voice would mean losing her translator position. Her voice meant everything to her since it was what pulled her out of poverty and earned her the respect of her government and peers.

The Chinese at that time were promoting the use of acupuncture and its benefits. Fortunately, Yali's doctor was involved in the acupuncture promotion and provided an alternative for her procedure. If she wanted to keep her voice, she could choose acupuncture instead of anesthesia. Acupuncture provided greater control during surgery, allowing the doctors to communicate with her. She was informed that this surgery would be broadcast on television live for the world to witness the marvels of acupuncture. She would keep her voice at the sacrifice of tolerating the unbearable pain. Yali Zou's doctors offered her this type of surgery and the accompanying promotion because they wanted someone who had experience with foreigners, could articulate their ideas and, more importantly, could eloquently answer reporter questions after surgery. Yali Zou was their perfect choice to promote surgery with acupuncture.

However, Yali, in her thirties, was in denial that she had a tumor and hesitated to agree to surgery. On the contrary, the leader of the medical team informed her that her tumor was serious and it needed immediate removal. He arranged for her to be admitted to one of the hospitals in Shanghai. The following day her father appeared in her hospital room as she lay overwhelmed by her pending surgery; his very appearance helped her believe that she had a serious problem. Her government leader would not have arranged for her father to be there had she not been seriously ill.

Yali's operation was broadcast for the world to see; she endured major surgery with only four acupuncture needles. Furthermore, a gallery was assembled above her operating table so that medical people and guests from the United Nations observed her surgery. The observers could verify that the surgery was not only real but was an astonishing medical feat for the Chinese doctors. Afterwards, news reporters interviewed Yali asking many questions about the surgery; she responded positively, singing the praises of her doctors. Her interview, too, was broadcast around the world. The medical world marveled at the apparent Chinese ability to control pain. However, the way Yali, only now, describes it is that she was in excruciating pain. To this day, she carries an eight-inch scar around her neck. Yali remembers that experience as a time when she behaved so as to please her leaders and her family.

MORE LIFE CHANGES

Other changes occurred in Yali's life rather quickly. She married a physics professor who she met after surgery and had a baby girl. Around the same time, she was appointed associate professor and chair of the Department of Foreign Languages at Changchun Science and Technology Institute in Jilin Province. Their school curriculum had not been changed for a decade; the faculty used only outdated textbooks. Yali brought new leadership and a new vision; she reworked the curriculum and improved on the contents of textbooks. She led the faculty in rewriting the textbooks. Yali Zou threw herself completely into this restructuring effort and it paid off with her students winning top academic awards in the government sponsored competition.

GOLDEN MOUNTAIN

The China Education Ministry awarded Yali's efforts by providing her with the opportunity to travel to the United States as a visiting scholar at the University of California at Davis (UCD) in 1988. This was a remarkable opportunity to be sent to the Golden Mountain to pursue the American dream. Chinese words that sound similar to San Francisco mean old golden mountain. With great confidence and big dreams, she arrived in beautiful America.

However, upon her arrival, Yali immediately realized that she was not prepared to function in this totally different socio-cultural environment. Once she stepped onto American soil, she became aware that she was different in many ways; she dressed differently, spoke differently and ate differently. Yali's English was not what the Americans spoke; she knew the homogenized English of the textbook. By trial and error, she was learning the American language and all the innuendos that went with it. There were times in her work and in her personal life where she was embarrassed by her lack of skill in English. In addition, she had to learn the American way of doing things in all aspects of university life. In other words, Yali was experiencing culture shock: American culture was an unanticipated stumbling block. As Yali tells it, these experiences helped shape her evolving identity. Yali Zou was gradually becoming a product of two cultures; she was developing a dual identity.

Yali recalls an incident where she was invited to a professor's house for dinner. Many foods were available for her; it was a smorgasbord of delicacies. Her host asked her what she wanted to eat. Observing her best Chinese manners, she requested the humblest food available—chicken noodle soup. Much to her surprise, she was served the chicken noodle soup, and nothing else, and went home hungry. In her home country, it would have been customary to give a guest the best of everything regardless of what a guest had requested. Unfortunately, Americans did not adhere to this expected pattern. Right off, it became one of many lessons that Yali Zou would learn: customs did not cross cultures, as Yali would later explain.

YALI'S GRADUATE DEGREES

Near the end of her first year at UCD, Yali attended the university's commencement ceremony. There, she witnessed this honorable tradition for the first time in her life and was mesmerized. After that, she told her advisor, Dr. Doug Minis at UCD, that she wanted to pursue an American diploma and experience the remarkable journey to a graduate degree. Dr. Minis told her anything was possible as long as she was prepared to work hard for it. His words were all Yali needed to hear.

In Dr. Minis, Yali had a powerful mentor who helped her through her college program at UCD. She wanted to stay in the United States to study because she saw the privileges and rewards of American life. Yali was on her way, or so one would think. She was intelligent, had learned how to navigate campus, and clearly she could study as hard as any other student. There was, however, one major drawback to this promising situation. The Chinese government allowed her to study at UCD, but they would not finance her studies. It was up to Yali Zou to find funds for her graduate endeavor.

By now, Yali Zou's struggles and successes brought her a new strength and maturity as she faced further challenges. Yali embraced her journey to a degree with vigor. To earn money, she taught Chinese during the day and attended classes; she obtained a second job of washing dishes in the faculty lounge at night. The time in between her classes and work was devoted to studying. Compounding the challenging nature of her situation was that Yali was taking classes and studying from materials that were not in her first language. Yet, she never wavered because she had that vision of her graduation and advanced degree. The one room that she and her roommate could afford contained only two beds, one table and two chairs, but that was all that she needed. Yali graduated from UCD in 1991 with an M.A. in Curriculum and Instruction. Her master's thesis was titled, *Healing Multicultural America: Minority Education*, which explored a case in the California courts that argued in favor of multicultural education for minority students' academic achievement. This court ruling on multicultural education was a groundbreaking decision in California that changed the way minority students were educated.

The contacts Yali made during her graduate years proved to be life-changing. As a highly-prestigious university, UCD attracted quality professors. For example, during Yali's time there, Dr. George Spindler, a Stanford professor, taught at UCD as a visiting professor and Dr. Henry T. Trueba, an influential scholar, was leading the Education Division. Yali worked with them and they became life-long friends. Dr. Spindler was a famous pioneer in educational anthropology; Dr. Trueba introduced ethnography to Yali Zou. Both scholars introduced a new field of study to her. Dr. Trueba's work reflected what Yali believed was critical to understanding dual cultures, minority education and immigration issues. These concepts then grew into Yali's main research interest.

A master's degree was not enough to satisfy Yali Zou. She stayed at UCD and pursued her Ph.D.; she had developed a secure support system and felt comfortable in her surroundings. However, her experiences in America while obtaining her schooling at UCD changed this Chinese woman's perspective. She observed how language and culture influenced one's life; she saw how all immigrants, regardless of their country, faced common problems adjusting to American life. At the same time, she was deeply motivated by the opportunities available to anyone who could overcome the challenges of a new culture, new language and new people. She knew firsthand that this transformation could happen since she had, herself, reinvented her life. She became very interested in exploring multicultural experiences and survival. In 1993, Dr. Yali Zou obtained her Ph.D. in Education in Sociocultural Foundations. She was honored by UCD at her graduation by being selected as the flag bearer for this ceremony. Her dissertation was titled, *Power in Education: The Case of Miao University Students and Its Significance for American Culture* (Trueba & Zou, 1994). This case study focused on the empowerment of some of the poorest Miao peasants who eventually became university students and obtained high prestige in mainstream Chinese society.

Yali's research illustrates the commitment that Miao students had to their villages, families and communities. It further demonstrates how they made sacrifices to reach academic excellence in school and thereby gained honor for their families and communities. Her dissertation covers the theoretical context of ethnic identity and academic achievement, the historical context of the Miao people in China, and the testimonies of students and their professors, relative to their university experiences. Finally, it provides a discussion of the ethnic motivation that drives students and examines the power of education in helping even the poorest peasants achieve highly in competitive society. Dr. Yali Zou's research became a small step in influencing multicultural awareness in America.

EARLY PROFESSIONAL WORK

This Chinese immigrant supervised graduate thesis work at California State University in Sacramento and later became a postdoctoral fellow and research associate at the University of Wisconsin at Madison. During this time, she honed her thinking about adaptive strategies necessary for immigrants to achieve success. Several of Dr. Zou's books were standard textbooks on campuses nationwide for multicultural studies and doctoral students' methodological training. Dr. Zou and Dr. Trueba collaborated on research that examined how to inspire immigrant children and how to achieve justice in society. Together, they edited two groundbreaking books, *Ethnic Identity and Power: Cultural Contexts of Political Action in School and Society* (Zou & Trueba, 1998) and *Ethnography and Schools: Qualitative Approaches to the Study of Education* (Zou & Trueba, 2002). Upon reviewing the first publication, Gilda Maria Bloom, a professor from San Francisco State University commented, "… [A] fascinating book on the role of cultural identity for political action as well as the educational implications of cultural identity. The authors weave the notion of ethnic identity and power throughout each article, thereby providing the reader with compelling evidence that these notions have serious implications for pedagogical praxis." A review of their second publication by renowned scholar Frederick Erickson stated, "This collection of essays is impressive for the range of approaches to ethnography that it covers, from classic interpretive ethnography through critical ethnography to action research." At that time, the exploration of cross-cultural experiences and the integration of recent immigrants into American society was a new area of study and publication. Dr. Yali Zou was on the cusp of this research.

THE UNIVERSITY OF HOUSTON

In 1995, Dr. Yali Zou was recruited as assistant professor and director of the Asian International Programs by the University of Houston (UH) Main Campus, where she remains a noted scholar today. At UH, her career moved rapidly. Dr. Yali Zou was totally immersed in building UH into a showcase for Asian American Studies. She recognized there was an urgent need for an Asian American Center after researching African and Mexican American Studies. After a campus-wide survey and interviews of faculty and students exploring the need for Asian American Studies, she developed a proposal for the establishment of an Asian American Studies Center (AASC). The center emphasized the study of Asians and Asian Americans both in the United States and abroad while exploring their social, historical, economic, political and linguistic characteristics and development at the university. She also focused the Center's mission on generating knowledge, increasing awareness and fostering appreciation of the Asian American experience. UH approved establishment of the Asian American Studies Center in 1995 and appointed Dr. Yali Zou as its founding director. Her founding of the Center came at a time when nationally, there were only a few Asian American studies programs in existence.

Dr. Zou quickly found career advancement and personal satisfaction at UH. She was promoted to Associate Professor with tenure in 1998. In 2002, she earned a full Professorship in Educational Leadership and Cultural Studies while retaining the positions of Director of the Asian American Studies Center and Director of Asian International Programs. In eight years, she developed six academic programs that quickly led to national recognition for UH. In 2010, her department was renamed and she became professor of Educational Leadership and Policy Studies while still retaining her other duties.

Publications flowed during these years. Dr. Zou co-authored *Successful Management and Operation in the Service Industry: A Cultural Perspective* (Stutts & Zou, 1997). With Henry T. Trueba, she edited the two books previously cited. With Fuling Yang and Rita Poimbeauf, she edited *Knowing China by Learning Chinese Culture and Chinese People* (Zou, Yang, & Poimbeauf, 2014), an award-winning book commissioned by Tianjin University in China to assist in the adjustment of their American foreign exchange students. In addition, still in progress is another editing project with Fuling Yang, *Chinese Society and Its Politics*, commissioned by Tianjin University as a sequel to their first book. Currently, she is writing *The Houston Chinatown: Its Origin and Transformation* with Zen Zeng, a newspaper journalist. Other works include 15 chapters; 13 articles, mostly in peer-reviewed journals; and conference papers and presentations too numerous to enumerate. Finally, Yali Zou has co-authored *Cross Cultural and Transnational Understanding: Cultural Bump and Cultural Therapy* and *Chinese Culture in America*. Both works were in collaboration with former graduate students and currently under review. Again, Yali Zou was paying back for the opportunities that she enjoyed at UCD. Dr. Zou did not forget the support that she received as she did her graduate work and she now chooses to provide this same support to her graduate students. These works stand as tribute to her work ethic and her commitment to multiculturalism and immigrant education. That young girl in the rice fields certainly found her calling in America.

Along the way, Dr. Yali Zou became an American citizen in 2000; this made her transformation into a Chinese American complete. She was successful and admired by her colleagues. Although she was dedicated to the AASC, she found that the attainment of her life-long goals did not bring her the happiness that she thought would come with success. Then, a guest lecturer she invited to her class discussed looking at the differences an individual can make on society, and how small contributions can multiply into big changes that benefit all peoples. This led Dr. Zou to realize that her life should be about inspiring others to contribute more to society.

Thus, in 2003 Dr. Zou started to focus her work on the hardships that exchange students endured, particularly students from Asian countries. She helped them with cultural therapy, a term she initiated. She knew the foreign exchange students that she encountered were undergoing the same cultural missteps that she struggled with in her younger days. Never forgetting her dinner experience at UCD, she wanted them to study without major hardships and misunderstandings arising from life in an unfamiliar place. The AASC was created in part to help these students cope in their new land. In other words, Yali aimed to help these students live and thrive in two cultures, while they developed their dual identities.

Sometimes, Dr. Zou helped her students financially and she allowed them to live with her. As Dr. Minis, her UCD advisor, helped her navigate the inner workings at UCD, Dr. Zou began to help graduate students understand the processes and procedures necessary for a degree. She became the go-to person when difficulties arose in maneuvering the UH system. At times, she found herself talking in the middle of the night to their concerned parents in China. She served as a mentor, counselor, and translator.

Along with students coming to the United States from Asia, the AASC also advised Asian/American youth who were born and raised in the United States. Although these students had Asian heritage, they had little or no contact with Asia. What they knew was what their parents had told them about their heritage, culture, and language: Her Asian/American students had lost their culture. As a result, Dr. Zou incorporated a study abroad aspect into her cultural program, which gave students an appreciation of their forgotten culture. To help them gain an understanding of what their parents experienced, she sponsored groups composed of students, faculty members and community leaders for summer study programs to China. The program was so successful that students of various cultures clamored to be in the program. Dr. Zou was pleased to accept them as well. To create a viable Asian and Asian American Studies Program, she partnered with Central University for Nationalities in Beijing along with eight other universities in China. Her students journeyed to various places in China and heard lectures by Chinese university professors. Dr. Zou made sure her charges got a close-up look at Chinese life, visited famous landmarks and temples, and tasted authentic Chinese food.

Much of what these Asian/American students experienced was astonishing to them. On one particular trip, one such student rather succinctly summed up his experience with Chinese food. When a dish he ordered was served to him, he blurted out, "This is not Chinese food. My mama cooks Chinese food." Although his comment was humorous, it was also very telling of the perception he possessed of his Chinese culture. Another American student, not of Asian background, was amazed to see Chinese dancing the polka which she thought was unique to her heritage. These personal stories validated what Dr. Zou believed. Her students had an unrealistic image of life in Asia that she attributed to media representation and elementary school geography lessons. She wanted to communicate to her UH students a truer picture of China and help students gain an appreciation for their heritage. She wanted her Asian/American students to understand that they were a product of two cultures; she assisted them in gaining a cross cultural and transnational understanding. In the last 20 years, Dr. Zou's China Study Abroad Program has hosted over 900 students, faculty, and community leaders. On two occasions, she traveled with two different mayors from Houston, Texas, to assist them in promoting friendship, economic development, and educational collaboration between Houston and various Chinese cities.

However, Dr. Yali Zou was not finished. Another aspect of her program was assistance to Asian scholars. Her center then hosted 86 Asian scholars who came to work and study at UH. They arrived from China, Japan, South Korea, India, Pakistan, Sri Lanka and Vietnam. In this manner, Dr. Zou was able to expose her Asian/American students to even more people of their culture. It brought a greater understanding of other cultures to both scholars and students. She hoped for mutual respect and multicultural acceptance. By the same token, she assisted these exchange scholars in a manner similar to the assistance she received when she arrived at UCD.

GLOBAL LEADERSHIP INSTITUTE

In 1996, Dr. Zou established the Global Leadership Program, designed to provide people from different countries with the leadership knowledge and skills necessary to interact with Americans in various endeavors. Since its inception, more than 2,500 public officials, business executives, and educational leaders from Asian countries have participated in the program. This program is individualized to meet the needs of each group who may be from the petroleum industry, education, public service, or other fields. These participants expressed gratitude in that the program enriched their knowledge, enhanced their skills, and helped them gain a better understanding of the American people and American culture. Now, many of the former participants play important roles in promoting relations between the United States and Asian countries.

UH recognized this outstanding achievement and bestowed on Dr. Yali Zou an Endowed Professorship in Global Leadership Studies in 2015. Upon acceptance of this honor, Dr. Zou remarked, "I am incredibly humbled by this endowed professorship. I will work very hard with the great team at Asian American Studies Center to ensure continued success of the AASC with this generous and invaluable gift which supports our cutting-edge research and academic excellence pursuits. The AASC is a place where we celebrate our cultural and linguistic diversity and enjoy an academic freedom to explore new professional opportunities. The center promotes academic excellence and equity for all through productive partnerships with the local, national and international community."

The AASC's former students, graduate scholars, and visiting foreign leaders are now university ambassadors who promote friendships between UH and several other countries; her students have become university presidents, faculty, government officials, business executives, and leaders in other fields. That is what

Dr. Zou is all about now, making the world a better place with the people that she has reached through the Global Leadership Program.

Her endowed professorship in Global Leadership Studies gives Dr. Zou opportunities to explore new ways to promote a better understanding of cross-cultural relations and effective communication skills. She has developed cultural therapy workshops for teachers and graduate students and written a handbook for international students about culturally relevant conversations.

Dr. Zou's life has been a classic example of what Confucius urged his followers to observe many centuries ago. Confucius (551 BC-449 BC) taught, "Whereso-ever you go, go with all your heart" (无论你去哪里，都要鞠躬尽瘁) ("Confucius Quotes," 2015). This girl from the rice fields opened her heart to all. Whether she was in a rice paddy or teaching class in an American university or hosting foreign dignitaries, she always threw her whole self into the work at hand. Dr. Yali Zou, a noted scholar, continues to work with all her heart at the University of Houston.

REFERENCES

10 Confucius Quotes That Will Change Your Life. (March 18, 2015). Retrieved from http://www.higherperspectives.com/confucius-quotes

Stutts, A., & Zou, Y. (1997). *Successful management and operation: In the service industry: A cultural perspective* (Chinese). Beijing: Central University for Nationalities Press.

Trueba, H. T., & Zou, Y. (1994). *Power in education: The case of Miao university students and its significance for American culture.* London: Falmer Press.

Zou, Y. (2017, May–July). Personal interview and telephone conversations.

Zou, Y., & Trueba, H. T. (Eds.). (1998). *Ethnic identity and power: Cultural contexts of political action in school and society.* Albany, NY: State University of New York Press.

Zou, Y., & Trueba, H. T. (Eds.). (2002). *Ethnography and education: Qualitative approaches to the study of education.* Lanham, MD: Rowman & Littlefield.

Zou, Y., Yang, F., & Poimbeauf, R. (Eds.). (2014). *Knowing China by learning Chinese culture and Chinese people.* Tianjin: University Publisher China.

CHAPTER SEVEN

The Scholar with Entrepreneurial Spirit

Professor Yong Zhao's Success Through Passion, Strength, and Value

YUROU WANG

文如其人 *wen ru qi ren* is an old Chinese saying that literally means "the writing mirrors the writer." Professor Yong Zhao writes about the entrepreneurial spirit (see Zhao, 2012) and he embodies that very spirit. Throughout his life he has practiced that which he preaches. He is a scholar with entrepreneurial spirit and it is this spirit that has taken him out of a tiny remote village in China and placed him on the world stage of education.

Professor Yong Zhao is a Foundation Distinguished Professor at the University of Kansas, a professorial fellow at the Mitchell Institute for Health and Education Policy at Victoria University in Australia, and a Global Chair at the University of Bath in the United Kingdom. He also holds visiting professorships at multiple universities in China. He has been invited to deliver keynote presentations in more than 20 countries, and he has worked with schools, educational organizations, and governments all across the globe. His writings, and there are lot of them—over 100 articles and 30 books—are read by people around the world. He was ranked in the top 10 most influential university-based education scholars in the United States by *Education Week* from 2013 to 2016.

"None of these prestigious positions were planned," Professor Zhao told me. "How can you plan for something that you don't know exists?" He did not know Kansas, Bath, Victoria, or many other places he has been to existed. He did not know educational research was a rewarding profession, nor did he know one can make a living by writing and talking. "I grew up in perhaps the most extraordinarily ordinary village with illiterate parents and siblings. The village is small and remote," said Professor Zhao. "It was the 1960s, China was going through the Cultural Revolution and was isolated from the rest of the world. So basically, the only world I knew was my village and the few other villages around me."

"What happened to me is a combination of good luck and my willingness to try everything that looks interesting," was his answer when I asked him how he transformed from a farm boy to an education scholar. The willingness to try interesting things is a significant element of entrepreneurship, which is fundamentally about the desire to solve problems creatively. The entrepreneurial spirit of being able to see opportunities in challenges, pursuing true passion, identifying one's own strength, being innovative, and creating value for others shaped his experience and research.

EVERY CHALLENGE IS AN OPPORTUNITY

There are always challenges, but every challenge to me is an opportunity. Challenges are unmet needs, unsolved problems, or unresolved issues. So they are great opportunities to make use of one's talents, passion, and efforts to make a contribution. So to me, there are no challenges. They are merely interesting opportunities to explore, to try out new ideas.—Professor Zhao

It would be misleading to say that Professor Zhao did not encounter any challenges on his journey from a village boy to a global scholar. He was born in a village tucked away in the remote part of China's Sichuan Province. He said: "In the village everyone was poor and hungry at that time. People died from famine in the village." Survival was a challenge but he was fortunate to have an entrepreneurial father who somehow managed to find enough food for the family. "I did not know that we were poor but I do remember every year my father would go out to borrow food from relatives living in better places." To supplement the poor diet, his father invented ways to catch fish and eels in the rice field. "I learned a lot from my father," Professor Zhao told me. "He taught me how to deal with challenges. He was always able to come up with some creative solutions."

Lacking reading materials and good instruction is a challenge to anyone who wants to learn to read. With virtually no books, illiterate parents and siblings, and a make-shift school in another village, Professor Zhao's early reading environment was certainly challenging. But he did not despair. Instead, he found creative ways to develop his reading ability, one of which was to read carvings on tombstones. In Chinese tradition, people carve sentences on gravestones that wish good fortune on the dead. During the Cultural Revolution, these stones were destroyed and removed, because they symbolized the legacy of old China that the new Communist government was eager to discontinue. Some were used as building materials by the villagers. The walls of his kitchen were built with tombstones, which became his early exposure to print. He read them every time when he helped power the coal stove with the wind box. The sentences on the stone were subtle, poetic, and elegant, but due to their age, some characters were missing or blurry, so he spent hours deciphering the "word puzzles." Guessing the missing part in a gravestone was his way of training himself to be creative.

He also loves to deal with challenges of others. In college, a professor of his was involved in an international study of learning behaviors of foreign language students in China, Japan, and Korea. The research team needed computer software to process the data and none was available at the time in his college. Professor Zhao volunteered to develop the software, although he had taken just one programming course and had no knowledge of statistics. It took him many sleepless nights to create the software because he had to study statistics on his own and improve his programming skills. "I learned a great deal about computers and statistics, which in the end secured the graduate assistantships that were essential to completing my graduate study at the University of Illinois at Urbana-Champaign (UIUC)," recounted Professor Zhao. "More important, it was the beginning of my interest in educational technology. The skills I learned were also very significant to my jobs at Willamette University, Hamilton College, and Michigan State University."

In a similar spirit, Professor Zhao volunteered to develop a computer program to convert emails into Web archives for his advisor Professor Gary Cziko in 1993. At that time, the Internet was in its infancy and Facebook and Twitter and web-based forums did not yet exist.[1] The most common way for professionals to exchange ideas was electronic mailing lists. His advisor was the leader of a mailing list group. In a casual conversation, Professor Cziko mentioned his interest in converting the email messages into threaded Web archives to make it easier for search and reading. Professor Zhao took up the challenge and developed a computer program called Eudora2HTML, which was later used by many professionals for similar tasks. This program may have even helped him in a small way to find his job at Michigan State University (MSU) because one of the search committee members was familiar with the program.

Perhaps one of the biggest challenges he volunteered to take up was the online submission system for the annual meetings of the American Educational Research Association (AERA). When he joined MSU, he met Professor Penelope L. Peterson, who was on the faculty and serving as President of AERA. Professor Zhao suggested that AERA consider electronic submissions for its annual meetings and volunteered to lead the effort. Most new assistant professors would be interested in focusing on tenure-related research, but when the opportunity at AERA arose, he saw it as both a challenge and a great opportunity to learn.

During the five years of developing and managing the online submission system, he learned the whole process of how articles were presented and how articles were submitted, which gave him a unique insight into the community of educational research. More importantly, the work taught him about innovation diffusion, which became part of his research. It also gave him the opportunity to work with AERA and to interact with senior researchers who were leaders at AERA, and this gave him a tremendous learning experience of how to conduct research.

The willingness to conquer challenges, as noted above, enables Professor Zhao to seize life-changing professional opportunities. He believes that every little thing you have done and every difficult problem you have attempted to solve in the past can be meaningful in the future. Just as he said: "When making decisions, we should look further and do not focus too much on the immediate value of certain things."

PURSUE WHAT YOU ENJOY DOING

You should pursue your passion, and move away from things that you are not interested in because if you are not interested, you will not put enough effort to it. If you are not interested, you're not going to pour your heart into it; you have to enjoy it. You should be intrinsically motivated. That's how I define passion.—Professor Zhao

Passion should be a core element of successful entrepreneurship, according to Professor Zhao. One should be driven by the intrinsic value of the process instead of extrinsic rewards that may or may not materialize. Professor Zhao's many endeavors were driven by passion, as exemplified by the projects he undertook for his major professor in China, his doctoral advisor at UIUC, and AERA. None of the projects were mandated to him, nor was there a promise of any extrinsic reward. He undertook them because he enjoyed the challenging process. In fact, his career has been fueled by his passion.

Upon entering graduate school, he was advised by many of his fellow Chinese graduate students at UIUC to change majors. They told him there would be no jobs for Chinese doctoral graduates in the field of education in the United States. They also told him that given his excellent English and computer skills, he should change to computer science, law, or business. But Professor Zhao did not take their advice. He was interested in education. "I did not enter graduate school in order to find a job," said Professor Zhao. "I had a job in China and I quit it because I wanted to study education." Professor Zhao's personal passion-driven career exemplifies what he advocates in his writings about a new paradigm of education. In his 2012 book *World Class Learners: Educating Creative and Entrepreneurial Students*, he argues that creative and entrepreneurial education should follow the children instead of imposing on all children the same set of knowledge and skills. Students should be given autonomy in deciding what they are interested in learning. He furthers this proposal in his 2018 book *Reach for Greatness: Personalizable Education for All* by adding that passion is essential for all children to achieve greatness in their unique ways. To encourage and enable students to discover their passion, education must be personalizable by students. That is, students should have control over their own learning.

He took control of his learning early in his life. Growing up without abundant books, he found reading materials in tombstones, government slogans painted on buildings and hillsides, newspapers used to wrap food, and used books collected as wrapping papers for dried noodles in his father's noodle shop. He followed the few people who could tell stories in his village. And he struck up conversations with traveling pot menders, bare-foot doctors, and photographers who would visit his village perhaps once or twice a year. In some sense, he managed to create his own learning environment.

This is also how Professor Zhao learned English. As someone who only began to learn English at the age of 14 in a rural high school, his English proficiency far exceeds many Chinese students who begin to learn English at a young age. He writes beautifully and speaks eloquent English. His English writings encompass multiple genres: academic papers, professional books, op-eds for well-known newspapers such as *The Washington Post*, and essays for popular magazines such as "The West and Asian Education: Fatal Attraction" in *New Internationalist*. He is also a globally sought-after speaker. "I learned English by escaping classes in college," said Professor Zhao when asked how he became so fluent in his second language. That was indeed what he did. Whenever possible, he spent most of his first and second years in college studying original English materials in psychology, education, linguistics, and other subjects instead of the textbooks assigned in his courses, which he found boring. Armed with content, he was able to discuss substantive matters with the foreign teachers instead of simply talking about superficial topics that typified conversations between Chinese students and foreign teachers for the purpose of practicing English.

He continued his habit of taking control of his own learning in graduate school. As a graduate student who finished his master's degree in one year and his Ph.D. in two years at UIUC, Professor Zhao had his own learning strategy. He believes people should become their own managers and owners of their learning. He always argues that schools should work for students and that students should not work for the schools. While in college he selected courses based on what interested him. What made him unique was that he was able to take the initiative with professors. He wanted to produce meaningful authentic works which aim to solve real-world problems instead of simply doing class assignments for his professors. As a student, everything he turned in to his professors was something that could help him gain valuable experience, such as a research proposal or a grant application—it was more than simply homework for a certain course. So during his graduate study, he worked with professors and other graduate students to write grant proposals and publish papers. He also led the development of a web-based magazine to publish news stories written by English Language Learners (ELLs) around the globe, which was one of the first efforts he undertook to create opportunities for students to create authentic works. This became his educational philosophy: learning should be driven by real-world problems and should be product-oriented.

All of his experience is passion-driven. When people are talking about balance in work and life, Professor Zhao suggests that there is no need for balance because when you are pursuing your passion, your work is your life and your life is your work. For him, they are the same.

REFUSE TO BE DEFINED BY DEFICITS

It is all right not to be good at everything as long as you are good at something; instead of trying to fix what may appear to be deficits and working hard to be the same as others, it may be fruitful to develop strength and be different.—Professor Zhao

Professor Zhao is always honest about his weaknesses. He concedes that he is not good at music, dancing, sports, math, and many other things, but he refuses to let these deficits define him. This honesty and comfort with his weaknesses helps him identify his strengths, as he does not waste too much of his time on what he cannot be very good at. He believes if one wants to be really great at something, he or she must be ready to let go of many other things.

One way to avoid putting efforts into something one cannot be great at is collaboration, which, in essence, is about outsourcing one's weakness. Professor Zhao practiced this early in his life. When he was young, he noticed that he was physically small which made farming hard for him, so he probably could not live successfully in a Chinese village. Because of his small size, he was also an easy target of bullying and harassment. To get out of this disadvantageous situation, he built an alliance with a big and strong boy who could protect him. In return, the young little Professor Zhao helped his "partner" with his homework and tests. "This alliance taught me a valuable lesson: what I am not good at can be made up with what I am good at. This lesson guided me through my life," Professor Zhao said.

His belief in admitting and outsourcing weaknesses led him to seek collaborators in his research. He has collaborated with many scholars who possessed the expertise that he did not. Upon arriving at MSU, he worked closely with

Professor Carol Sue Englert, a respected scholar in literacy and special education. He later collaborated closely with Professor Ken Frank, a specialist in methodology and social networks. Together they produced some of the most influential works in his career. One of them is a study of teacher adoption of technology from an ecological perspective that appeared in *Pedagogies: An International Journal* (see Zhao, Lei, & Frank, 2006).

Apart from moving away from his deficits and finding alliances, he is great at recognizing his potential strengths, which are always associated with his passion. He was not very good at math, but his English was better, so he chose English as his major. After that, he found he might not become the greatest English major student since he did not have as strong a background as his peers. But he was a great reader, so he read various authentic English books covering a wide range of topics: education, anthropology, psychology, and sociology, other than his textbooks. By taking some computer courses in college, he found out computer programing fascinated him; then he started writing software. To summarize his experience, he said, "To avoid my physical disadvantage in my village, I became interested in academic pursuits. To avoid my comparatively weak English background, I became interested in education, psychology, and computers. Trying to avoid comparative weaknesses meant avoiding things that the majority of the people are very good at doing. As a result, I have always ended up doing things that seemed out of the ordinary, which is synonymous with innovation and uniqueness."

He is also very good at reflecting on and learning from his experiences. In his most recent book *Reach for Greatness: Personalizable Education for All* (2018), Professor Zhao argues that today's educational system is focused too much on what children do not know or are unable to do. The educational system has even created different ways to verbalize children's deficiencies, in the forms of tracking, grade retention, and sorting into different programs such as special education, summer remediation, and extra tutoring. The current education paradigm does not encourage individuals to become great in a unique way. It produces mediocrity by pushing all students to learn the same thing. Professor Zhao believes deeply that educators should have the mindset to look for the strengths in each child because every one of them has a combination of innate qualities and environmental experiences that help turn them into a unique individual. These qualities distinguish them from others, making them above the average in some way.

THE COURAGE TO CREATE

One way to be creative is to develop unique combinations, which is essentially about cross-fertilization of ideas. Entrepreneurially spirited scholars go beyond one discipline or domain and seek to come up with novel ideas and solutions by combining ideas from different disciplines and domains. Because such combination may not fit into one discipline or domain, it can be rejected easily. So it takes courage to be creative.—Professor Zhao

According to Professor Zhao, creativity is a threefold construct. The first level is the ability to create, which means the ability to come up with new things based on what already exists. The second level is the courage to create, which is associated with the willingness to deal with challenge, uncertainty, and emotional vulnerability. The third level is social value. Professor Zhao believes that when we create a certain thing, it should have value to other people, and this has also become his working philosophy.

Throughout Professor Zhao's life, he has never stopped combining things from different domains and disciplines. His scholarly work has crossed many traditional disciplines. His major was English, but he crossed over to educational psychology, technology, and education. As a result, a significant part of his work has been in computer-assisted language learning, online second language education, and language policies. Besides numerous research publications, he has developed technology-based English textbooks and multimedia materials and online games for learning Chinese.

His doctoral specialization is educational psychology, but he also added second language education, and later educational technology. His research topics range from educational technology, teacher adoption of technology, online learning, educational policy, comparative and international education, creativity and entrepreneurship, language learning, special education, globalization, global competency, digital competency, and many more. Consequently, it is difficult to place his work in one academic domain. It is also why he has held positions in different departments: Department of Counseling, Educational Psychology, and Special Education at MSU, Department of Educational Methodology, Policy, and Leadership at the University of Oregon, and Department of Educational Leadership and Policy Studies at the University of Kansas, where he also has courtesy appointment in the School of Business.

Besides disciplinary boundaries, Professor Zhao also crosses national and cultural boundaries to seek new ideas. He sought funding and established the U.S.-China Center for Research on Educational Excellence at MSU. With a generous investment from Sunwah Education Foundation in Hong Kong, the Center distilled and combined the best ideas from Eastern and Western education traditions and developed a unique model of education that features bilingual, bicultural, and dual-pedagogical education. The model has been implemented in schools in China and the United States.

It is through looking across cultural and national boundaries that Professor Zhao developed some of his most influential ideas. Observing that the growing enthusiasm for standardization and centralization in America and the No Child Left Behind Act (NCLB) was making education in the United States more like that in China, he wrote *Catching Up or Leading the Way: American Education in the Age of Globalization*, in which he warned the following: "American education is at a crossroads. There are two paths in front of us: one in which we destroy our strengths in order to 'catch up' with others in test scores and one in which we build on our strengths so we can keep the lead in innovation and creativity" (Zhao, 2009, p. xii).

Noticing that international testing programs, which aim to evaluate different countries' education systems—such as the Program for International Student Assessment (PISA) and Trends in International Mathematics and Science Study (TIMSS)—erroneously point to East Asian education systems, particularly Chinese education, as the model of educational excellence, he wrote *Who's Afraid of the Big Bad Dragon?: Why China has the Best (and Worst) Education in the World* (2014). In the book he argues that Chinese education is the best at cultivating a homogenous and compliant workforce, but it is the worst in developing a diverse and creative citizenry.

Professor Zhao (2014) writes,

> The Chinese national educational system has won high praise as an efficient system with national standards, a national curriculum, a high-stakes test (the college entrance exam), and a clearly defined set of gateways to mark students' transitions from one stage to another. Admirers note that every Chinese student has a clear and focused goal to pursue; Chinese teachers and parents know exactly what to do to help their students, and the government knows exactly which schools are doing well. What those admirers ignore is the fact that such an education system, while being an effective machine to install what government wants students to learn, is incapable of supporting individual strengths, cultivating a diversity of talents, and fostering the capacity and confidence to create. (p. 9)

Zhao's creativity enables him to identify unique combinations. He is not only a successful educational researcher, but also computer programmer, writer, and teacher. He is always doing things out of the ordinary. Studying education as an English major is nontraditional. Doing computer programing for an education researcher is unique. For him, all of the odd things he did in the past became fruitful. In his opinion, when a person is not good at either one of two disciplines, they could do cross-disciplinary work and create a great bridge between them.

BE OF VALUE TO SOMEBODY

You should always think how you can be of service, of value to others. How are you making contributions to another person's life?—Professor Zhao

Professor Zhao's life also exemplifies another element of the entrepreneurial mindset: creating value for the world, for others. He has been tackling important, relevant, and meaningful problems that matter to others. His work in research and development attempts to address problems that matter to organizations, teachers, parents, students, and policy makers.

One of the most important problems Professor Zhao has been trying to address is the massive job loss and youth unemployment around the world that has resulted from recent technological changes (Zhao, 2012). His proposed solution is a paradigm shift in education. Professor Zhao argues that there are two educational paradigms discussed: the employee-oriented and the entrepreneur-oriented. The first paradigm assumes that "a body of knowledge and skills can be decided based on predictions of needs of the society," while the second "assumes if a child's potential is developed she will become valuable in her own way" (Zhao, 2012, p. 5). The old employee-oriented paradigm served the industrialized society by preparing employees for existing jobs and fitting them into the existing social order. However, in the environment of globalization and booming technology, we need people who have their own talent, who are creative and hold an entrepreneurial mindset to create a job. Thus what we need in the 21st century is the entrepreneur-oriented paradigm, which supports the development of diverse talents, deliberately cultivates creativity and individual differences, intentionally encourages children to be entrepreneurial, and fosters global perspectives and competence.

The new paradigm should not be deficit-driven. Instead it be should strengths-driven. "Schools and teachers should work to encourage students to explore their interests, passions, and strengths as well as recognize their accomplishment, instead of fixing their deficits" (Zhao, 2016, p. 720). He also argues that the project-based learning model should be replaced by the product-oriented model, in which students need to identify real-world needs, come up with ideas, assess strengths and resources, convince others of the value of their product/service, build the product/service, market the product/service, and, at last, do the post-product management and maintenance. By implementing the product-oriented model, students' role shifts from passive consumers and recipients to makers, creators and entrepreneurs. This new paradigm can better guide the use of technology in education and the needs to support such technology.

Zhao et al. (2015) believe,

> To better capitalize on the potential of technology, schools and teachers need to reimagine the relationship between technology and human educators so as to determine what can be delegated to technology and what must be done by human educators [...] A realigned teacher-machine relationship is essential for realizing the reimagined paradigm of schooling. A personalized curriculum and product-oriented pedagogy require

schools to transform from one-size-fits-all factories into personal learning ecosystems. (p. 123)

Professor Zhao believes that this new education paradigm is not only necessary, but very possible: "As the numerous education innovators have demonstrated, education can be changed. It can be made personalizable so as to help each and every student to actualize his or her potential and become great. To turn pockets of success demonstrated by the courageous and innovative educators, who have done it regardless of the constraints, into a full paradigm shift for all children requires the actions of everyone involved" (Zhao, 2018 p. 47). Again, the key of the new paradigm is about encouraging students to learn to solve problems worth solving and create value for others, a philosophy he has practiced in his life.

Professor Zhao does not limit himself to ideas and theories. He loves to put his ideas into practice. In 1998, with a group of educators from MSU, Professor Zhao built a program called Kids Learning In Computer Klubhouses (KLICK!) aimed at providing safe and engaging learning opportunities to students during out-of-school hours. In KLICK!, middle school students were encouraged to use technology to create value for others. They helped teachers conduct online research and create PowerPoint slides, helped schools manage their networks, built websites for local businesses, and created video yearbooks.

He was instrumental in the founding of 3e International Kindergarten in Beijing, as a site to pilot a bilingual, bicultural, and dual pedagogical immersion program. After 10 years, 3e has become one of the most successful international schools in Beijing. Recently he has put his new ideas to the test by working with schools and teachers. He has been working with schools in Australia, China, and the United States to implement a new paradigm of education. Students in these schools are enjoying more autonomy, working on making products that matter, and learning from, with, and for others around the globe.

CLOSING

Professor Zhao is a scholar with entrepreneurial spirit. When you put his studies and his practices together, you will see the future of education through his splendid vision. His success comes from his passion, openness, strength, uniqueness, and great heart. He does not prejudge people. Instead, he reads people like a book. The first time I met him, he asked lots of questions about me and about my studies. I felt he was really trying to know and care about me, but it really made me nervous. After the first meeting, when I was working with him I felt much more relaxed. He has high standards, but he is also quite understanding. Once he comes to know you, he will try to think from your perspective. He is a great mentor for me, and provides clear professional guidance. The willingness to provide opportunities for students and young professors is another precious trait of his. I really love to meet with him, because every time I can learn something from him. He provides me the inspiration, the passion and the confidence that I need to dedicate myself to the things that I like. It is an honor and privilege for me to write about him for this volume. He made me understand what it takes to be a real education scholar and leader. The passion he holds for his studies, the ability to maximize his own strengths, the belief of always creating values for other people will guide me throughout my life.

NOTE

1 Facebook was launched in February 2004 and Twitter in March 2006.

REFERENCES

Zhao, Y. (2009). *Catching up or leading the way: American education in the age of globalization.* Alexandria, VA: ASCD.

Zhao, Y. (2012). *World class learners: Educating creative and entrepreneurial students.* Thousand Oaks, CA: Corwin Press.

Zhao, Y. (2014). *Who's afraid of the big bad dragon? Why China has the best (and worst) education system in the world.* San Francisco, CA: John Wiley & Sons.

Zhao, Y. (2016). From deficiency to strength: Shifting the mindset about education inequality. *Journal of Social Issues, 72*(4), 720–739. https://doi.org/10.1111/josi.12191

Zhao, Y. (2018). *Reach for greatness: Personalizable education for all.* Thousand Oaks, CA: Corwin Press.

Zhao, Y., Coates, K., Gearin, B., Shen, Y., Soltz, S., Thier, M., ... Anderson, R. C. (2015). *Counting what counts: Reframing education outcomes.* Bloomington, IN: Solution Tree.

Zhao, Y., Lei, J., & Frank, K. A. (2006). The social life of technology: An ecological analysis of technology diffusion in schools. *Pedagogies: An International Journal, 1*(2), 135–149. https://doi.org/10.1207/s15544818ped0102_5

CHAPTER EIGHT

Analogies of a BlackBerry

The Foundation and Impact of the Inaugural Morgan and Helen Chu Endowed Chair in Asian American Studies at UCLA

BACH MAI DOLLY NGUYEN AND CYNTHIA MARIBEL ALCANTAR

If you know Dr. Robert T. Teranishi, Professor of Social Science and Comparative Education (SSCE), the Morgan and Helen Chu Endowed Chair in Asian American Studies, and co-director of the Institute for Immigration, Globalization, and Education (IGE) at the University of California at Los Angeles (UCLA), you know that he uses a BlackBerry phone, which is a smartphone that has been unfairly discounted given the craze over Android and Apple. However, in the most recent reviews, BlackBerry was praised for being "a great productivity device" in an online article titled, "While No One was Looking, BlackBerry Built a Damn Good Phone" (Hruska, 2017). Despite the BlackBerry's legacy as being a leading product for work applications, those *choosing* to stay devoted to this mobile option are typically the focus of great curiosity, or in the IGE team's case, relentless teasing because BlackBerry stands outside the mobile norms. Dr. Teranishi has, nonetheless, remained resolute in his commitment to his BlackBerry. Despite backhanded comments from his advisees that the BlackBerry cannot receive pictures or download software applications, and a joke from a college dean who stated, "You and President Obama are the only two still using BlackBerries!" (the federal government has since transitioned to iPhones), Dr. Teranishi maintains his smartphone choice. Although we cannot claim innocence in the teasing as iPhone and Android users, we do find a compelling analogy in this smartphone debacle.

The analogy is between Dr. Teranishi's work and the BlackBerry. In more ways than one, the BlackBerry has features that are characteristically representative of our advisor, mentor, and colleague. First is the matter of the keyboard—a feature other phones moved away from years ago. This is the one central feature, however, that keeps Dr. Teranishi coming back to the BlackBerry, stating that it allows for precision that on-screen keyboards lack. Precision, we have learned, is one of Dr. Teranishi's greatest strengths. As a scholar who sits at the intersection of research, practice, and policy, it is precision that has foregrounded his impact—precision in how he constructs research studies, approaches his work with institutional partners, offers advisement for federal and state policies, and deliberates strategies as a public scholar for addressing inequality in postsecondary education. Dr. Teranishi's sharp focus on improving the college system is apparent in both broad-reaching ways, such as the publication of his book *Asians in the Ivory Tower: Dilemmas of Racial Inequality in American Higher Education* (2010), and in small and meticulous manners, such as his detailed time and attention to each and every PowerPoint that he presents. Like the BlackBerry, precision is a main feature of Dr. Teranishi's work.

A second analogy that can be drawn between the two lies in the software. Unlike the more popular smartphones, BlackBerry has stuck to what matters most—the utility of applications for users, which is what has preceded its standing as the best productivity device. It has not turned its attention toward generating excessive options or keeping with the current trends. Instead, it has remained squarely focused on serving its users to the fullest extent possible. Likewise, Dr. Teranishi has maintained a research agenda that is cohesive, committed, and consistent because he has never turned his attention away from what matters—addressing inequality in higher education. As the field of education has ebbed and flowed in terms of the most recent areas of focus and research trends, Dr. Teranishi's work has tirelessly aimed its attention at race, ethnicity, and the stratification of college opportunity—forms of inequity that have continued to persist in higher education. Although focused, his research has also been flexible enough to capture shifting demographics (e.g. greater attention to within-group heterogeneity), changing demands (e.g. fluctuating time and attention to urgent calls for reliable research, such as on affirmative action), and varying institutional contexts (e.g. partnering with community colleges, and public and private four-year institutions). Despite the varying student populations or settings for his work, the heart of his scholarship is grounded in a commitment to achieving equity. Like the BlackBerry, there has never been a need for bells and whistles because it has always been about doing good work that addresses inequities in higher education.

Finally, the primary color for BlackBerry and the one Dr. Teranishi uses is black, which is a classic and timeless color, similar to his work. Given the anchor his scholarship has in addressing inequality, his research has transcended both time and sector. The answers he has provided about barriers to Asian American college access, transfer pathways from two-year to four-year institutions, and degree attainment are as relevant today as they were when he wrote them, as they continue to be applied to other student groups, and put into conversation with new texts to understand the intricacies of inequality. It is also timeless in a variety of sectors, making Dr. Teranishi a public scholar who conducts research that truly plays a role in theory, in practice, and in policy. Put together, the precision, commitment, and timelessness of Dr. Teranishi's work are the foundations for his ongoing legacy as an education and Asian American Studies scholar. This is why, we believe, he was chosen as the inaugural Morgan and Helen Chu Endowed Chair in Asian American Studies. The influence of his work is readily apparent today and will continue to extend itself in both breadth and depth.

The remainder of this chapter will focus on our rationalization of his Endowed Chair appointment through a discussion of the impact of his work on the field of higher education, Asian American Studies, and individuals with whom he has worked, including mentors, colleagues, and students. First, we will provide a brief history of Dr. Teranishi's educational trajectory as context.

DR. TERANISHI'S EDUCATIONAL AND CAREER TRAJECTORY

Born in Northern California, Dr. Robert Teranishi began his academic career in public education. He was not always the stellar academic he is now, as he struggled through schools that were severely underfunded and was challenged to develop the reading and writing skills that would eventually lend themselves to his remarkable career. Despite his K–12 school context, Dr. Robert Teranishi was accepted to the University of California at Santa Cruz (UCSC) where he blossomed as a critical thinker and a writer while majoring in sociology. It was at UCSC where he met a mentor who encouraged him to consider graduate school and motivated his future path to UCLA. Under the advisement of Dr. Patricia McDonough, and with an incredible committee made up by Drs. Walter Allen, Mitchell Chang, and Daniel Solórzano, who are influential scholars in their own right, Dr. Teranishi received his Master of Arts and Doctor of Philosophy in Higher Education and Organizational Change. By that time, Dr. Teranishi had gained experience on several nationwide research projects, published with his committee members, and began to make an indelible mark on the field of higher education.

In his first position post-graduate school, Dr. Teranishi was a National Institute of Mental Health Postdoctoral Fellow in the Center for Health, Achievement, Neighborhood Growth, and Education at the University of Pennsylvania. After one year, he moved to New York University (NYU) where he began his role as an Assistant Professor in the Steinhardt School of Culture, Education and Human Development in the Higher Education and Student Affairs program. It was during his 12-year tenure at NYU that he started the National Commission on Asian American and Pacific Islander Research in Education (CARE). CARE aims to increase awareness about the needs and challenges facing Asian American and Pacific Islander (AAPI) students in U.S. higher education. It conducts applied research on the demography of AAPI students, their educational trajectory, and their barriers to college access and success. CARE has produced a vast number of briefs and reports that have been used in both practice and policy, and has expanded to work directly with institutional and federal partners. Additionally, during his time at NYU, he was a Strategic Planning and Restructuring Consultant for the Ford Foundation's Educational Opportunity and Scholarship program. He was also Co-Director of the Institute for Globalization and Education in Metropolitan Settings, broadening work on immigrant-origin and community college students. Further, in line with his commitment to public scholarship, Dr. Teranishi was appointed by Arne Duncan, U.S. Secretary of Education, to the United States Department of Education's Equity and Excellence Commission. Upon Dr. Teranishi's move to UCLA, where he now resides as a Professor of Education in the Graduate School of Education & Information Studies, he relocated CARE and continues to be the principal investigator of the research organization. He is also the Morgan and Helen Chu Endowed Chair in Asian American Studies, and Co-Director of the Institute for Immigration, Globalization, and Education (IGE).

IMPACT ON THE FIELD OF HIGHER EDUCATION

Referring to the deep impact Dr. Teranishi's work has had on the field of higher education, one of his colleagues[1] expressed:

> In the 20 years I have known Rob, his scholarship has evolved into one that is not only useful for the field of education and mainstream thinking, but his work also challenges the status quo, which ultimately has led to some transformational changes in the topic of equity and diversity particularly for the Asian American, Pacific Islander populations and undocumented students.

This individual goes on to share, "Rob's contributions to the field of education are many. One of them would include his persistence toward bringing the topic of Asian American educational disparities to the forefront in the discourse of education." It is no doubt that Dr. Teranishi has been a leading scholar on AAPIs in higher education, bringing attention to the stratification of within-group heterogeneity (Nguyen et al., 2017), countering the misconceptions of their universal success (Teranishi, Lok, & Nguyen, 2013), and highlighting where and for whom inequality continues to be a barrier to achievement (Teranishi, 2010). As another colleague rightly commented, "He has added significantly to documenting and understanding what disadvantage looks like for Asian American students and why that disadvantage is consequential in one's educational trajectory."

The scope of his research, however, is broader than on AAPI students singularly. When asked, what is the most significant contribution of Dr. Teranishi's work to the field of education, a former student aptly responded:

(1) Demonstrating the pernicious effect of lack of disaggregated data on AAPIs in a variety of contexts and subsequent engagement with institutional and system leaders and policymakers to revise data collection and reporting practices; (2) Studying the newest group of Minority Serving Institutions (MSIs), Asian American Native American Pacific Islander Serving Institutions, to discern their impact on low-income AAPI students while contributing to the base of knowledge on MSIs more generally; and (3) Providing a clearer portrait of undocumented students, a stigmatized group that is difficult to study, busting myths about their demographics and aspirations, and developing a basis for institutional and state policy changes grounded in evidence.

In addition to the range of his research within education, Dr. Teranishi's work has reached beyond the borders of his own discipline, as his colleague points out:

I think he has an extraordinary capacity to conduct and apply research in a way that makes sense for those outside of the academy. Many scholars get too buried in their own small insular academic circle, but Rob is always reaching outside of his core scholarly community to make research matter in the real world. His research is not driven only by what matters for knowledge production within a field, but also takes into account the interest of solving real world problems and issues.

Dr. Teranishi always reminds his students, "Education is an applied field," a principle he takes to heart in his research, as this comment clearly demonstrates. As opposed to working in isolation, Dr. Teranishi deepens the impact of his work by engaging with practitioners, policymakers, community organizers, and students, which simultaneously strengthens the field by demonstrating its functionality as an applied discipline. In combination, his research has developed a strong legacy and contributed to the field by bringing attention to understudied and overlooked populations and issues, and by reinforcing the role of the field to apply such research in practical ways that influence tangible change.

IMPACT ON ASIAN AMERICAN STUDIES AND EDUCATION

Dr. Teranishi's appointment as the inaugural Morgan and Helen Chu Endowed Chair in Asian American Studies is symbolic of the influence his research has had on the study of Asian Americans. It also signifies the acknowledgment of research on this population as one of significance by the academy. To this point, a former student ruminates:

Asian American Studies is a field that tends to be under pressure to justify its existence due to a mix of philosophical and political concerns. Yet, the field provides intellectual sustenance for students interested in exploring the role of racial/ethnic identity in American life from a variety of disciplinary perspectives. Having a named chair for Asian American Studies is a win not only for the institution housing the appointment, but also for the field as a whole, as it signals external support for teaching, learning and research in a contested arena. As a scholar who has pushed heavily against prevailing norms (e.g. the perception that AAPIs are a uniformly socioeconomically advantaged group) throughout his career, it is only appropriate for someone like Rob to serve as the inaugural chair.

The matter of acknowledgment and representation is central to why it is significant that Dr. Teranishi holds this seat, as one of his colleagues states:

> It goes without saying that his role as one of the few Asian American endowed professors, is one to be acknowledged—not only because he is one of the few, but it is also an indication that the field of education has a long way to go in recognizing important scholarly contributions by Asian Americans; Asian American scholars whose intentions are not self-serving, but truly serving and advancing the Asian American community in positive ways.

This appointment, then, is a pathway for future Asian American scholars who conduct research within the discipline of ethnic studies, and Dr. Teranishi is a role-model for future possibilities in acknowledging the significance of the field. Additionally, the appointment represents a historical legacy of Asian American influence, as the late Dr. Don Nakanishi was involved in helping to secure the funding. A colleague expressed the links between the past and present, "For me, the Chair is another reminder of [Dr. Nakanishi's] impact on our School, and I was thrilled that it was secured by one of our former students who is a direct beneficiary of [Dr. Nakanishi's] legacy." How fitting, then, that Dr. Teranishi's work continues to advance Asian American Studies and honor Dr. Nakanishi's legacy, which established the relevance of Asian American Studies as a field for scholarship, teaching, discourse, and advocacy.

IMPACT ON INDIVIDUALS

Beyond influencing the fields of education and Asian American Studies, Dr. Teranishi's work, and his personal character, have touched the lives and scholarship of students and colleagues—a final seal to his legacy. This is particularly clear when it comes to his mentorship style, one that is well-received by his advisees, as there is an intentional lack of formality that puts students at ease in the demanding graduate school environments in which Dr. Teranishi's students are enrolled. One former student stated it well, as she remembered:

Rob treated me as a colleague from the beginning and trusted me with challenging projects even as a first-year student. The combination of challenge and trust was immensely valuable because it stretched me professionally, gave me some faith when I doubted myself, and made me feel I would be supported even if I failed.

She goes on to share, "Rob was generous not only with his mentorship, but also with his support in other tangible ways. For instance, he regularly supported travel to professional conferences, made introductions to key figures, and steered publishing and presenting opportunities my way." This important note speaks to the intentionality of his mentorship, and the commitment he makes to students to support their learning above and beyond his direct work with them. He also thoughtfully fosters opportunities to instill mentorship and growth among his team members using the environment of CARE and IGE to encourage collaboration. To this point, the former student comments, "Anyone who has worked with Rob knows that he loves teamwork—he is wonderful about organizing his research teams, so they meet shared goals but also build camaraderie," which is an example of why his research teams have maintained professional connections and friendships beyond their time together at NYU and UCLA.

Furthermore, Dr. Teranishi's mentorship reaches individuals who are not designated as formal advisees. This is demonstrated by a colleague's remarks:

One of the many ways that Rob has shaped my thinking and scholarship about Asian American students and education has had more to do with his role-modeling and mentoring for his peers, like myself. In the early stages of my career, he helped me with some doubts I had as a scholar. He took time to have critical conversations with me about the validity of my scholarship and my role as a scholar.

As this statement reveals, role-modeling the virtues of being a committed scholar of, and contributor to, the field is a clear characteristic of Dr. Teranishi's impact. To this point, a former student summarizes:

Rob has been a creative and resourceful researcher, instructor, fundraiser, adviser, and advocate. He models the work involved in being a good scholar and citizen, not just in his home department but at the world at large. And he's not afraid to model how to give yourself a break once in a while, even if it's getting a burrito from a food truck.

As his most recently graduated students, we can attest to this last comment. In the many meals we have shared as a team from ramen to enchiladas, and tacos to Shake Shack—a team staple—Dr. Teranishi's calm demeanor and steady focus have communicated that it is not the flash and flare of the academy that bodes well over time, or the title of your position, it is in maintaining a clear agenda that persistently and unfailingly aims to lift others around you. In this way, Dr. Teranishi has not only contributed to the fields of education and Asian American Studies, he has impacted much more lasting change, as he transformed those with whom he has worked.

CONCLUSION

Writing a chapter in this volume, which focuses on the accomplishments of Asian American endowed professors as written by their students, demands a flawless balance between overstated glorification and disregarded success because there is a boundary between advisor and student, which limits our knowledge about the full scope of their achievements. We are fortunate, however, to have bypassed this conundrum, as Dr. Teranishi's work speaks for itself. As such, we were not compelled to exaggerate any personal characteristics, and were able to let the statements of those he has worked with in the past, and the merits of his scholarship, do the work for us. As this chapter clearly reveals, the appointment of Dr. Teranishi as the inaugural Morgan and Helen Chu Endowed Chair in Asian American Studies at UCLA is grounded in the precision, commitment, and timelessness of his work, and the impact of his research on a broad policy level down to an individual level is unquestionable. It was, therefore, more than fitting for Dr. Teranishi to receive the honor of Endowed Chair. In keeping with his personal style, he has no intentions of slowing down because there is more good work to be done. You can find him on campus doing that work with his handy BlackBerry by his side.

NOTE

1 Mentors, colleagues, and students who shared their comments for the purpose of this chapter are not identified for the purpose of confidentiality.

REFERENCES

Hruska, J. (2017). While no one was looking, BlackBerry built a damn good phone. *Extreme Tech.* Retrieved from https://www.extremetech.com/mobile/248989-blackberry-keyone-review-roundup.

Nguyen, B. M. D., Alcantar, C. M., Curammeng, E., Hernandez, E., Kim, V., Paredes, A. D., ... Teranishi, R. (2017). *The racial heterogeneity project: Implications for educational research, practice, and policy.* Los Angeles, CA: Institute for Immigration, Globalization, and Education (IGE).

Teranishi, R. (2010). *Asians in the ivory tower: Dilemmas of racial inequality in American higher education.* New York, NY: Teachers College Press.

Teranishi, R., Lok, L., & Nguyen, B. M. D. (2013). *iCount: A data quality movement for Asian Americans and Pacific Islanders in higher education.* New York, NY: National Commission on Asian American and Pacific Islander Research in Education (CARE). Retrieved from https://files.eric.ed.gov/fulltext/ED573772.pdf

CHAPTER NINE

The Development of a Legacy

Paying It Forward[1]

SHEETAL SOOD AND AMY E. LEIN

INTRODUCTION

Professor Asha K. Jitendra is the Rodney Wallace Endowed Professor for the Advancement of Teaching and Learning in the College of Education and Human Development (CEHD) at the University of Minnesota, Twin Cities (UMN). Before moving to Minnesota, Dr. Jitendra served as a faculty member for 14 years in the Department of Education and Human Services at Lehigh University, located in Bethlehem, Pennsylvania. During her academic career, Dr. Jitendra has received numerous honors and awards in recognition of her contributions as a researcher and mentor. In 2016, she received the Distinguished Researcher Award from the Special Education Special Interest Group (SIG) of the American Educational Research Association (AERA) and the Distinguished Alumni Award from the College of Education at the University of Oregon. In addition, Dr. Jitendra was recognized by the University of Minnesota, Twin Cities with the College of Education and Human Development Excellence in Research Award in 2012 and the Distinguished Faculty Mentor Recognition Award in 2011. She has received several grants, totaling approximately $9 million, from federal agencies including the U.S. Department of Education's Institute of Education Sciences (IES), the National Institute of Mental Health (NIMH), the Office of Special Education Programs (OSEP), and the U.S. Department of Health and Human Services (HHS) to support her scholarship.

Dr. Jitendra's research focuses on instructional design, specifically mathematics word problem solving; reading interventions for students with learning disabilities; assessment; and textbook analysis. Her work appears in prestigious education journals, including *Elementary School Journal, Exceptional Children, Learning and Instruction, Journal of Abnormal Child Psychology, Journal of Educational Psychology, Journal of Learning Disabilities, Journal of School Psychology*, and *Journal of Special Education*. Her scholarship also includes textbooks, mathematics curriculum programs, several book chapters, and a well-respected Institute of Education Sciences (IES) Practice Guide. In addition, Dr. Jitendra has disseminated her work broadly, both nationally and internationally to include Australia, Canada, Cypress, India, Slovenia, and Taiwan among other countries.

Dr. Jitendra is best known for her research on Schema-Based Instruction (SBI) for solving word problems. In this line of inquiry over the last 25 years, her articulation of SBI evolved over time to incorporate curriculum design theory and combine best practices in special education and contemporary mathematics education to yield a curriculum on ratios and proportions that is considered a significant contribution to the broad area of education.

The field of special education has several individuals who are distinguished for their research scholarship. However, it is not scholarship in itself, but stellar mentorship of students in terms of knowledge and implementation of research and practice that leaves a lasting legacy. A large part of fostering a lasting legacy takes the shape of mentoring future educators and researchers so that they can then impact those in their circle of influence and ensure continual positive momentum. To chronicle Professor Jitendra's journey to success, we interviewed her about her background and experiences, and reflected on our experiences when she mentored us, Sheetal Sood and Amy E. Lein, who studied with her from 2001 to 2009, and from 2010 to 2016, respectively. In our current positions as professors, we draw upon some of our own experiences to shed light on her influence in our interactions and experiences with our students, and we illustrate how her generous support and mentoring formed the foundation of her legacy.

Dr. Jitendra grew up in Chennai, India and moved to the United States to pursue a master's degree in special education with a personal goal of helping her daughter, who was diagnosed at the age of four months with a developmental disability. Although the medical profession was quick to provide a prognosis of her daughter's condition (i.e., mostly bleak), it was not as ready to explain the cause or the ostensible effect that education may have in developing her individual potential. As Dr. Jitendra tried to cope with the reality of the situation, she groped for ways to foster her daughter's intellectual growth. Her efforts to educate her daughter who has survived numerous labels (e.g., "mildly mentally retarded," "autistic," "communication disordered," "language impaired," "pervasive developmentally disabled") were instrumental in shaping her views and values of how best to serve historically underserved children. It was intriguing that despite a significant language delay, it became clear around age 10 that her daughter understood the logic of mathematics. She learned the multiplication tables in three trials, responded instantly with the day of the week when given the month, date, and the year, and figured out that every 28 years the calendar repeats itself. Despite her prodigious ability with numbers, her daughter struggled with math word problems. Dr. Jitendra's personal interest in unlocking her daughter's potential unfolded into the need to educate children with special needs and compelled her to enter the field of special education, after a lapse of eight years from formal education. Undoubtedly, her daughter was the driving force for Dr. Jitendra's interest in special education and the inspiration for her work in mathematics, and word problem solving instructional strategies in particular.

Dr. Jitendra chose Purdue University to pursue a master's degree in special education because it afforded her family support; her sister and family resided in West Lafayette, Indiana. She received her master's degree in special education from Purdue University in 1986, but she felt that her education and experiences were not sufficient to fully understand what it took to enhance the learning potential of children with disabilities. As such, her search for advanced knowledge about special education led her to pursue a doctoral program in special education. She was the first person in her family to pursue a Ph.D. and felt fortunate to have Dr. Edward Kame'enui as her advisor both at Purdue University and later at the University of Oregon where she completed her Ph.D. in 1991. Dr. Kame'enui is currently the Dean-Knight Professor of Education Emeritus and Founding Director of the Center on Teaching and Learning at the University of Oregon. Dr. Kame'enui is a renowned researcher in reading interventions. He has published over 150 journal articles, 50 book chapters, and has co-authored 20 college textbooks focusing on teaching reading, curriculum design, vocabulary instruction, higher order thinking, and classroom management—see *Direct Instruction Reading* (6th ed.); *Reading Vocabulary Instruction: Research to Practice* (2nd ed.); *Effective Teaching Strategies that Accommodate Diverse Learners* (4th ed.); *Teaching Struggling and At-Risk Readers: A Direct Instruction Approach.*

CHAPTER PURPOSE

Our chapter conceptualizes Dr. Jitendra's mentorship as informed by a cognitive apprenticeship model (Collins, Brown, & Holum, 1991), wherein she provides support and feedback as she creates opportunities for authentic participation in research activities to acculturate students to the values and norms of academia. She also provides explicit instruction to her students, and cares about her students' growth, and uses teachable moments to integrate something extra into the lesson to make every moment count. As she works with her students, she is responsive, reading each situation, each moment, and determining the best action—what does that student need from me at this time? How can I best help?

DEVELOPING PERSONAL CONNECTIONS

A critical first step in an apprenticeship is developing relationships and rapport (Golde, Bueschel, Jones, & Walker, 2008). Dr. Jitendra's initial effort to connect with her students includes inviting them to her home and sharing a meal to get to know them. Sheetal recalled:

I first met Dr. Jitendra when I came to the United States from India to pursue my dream of becoming a special educator. Having come from a completely different cultural and academic background, settling in a new country and experiencing a new way of learning was very challenging. In the midst of all the faculty members at Lehigh University, the one face that stood out was that of Dr. Jitendra. Being a quiet student myself, I remember not talking to anyone unless I was asked a question. A few months went by and my only interaction with Dr. Jitendra was a smile, until one day Dr. Jitendra called me to her office. To be honest, I was overwhelmed as I was not sure why she had called me. I hesitantly went to her office and was surprised when she asked me about my family and where I was from and then invited me to her house for Thanksgiving. I share this story because this was one of the first lessons I learned from Dr. Jitendra. I learned from Dr. Jitendra the importance of being compassionate and to make students feel like there was a home away from home.

At the University of Minnesota, Twin Cities, it remains commonplace for Dr. Jitendra to invite her advisees to join her for lunch to continue a conversation, or to meet for a working lunch. Further, Dr. Jitendra maintains rapport by always taking time to show interest in her advisees' lives beyond the University. She honors special occasions with thoughtful gifts and personal cards and always expresses gratitude with a thank you note when she has received a gift.

THE PURSUIT OF KNOWLEDGE

Dr. Jitendra guides her students to develop their knowledge base and experience as teacher educators, scholars, researchers, and leaders. Through a scientific inquiry approach, she promotes critical thinking in her students and her students learn to construct and critically evaluate arguments in relation to bodies of evidence from different perspectives. While preparing for an academic position in higher education, she recalls her mentor, Dr. Kame'enui, promoting critical thinking and providing her with several opportunities to engage in research throughout her doctoral program, starting with a textbook analysis research project. The intent of this analysis was to examine the extent to which the structure of information presented in textbooks adheres to the selected theoretical models that deal with the coherent organization and structure of information. Since that study was published, Dr. Jitendra conducted several studies related to materials analysis, including editing a special issue of *Reading & Writing Quarterly* in 2001 on "Textbook Evaluation and Modification for Students with Learning Problems." She acknowledges the importance of her experiences, which led to the development of a research program of inquiry, and provides similar opportunities for her students to get immersed in research from the beginning of their doctoral programs. Under Dr. Jitendra's mentorship, we each co-authored a number of publications with her as the lead author and had at least one first-author publication before completing our doctoral programs (see Lein et al., 2016; Sood & Jitendra, 2007). In addition, we had the opportunity to present at various regional, national, and international conferences.

THE GENEROSITY AND STRENGTH OF ELABORATE FEEDBACK

Dr. Jitendra fondly recalls how generous her adviser was with his time, always giving prompt and elaborate feedback on assignments. She and her peers used to joke about Dr. Kame'enui's red pen, but noted that his constructive feedback helped immensely in honing her technical writing skills. Given her success, she decided to emulate his model of leadership and mentorship as she worked with her own advisees. When we were her students, we also joked about the way a paper looked after Dr. Jitendra had given feedback—covered with tracked changes, comments, and questions designed to challenge our thinking about the topic as well as refine our writing and communication skills. We often reminisce about our experiences of receiving her feedback, and how the swiftness of this response kept us from losing our focus on the assignment. It seems that she was always mindful of what role she might need to play in helping us succeed. We realized the amount of work it takes to not only provide comprehensive feedback but also respond quickly. Dr. Jitendra modeled for us the determination and perseverance we would need to be successful. These practices communicate the high expectation she has of her students and illustrate the high expectations she holds for herself.

In reflecting on our experiences with our mentor, we now find ourselves in our roles as professors providing feedback to our own students with the same attention to detail and timeliness. Our students also comment on the value of our extensive and prompt feedback. Amy shared:

One of my students wrote on my midterm evaluation: "I feel as though you really care about our success. You are always willing to help us with this class and others." To me, that is a high compliment because it suggests that I am embodying what Dr. Jitendra taught me and moving her legacy forward.

SUPPORTING STUDENT INTERESTS

Learner interest matters, because when students choose a topic that is of interest, it is likely they will be engaged and will spend time thinking and creating ideas in meaningful ways. Far from the "sage on the stage" stereotype of professors, Dr. Jitendra models a sense of humility and is forthcoming about her limitations; and then she uses student interests to help her expand her knowledge base in diverse areas of educational research. When talking about her adviser Dr. Jitendra remembered him as being very open; even though his specialty was in reading, she was able to explore math and he could still offer help as an adviser. This modeled for her that she could help students with different interests and areas of focus. She effectively does so by applying common research methodology and keeping up with the literature across varied content areas. Further, she connects her students with other professors whose areas of expertise differ from hers.

FOSTERING COLLABORATION

Through her mentorship, Dr. Jitendra taught us that connecting and collaborating are highly beneficial in one's pursuit of knowledge. She shared with us her own experiences as a doctoral student and how she survived the hurdles of her doctoral program by having a support group of other doctoral students who collaborated on research projects, collected data for dissertations, and participated in social events that led to lasting friendships. She emphasizes the importance of peer support and notes, "completing the doctoral program is not something you can do alone."

Dr. Jitendra extends the opportunity to be involved in her research projects and to co-author papers for presentations and publications to graduate and doctoral students across disciplines (e.g., special education, school psychology, psychological foundations). As the culminating project of her special topics doctoral seminar course on mathematics interventions for students with or at risk for mathematics difficulties, which is offered every alternate year in the special education program at the University of Minnesota, Twin Cities, Dr. Jitendra has students work collaboratively on a research project. She involves students in all phases of the research, including conceptualizing the study, developing a coding scheme for synthesizing research, writing, and submitting for publication. Dr. Jitendra taught this seminar course in 2011, 2013, 2015, and three papers based on the class projects have been presented at several national conferences and published in prestigious journals in special education such as *Exceptional Children* and *Journal of Learning Disabilities* (Jitendra et al., 2015, 2018; Jitendra, Nelson, Pulles, Kiss, & Houseworth, 2016). She supported a total of 16 doctoral students in the seminar course by providing them with critical first-hand experience in conducting research early in their programs. Such experiences hone her students' research and writing skills, work-ethic, and perseverance while giving them a professional edge on the upcoming job market and a head start toward earning tenure as a professor.

By fostering collaboration among her students, Dr. Jitendra extends her net of support beyond what one person could possibly provide, thus intensifying the positive impact she makes in her students' lives. For example, Amy reflected:

> In the year after I received my Ph.D., Dr. Jitendra encouraged me to collaborate with her current doctoral advisee to work on some research projects. As a result, we are currently preparing two manuscripts, with each one of us being a primary author on these papers. Further, she would suggest to her current advisee about connecting with me to learn about research in areas she felt I was knowledgeable, which allowed me a terrific opportunity to practice advising a doctoral student.

Dr. Jitendra's ongoing generosity in terms of collaboration built a foundation for the creation of lasting partnerships and friendships. Even now, we, her former students, know we can pick up the phone or send her an email and she will be there to guide us. Because of her generosity, we reach out in our positions as tenure-track faculty to collaborate with our students, inviting them to co-author papers with us for presentation and publication.

BRINGING AN ACADEMIC PROFESSION TO LIGHT

Student Induction

On her own academic journey, Professor Jitendra experienced a distinct challenge when her adviser, Dr. Kame'enui, left Purdue University in 1987, a year after she started the doctoral program, for a privileged position in the U.S. Department of Education (USDOE). Dr. Jitendra was assigned a new advisor. This advisor's laid-back mentoring style and expectation that doctoral students should work independently was contrary to the explicit direction and support she received from Dr. Kame'enui. After a semester of working with the new advisor, she felt that his advising style did not match her needs. Around this time, her husband wanted to move back to Bangalore, India and she dropped out of the doctoral program.

After a year and a half of working as a special education teacher and administrator in Bangalore, she returned in 1989 to the United States and worked with her former advisor, Dr. Kame'enui, who provided her with financial support in terms of a graduate research assistantship in order to finish her Ph.D. at the University of Oregon. Sheetal had a similar experience when Dr. Jitendra accepted a prestigious endowed chair position at the University of Minnesota, Twin Cities. Sheetal's comments illustrate how Dr. Jitendra supported her during this time:

I was in the final stages of writing my dissertation when Dr. Jitendra decided to move from Lehigh University to the University of Minnesota. I was devastated when she told me about her decision to move, but every time I met with her she assured me that even though she would not be my adviser on paper nothing would change—she would continue to work with me to complete my Ph.D. I remember meeting with her numerous times to discuss the situation and even though Dr. Jitendra moved, she was always available to support and guide me through the process.

The traditional "sink-or-swim" model for beginning assistant professors may not always be effective. New professors often face challenges as they are immersed in a culture of teaching, research, and service and without sufficient support, they may struggle to succeed. Dr. Jitendra's support of her advisees extends even beyond graduation. First, she explicitly scaffolded and coached us through the job search experience. Amy recalled:

In the year before I graduated with a Ph.D., Dr. Jitendra offered me the opportunity to serve on the job search committee as a student member so I could become familiar with the process. When I graduated, I applied to a select few positions, but disappointingly, I did not get a job offer. During this time, Dr. Jitendra supported me in a number of ways. She encouraged me to work on preparing a manuscript based on my dissertation study for submission to a journal, wrote letters of recommendation for me, and counseled me on how to navigate the job search that year. She also found funds to support me during this time—I worked with her on the revision of a mathematics curriculum program. Furthermore, she provided me with the experience to work with and guide one of her doctoral students, while also building my portfolio of publications. She even handed down beautiful work clothes to help me build my professorial wardrobe and have appropriate things to wear to job interviews.

Second, and perhaps the clearest mark that Dr. Jitendra is developing a legacy of lifelong learning, is the fact that her guidance and support have not ceased even though her advisees have moved on to take academic positions in other states.

In closing, it is clear that Dr. Jitendra used her own array of experiences, which ranged from good to challenging, to distinguish herself as an extraordinary researcher, teacher, and mentor. She encourages her advisees to use the practices she learned and taught us and to carry them forward with our own students. Also,

Dr. Jitendra never pretends to be perfect. Rather, she uses her own setbacks and how she dealt with them as opportunities to relate to her students. This motivates her students because we can see how she was once in our shoes and effectively applied strategies to triumph over what seemed, at the time, an insurmountable obstacle. Furthermore, Dr. Jitendra does not shy away from difficult discussions about complicated issues. For example, she shared this reflection about cultural differences:

> As someone who grew up in India before coming to the United States, I came to understand what it feels like to find myself outside the dominant culture, but also to identify and value both the commonalities and differences in the cultures of the two countries. At the same time, *I* believed people who are different (culturally and linguistically) must prove that we are just as good or better than those from the dominant culture to earn their respect. As such, I learned early in my career the importance of diligence and perseverance and pushed myself to be an overachiever.

Interestingly, Dr. Jitendra's self-identified perfectionism does not mean that she is flawless. By embodying the ideal of a lifelong learner, she models for those around her that one should not feel disheartened when they do not attain that perfection. Rather, the goal *is* the struggle, the constant learning and growing. And what better way to remind oneself of that than by helping others learn to see life that way in their journey to academic success.

CONCLUSION

This book chapter gave us the opportunity to sit down with Dr. Jitendra to learn more about the details of her journey, which has motivated and inspired us in new ways and sharing that with others is an honor. There is no doubt that Dr. Jitendra brings integrity and full commitment to her work and her professional contributions are substantive. She takes great care to ensure meaningful, far-reaching dissemination of her work. Her presentations at conferences, papers published in peer reviewed journals, working on federally funded research projects, service and teaching at her university, and outreach to teachers and schools illustrate Dr. Jitendra's dedication to the application of research and scholarship in a variety of settings. As a mentor, Dr. Jitendra always seems to know exactly when students need to be challenged and when they need to be guided through the process.

Under Dr. Jitendra's guidance, we, her former advisees, have continued to grow as educators and researchers. We learned from her the importance of being patient, supportive, and to believe in others even when they do not believe in themselves. We learned from her to understand social complexities that students might encounter and support them. This is a skill that has helped us be successful in responsibilities that we take on as faculty members.

Dr. Jitendra was deeply influenced by her advisor, Dr. Kame'enui and, in turn, she inspired us by being our adviser. Dr. Jitendra's mentorship allowed us to become diligent and conscientious individuals, who embody lifelong learning by continually monitoring, reflecting, revising, and adjusting our pedagogy, research, writing, and advising of our own students. Our goal has always been to take what we learned from her and move it forward to make a difference in the lives of our students just as she did for us, and her adviser did for her.

NOTE

1 Effective July 1, 2018, Dr. Asha Jitendra holds the Peloy Endowed Chair in Learning Disabilities in the Graduate School of Education at the University of California, Riverside.

REFERENCES

Collins, A., Brown, J. S., & Holum, S. (1991). Cognitive apprenticeship: Making thinking visible. *American Educator: The Professional Journal of the American Federation of Teachers, 15*(3), 6–11, 38–46.

Golde, C. M., Bueschel, A. C., Jones, L., & Walker, G. E. (2008). Advocating apprenticeship and intellectual community: Lessons from the Carnegie initiative on the doctorate. In R. C. Ehrenberg & C. V. Kuh (Eds.), *Doctoral education and the faculty of the future* (pp. 53–64). Ithaca, NY: Cornell University Press.

Jitendra, A. K., Lein, A. E., Im, S.-H., Alghamdi, A., Hefte, S., & Mouanatoua, J. (2018). Mathematical interventions for secondary students with learning disabilities and mathematics difficulties: A meta-analysis. *Exceptional Children, 84*(2), 177–196. Doi: https://doi.org/10.1177/0014402917737467

Jitendra, A. K., Nelson, G., Pulles, S. M., Kiss, A. J., & Houseworth, J. (2016). Is mathematical representation of problems an evidence-based strategy for students with mathematics difficulties. *Exceptional Children, 83*(1), 8–25.

Jitendra, A. K., Peterson-Brown, S., Lein, A., Zaslofsky, A., Kunkel, A., Jung, P.-G., & Egan, A. (2015). Teaching mathematical word problem solving: The quality of evidence for strategy instruction priming the problem structure. *Journal of Learning Disabilities, 48*(1), 51–72.

Lein, A. E., Jitendra, A. K., Starosta, K. M., Dupuis, D. N., Hughes-Reid, C. L., & Star, J. R. (2016). Assessing the relation between seventh-grade students' engagement and proportional problem solving performance. *Preventing School Failure, 60*, 117–123.

Sood, S., & Jitendra, A. K. (2007). A comparative analysis of number sense instruction in first grade traditional and reform-based mathematics textbooks. *Journal of Special Education, 41*(3), 145–157.

CHAPTER TEN

From Dreaming of Being a Biologist to Becoming an Endowed Professor in Higher Education

When Passion and Diligence Meet Opportunity

XINYE HU AND YANLI MA

INTRODUCING DR. SHOUPING HU

Dr. Shouping Hu is currently the Louis W. and Elizabeth N. Bender Endowed Professor of Higher Education, as well as the founding director of the Center for Postsecondary Success (CPS) at Florida State University (FSU). Dr. Hu received this endowed professorship because of his commitment to scholarship and teaching in higher education. The Louis W. and Elizabeth N. Bender Endowed Professorship was created by family, friends, and former students to honor Lou Bender. Professor Bender gave 40 years of service to FSU as an educator and administrator, with the last 21 years of service as Professor of Higher Education.

Dr. Hu's story began in China. In 1992, Dr. Hu graduated from Peking University in Beijing, China with a bachelor's degree in Geography. He started his master's degree in Higher Education at the same university a year later, and in 1995 continued his graduate studies at Indiana University in Bloomington. While at Indiana University, he obtained a master's degree in Economics in 1998 and a Ph.D. in Higher Education in 2000. After earning his Ph.D., Dr. Hu worked as an Assistant Professor of Higher Education at Seton Hall University in New Jersey from 2000 to 2004. In fall 2004, he joined FSU as an Associate Professor of Higher Education in the Department of Educational Leadership and Policy Studies.

Research and Teaching Achievements

Dr. Hu's main research focus is student success in postsecondary education, which includes studying student college access, student engagement, student persistence, and educational attainment. Dr. Hu has published numerous studies in top peer-reviewed journals such as *Research in Higher Education*, *Journal of Higher Education*, and *Review of Higher Education*, among others. His research in the field of higher education is widely recognized; for example, Google Scholar shows that his publications have been cited more than 5,000 times. Dr. Hu's research impact is tremendous in higher education.

As a faculty member at FSU, Dr. Hu has devoted himself to helping students succeed. He has enhanced students' learning opportunities by developing various new courses, such as Research on College Students, Higher Education Finance, Student Success in College, and Public Policy and Higher Education. Through his courses, he responds to students' diverse interests and needs by balancing the breadth and depth of subject matter as well as connecting theory, research, and practice. Dr. Hu receives overwhelmingly positive student evaluations in his courses. While pursuing his Ph.D. at FSU, Yanli Ma, the second author of this chapter, took several of Dr. Hu's courses. He was impressed by the professor's in-depth knowledge of numerous subjects such as Economics and Finance. He recalled that Dr. Hu encouraged class discussions and was very responsive to a range of questions.

As a mentor, Dr. Hu has chaired more than 20 doctoral dissertation committees and served as a committee member for more than 30 others. As he puts it, he has established "a trusting intellectual relationship" with his students. Through this approach, he has helped students explore the frontiers of research in higher education and inspired them to realize their full potential. To cite just one example, Kristina Cragg wrote Dr. Hu a letter thanking him for "the guidance, advice, and mentoring" he offered her while she was a student at FSU. She also commented that Dr. Hu is an "extraordinary" faculty member who "makes FSU a special and nurturing university." Cragg is now a research fellow on student achievement in the Western Association of Schools and Colleges.

This chapter focuses on Dr. Hu's pathway from China to becoming an endowed professor in Higher Education in the United States. The chapter will first introduce Dr. Hu's educational experiences in both his home country and the United States and then highlight his research contributions. The Center for Postsecondary Success, which Dr. Hu founded and currently leads, will be addressed. Finally, we will discuss our personal experiences with Dr. Hu.

FORGING A PATHWAY FROM BIOLOGY TO HIGHER EDUCATION

The claim that "the 21st century is the century of biotech" was widely heard in China in the 1980s. As a high school student during that period, Dr. Hu was influenced by this narrative and dreamed of becoming a biologist. After he finished his college entrance exam, he applied to study biology at Peking University (PKU). However, he was not accepted to PKU's Biology department. Instead, the PKU admissions office assigned Dr. Hu to the Geography department. Although he had no interest in geography, he accepted the offer, and studied diligently. During his four years in the program, he traveled across China and gradually became interested in the field of Geography.

Dr. Hu was participating in field research in Yunnan Province for his capstone project when he received notification that he had been recommended for admission as a master's student in the Institute of Higher Education at Peking University. At that time he knew little about the field of Higher Education, but he knew that there was a famous professor at that institute who had graduated with a Ph.D. from Stanford University and worked in the World Bank. Because of the reputation of this professor, Dr. Hu was enthusiastic and looking forward to entering the Higher Education program.

In 1994 while Dr. Hu pursued his master's degree at the Institute of Higher Education at PKU, he attended a lecture on educational planning at Beihang University. The main presenter was Dr. Donald Warren, the Dean of the School of Education at Indiana University. Dr. Hu was taking courses in economics of education at that time and, thus, was quite familiar with the lecture topic. At the end of a conversation with Dr. Warren, the lecturer gave young Dr. Hu his business card and asked him to stay in touch. Dr. Hu followed up, and Dr. Warren wrote advising him to meet Dr. Donald Hossler, who was scheduled to visit Beihang University in the early part of 1995.

Dr. Hossler met with Dr. Hu and brought him an application for the graduate program at Indiana University. Dr. Hu was excited at the prospect of studying abroad, something most Chinese students only dreamed about at that time. However, he realized that he had not taken the Test of English as a Foreign Language (TOEFL) or the Graduate Record Examination (GRE), and he had no money to prepare for these tests. Worse yet, he was running out of time to take the exams: it was already April and he was expected to enroll at Indiana University in the fall. Dr. Hossler advised Dr. Hu that the GRE could be postponed until he arrived at Indiana University, but the TOEFL was required. Dr. Hu explained his situation to some friends he had known since high school. They generously raised money for him to take the TOEFL. It was in June 1995, two months after Dr. Hu took his TOEFL, that he received an acceptance letter to the graduate program at Indiana University. With the money from his friends and one of his professors at PKU, Dr. Hu paid off his remaining academic-related debts, and bought a plane ticket to the U.S.

After intense personal and logistical preparation, Dr. Hu arrived at Indiana University and began his program in August 1995. He dreamed of working as an economist in the field of higher education based on his background at PKU's Institute of Higher Education. However, he gradually found that instead of Educational Economics, the strongest area of Indiana University's Higher Education program was Student Affairs Administration. Dr. Hossler realized Dr. Hu's interests, and advised him to choose Economics as his minor for his doctoral program of study. The combination of Indiana University's strong student affairs-based Higher Education program and his personal interests in economics and public policy shaped Dr. Hu's research agenda, covering both higher education policy and student affairs. He has maintained a primary research focus on these two areas since then.

Dr. Hu's first research report, *Crossing the River by Touching the Stones: The Experiences of First Year Eastern Asian Graduate Students at a Midwestern Research University*, was presented at the 1997 annual meeting of the American Educational Research Association (AERA) in Chicago, Illinois. While Dr. Hu applied qualitative research methods in this specific paper, he was generally more interested in quantitative research methods.

In 1997, the College Student Experiences Questionnaire Assessment Program, the predecessor of the National Survey of Student Engagement, was transferred from the University of California at Los Angeles to a team at Indiana University, led by Dr. George Kuh. At the same time, Dr. Edward St. John, an expert in educational finance, joined Indiana University. Dr. Hu seized the opportunity and began to work with these two professors on projects related to higher education policy and college student experiences while also continuing his work with Dr. Hossler. Through these efforts, Dr. Hu became more accomplished and prolific in his research and began to publish in respected, high impact educational journals.

While Dr. Hu's research and publishing confidence was growing, becoming a professor was still a faraway dream for him at that time. Among other reasons, his spoken English impeded his professorial career significantly. As he joked: "When I spoke in English, American people thought I was speaking in Chinese, Chinese people thought I was speaking in Hubei-accent Chinese, and my wife, who is also from Hubei province, had no idea of which language I was speaking in." His advisor and professors also suggested that becoming a full-time researcher, rather than a professor, would fit his background and situation well. They even hired Dr. Hu as a research analyst to continue to work on a number of research projects at Indiana University. However, Dr. Hu told them frankly he wanted to pursue a career as a university professor, and they were very supportive. Dr. Kuh reviewed Dr. Hu's cover letter. Dr. Hossler, who was the Vice Chancellor for Enrollment Service at that time, provided assistance with Dr. Hu's job applications and interview skills. With substantial support from Dr. Kuh, Dr. Hossler, and other professors, Dr. Hu obtained an assistant professorship in Higher Education at Seton Hall University in 2000, before he graduated from Indiana University. When Dr. Hu received the offer phone call from the Dean of the College of Education and Human Services at Seton Hall, he accepted the position without hesitation.

After his dissertation defense in June 2000, Dr. Hu and his wife left Indiana, where they had lived for five years, and moved to New Jersey. Taking his experiences and practical situation into consideration, Seton Hall University arranged for Dr. Hu to forgo teaching in the first semester. "[Although] I did not face the role-change challenge in my first semester as assistant professor," said Dr. Hu, "[honestly], I wished to start teaching as soon as possible." He made great progress in his scholarship during his time at Seton Hall University. After getting familiar with the new working atmosphere, he also began to teach from the second semester on. With his passion and interests in teaching, Dr. Hu became comfortable with the teaching load and expectations at Seton Hall.

The four years he spent at Seton Hall improved Dr. Hu's teaching skills dramatically. "If there was anything concerning me at that time," said Dr. Hu, "it might be how to move up the career ladder, and become a more successful scholar and professor." While Dr. Hu enjoyed being at Seton Hall, he wanted to work at a more highly ranked institution. In 2004, Dr. Hu joined Florida State University as an associate professor of higher education. FSU is an outstanding research university, and its higher education program has a long-standing history and respectable reputation. With his excellent teaching and research qualifications, Dr. Hu was granted tenure in 2007, and promoted to full professor in 2010 at Florida State University.

Research Contributions

Dr. Hu's research interests center around college access and success, student engagement and learning, and higher education policy. He has published more than 60 journal articles and book chapters. He is the author of *Beyond Grade Inflation: Grading Problems in Higher Education* (Jossey-Bass, 2005), the lead author of *Reinventing Undergraduate Education: Engaging College Students in Research and Creative Activities* (Jossey-Bass, 2008), a co-author of *Breaking Through the Access Barrier: Academic Capital Formation Informing Policy in Higher Education* (Routledge, 2011), and a co-author of *Cultivating Leader Identity and Capacity in Students From Diverse Backgrounds* (Jossey-Bass, 2013). Dr. Hu is also the lead editor of the *New Directions for Institutional Research* volume titled *Using Typological Approaches to Understand College Student Experiences and Outcomes* (Jossey-Bass, 2011).

Dr. Hu believes that ensuring students have access to higher education, and are able to become their optimal selves as a result of their college experiences, is key to maintaining the high quality of the American postsecondary education sector, enhancing the quality of life in the United States, and sustaining its competitive standing in the world. Based on these beliefs, he has conducted his research on two themes for over a decade: the first is student decisions about participating in higher education, including college access, choice, persistence, and educational attainment while the second theme is student engagement in educationally purposeful activities including research and creative activities.

Understanding Financial Influences on Student College Decisions

Dr. Hu has devoted much time to understanding financial influences on student college decisions; especially the influence of two prominent scholarship programs on student college access and success: the Gates Millennium Scholarship (GMS) program and the Washington State Achievers (WSA) program. The Bill & Melinda Gates Foundation underwrote both scholarships in an attempt to promote postsecondary access and success. The results from Dr. Hu and his colleagues' study of the GMS and WSA programs revealed that financial assistance is critical to equalizing educational opportunities for low-income minority students. Students who received financial assistance were more likely to go to college and more likely to persist in college (St. John & Hu, 2006, 2007). This line of research has informed policy discussions about student success and equity in educational opportunities. In 2004, *The Chronicle of Higher Education* highlighted Dr. Hu's research regarding the impact of the WSA program on student college access and choice.

In 2005, Dr. Hu published a single-authored monograph titled *Beyond Grade Inflation: Grading Problems in Higher Education* in the *Association for the Study of Higher Education (ASHE) Higher Education Report* series (Hu, 2005), widely considered "one of the most peer reviewed in higher education" (from the ASHE Higher Education Report Statement). In *Beyond Grade Inflation*, Dr. Hu empirically studied how college grading policies and practices could affect student choice of major fields and discourage students from choosing programs such as science and engineering. In particular, he pointed out that academic programs which are graded more stringently might attract fewer students, because state-funded, merit-based financial aid programs often tie college grades to eligibility. Dr. Hu conducted an empirical study to support this supposition using a sample of Florida's Bright Futures scholarship recipients. The study was featured in *Inside*

Higher Ed (Doug Lederman, 2008) along with other media outlets and received inquiries from the Florida Legislature, the governor's office of Florida, and many other interested groups and individuals.

Identifying Student Engagement Conducive to Desirable Outcomes

As student engagement is an important factor for student development and college success, it is instructive to examine which types of engagement may increase positive educational outcomes for diverse students. Dr. Hu has spent a considerable amount of time studying undergraduate engagement in research activities. Using National Survey of Student Engagement data, he conducted several studies examining the effects of undergraduate research engagement on a variety of college outcomes. He also investigated how institutional characteristics are associated with such engagement. Dr. Hu and his colleagues found student engagement in undergraduate research activities has positive effects on student overall gains in science and technology, vocational preparation, and intellectual development, but the effects are moderated by student background characteristics (Hu, Kuh, & Li, 2008). In terms of institutional characteristics, they also found that undergraduate students at research universities have a lower level of engagement in research activities than students at selective liberal arts colleges, although research universities are known for their research emphasis (Hu, Kuh, & Gayles, 2007).

In 2008, Dr. Hu published a monograph—*Reinventing Undergraduate Education: Engaging College Students in Research and Creative Activities*—in the prestigious ASHE Higher Education Report Series to examine the theories, research, policy, and practices related to undergraduate engagement in research activities (Hu, Scheuch, Schwartz, Gayles, & Li, 2008). In 2009, Dr. Hu co-authored an article titled "The Influence of Faculty on Student Participation in Research and Creative Activities" in *Innovative Higher Education*. This research identified faculty activities that can contribute to student engagement in research and creative activities (Hu, Scheuch, & Gayles, 2009). The results showed that an increase in faculty's research orientation significantly improves students' likelihood of engagement in hands-on research activities. Also, the more external funding support professors have, the more likely a student in that department will participate in research and creative activities. Dr. Hu's research in this area has made a noteworthy contribution to the knowledge base of student engagement and success as well as institutional programming and practice (Pascarella & Terenzini, 2005).

Connecting Financial Factors and Student Engagement

Financial impacts on student college attendance and engagement in college activities are arguably two of the major topical areas in higher education research.

Dr. Hu has been developing studies to investigate how financial factors relate to student engagement in college activities (e.g., academic and civic engagement) and student outcomes (including students' leadership development and democratic values). With funding from the Bill & Melinda Gates Foundation through the Institute of Higher Education Policy (IHEP) in Washington, D.C., and the use of high-quality longitudinal data from the National Opinion Research Center (NORC) at the University of Chicago, Dr. Hu has examined how scholarship programs such as the GMS and WSA affect student engagement in college activities. In a series of studies, Dr. Hu found that financial aid awards promote academic and social engagement during college (Hu, 2008b). Those types of engagement in turn have a positive impact on a range of desirable college outcomes, such as the development of democratic values, leadership development, and civic engagement after college (Hu, 2008a, 2008b). *The Chronicle of Higher Education* and several other news outlets featured the findings of his research in March 2008.

Evidence for the importance of student engagement on learning and personal development is well-established (Pascarella & Terenzini, 2005). However, it is less clear how student engagement would translate into success in the labor market, perhaps due to the lack of suitable data. With the availability of the longitudinal data collected by NORC for the GMS program, Dr. Hu and his collaborator, Dr. Gregory Wolniak, examined the relationships between student engagement in college activities and early-career earnings of college graduates in the labor market. They found that student academic and social engagement function differently for students of different backgrounds and in different major fields. For example, they found that students in the science, technology, engineering, and mathematics (STEM) fields benefitted more from their engagement in social activities than non-STEM students (Hu & Wolniak, 2010, 2013). Evidence like this could help shed light on the importance of developing not only the hard skills of college graduates, but also their soft skills, which likewise translate into success in the labor market.

The Center for Postsecondary Success

Dr. Hu founded the Center for Postsecondary Success (CPS) at Florida State University in 2014. The CPS aims to enrich the conversation on promoting student postsecondary success, both in the state of Florida and the nation overall. Also, Dr. Hu and his colleagues at the CPS hope its establishment helps move FSU into the ranks of the top public research universities in the country. The general mission of the CPS is to provide support for, and foster collaboration among, those who are interested in studying student success in postsecondary education, and to identify and evaluate institutional, state, and federal policies and programs that may serve to improve student success. In addition, the CPS' goals are to foster a culture and create a structure where researchers, policy makers, and practitioners can come together to find solutions that address issues facing postsecondary success through rigorous and timely research and evidence-based policy and practice.

Since 2014, the CPS has received more than $5.5 million dollars, mostly from the Bill & Melinda Gates Foundation and the U.S. Department of Education Institute of Education Sciences. Projects in the CPS include research on college readiness, higher education finance and policy, institutional effectiveness, student engagement and outcomes, technology in higher education, postsecondary STEM education, college opportunity and success for diverse student populations, and community colleges. The CPS has prominently researched developmental education reform in Florida. One of the most comprehensive studies addressing developmental educational reform is the report *Probability of Success: Evaluation of Florida's Developmental Education Redesign Based on Cohorts of First-Time-In-College Students from 2009–10 to 2014–15* (Hu et al., 2016). In this report, Dr. Hu and his colleagues "compared enrollment and passing rates of Developmental Education (DE) courses and gateway courses for first-time-in-college (FTIC) students before (2009–10 and 2013–14) and one year after the reform was implemented (2014–15)" (Hu et al., 2016). They also examined the association between student characteristics and DE course modality as well as the relationship between DE course modality and early student success. They found that when examining FTIC students' first-semester passing rates, the legislation has a positive impact on the performance of Hispanic and Black students who performed just as well, and in some cases better, than similarly prepared White students (Hu et al., 2016).

The latest report from the CPS relates to implementing developmental educational reform in the Florida College System after 2013. Through site visits to nine college campuses from November 2016 to April 2017, the study focuses on how institutions implemented the legislation on the ground. The report indicated unexpected positive outcomes from the legislation. Specifically, collaboration and coordination improved across campuses, although collaboration challenges remained within colleges at early implementation stages (Hu et al., 2017). Also, students in this study reported lacking clear guidance on selecting gateway or DE courses (Hu et al., 2017). The CPS is dedicated to continuously studying developmental education reform in Florida to help expand the understanding of the influence of DE courses on student achievement and development. This research has implications for both the state of Florida and the country.

The work done by Dr. Hu and his colleagues at the CPS has attracted attention from the media and policy circles. *The Chronicle of Higher Education*, *Inside Higher Ed*, and many major press outlets in the state of Florida such as the *Orlando Sentinel*, *Tampa Bay Times*, and *Miami Herald* have interviewed Dr. Hu on various higher education topics including the Bright Futures program and developmental education reform in Florida. Dr. Hu has been invited to testify in front of the Florida legislature and attended higher education convenings at the White House and the headquarters of the Bill & Melinda Gates Foundation.

OUR EXPERIENCES WITH DR. HU

From Xinye Hu

I am a second-year doctoral student in the Higher Education program at FSU. I first met with Dr. Hu during the last semester of my master's program in Educational Policy and Evaluation at FSU. At that time, I was planning to apply to a doctoral program at FSU and sought the advice of one of my professors in the class I was taking. The professor suggested that I talk with Dr. Hu in order to get more specific information about the higher education program. Dr. Hu gave me an overview of the program, as well as its requirements and application process. He was nice and friendly, and encouraged me to pursue my passion in the field of education.

In December 2016, I applied to the doctoral program in Higher Education and was offered admission to the program. After that, I applied for a graduate assistantship in the CPS and received the position. I feel grateful to Dr. Hu for his help and the opportunity to work with his team in the CPS. Dr. Hu advises me in both my academics and professional work. He helps me build my course plan and discusses potential dissertation topics with me. Dr. Hu also gives me feedback on papers and proposals, and assists me with building a strategic plan for my future work in the CPS.

Dr. Hu helped me identify my research interest in student math pathways in Florida. Since Fall 2014, Florida's 28 state colleges have allowed many students to have the option of bypassing DE courses regardless of their prior academic preparation and enrolling directly in gateway courses. Given that background, I am interested in what influences students' decisions to enroll in gateway/DE math since the prior academic preparation is less decisive; what students would do if they took and failed the gateway math courses; and how students perform in different math course decisions.

As an international student from China, I see Dr. Hu as a role model in both career and spirit. I dream of one day becoming a professor. Working with Dr. Hu gives me a chance to improve my research skills and understand the job of being a professor. Dr. Hu's success inspires me to be a diligent, modest, and amicable researcher who will contribute to the study of higher education and the success of college students.

From Yanli Ma

I have known Dr. Hu since I joined the Higher Education program at FSU as a doctoral student in fall 2005. I took several of his graduate courses and worked as his graduate assistant for one year. He was also my major professor and supervised my Ph.D. dissertation research. Undoubtedly, his excellent teaching, advising, and supervision significantly influenced my academic and professional development. With his strong support, I was able to win two competitive national fellowship/scholarship awards and complete my degree on time.

I have collaborated with Dr. Hu on several research projects before and after my graduation. Most of these projects have been published in leading higher education journals and presented at national conferences. While working on these projects with Dr. Hu, I learned a lot from his research acumen, his subject matter expertise, and his sound advice and guidance. Consequently, these collaborations have helped shape my research interests and enhance my research and writing skills.

I think I can also testify to Dr. Hu's passion for Asian/Chinese higher education as an Asian/Chinese American professor. He, together with me or others, has published about ten articles on U.S. higher education in Chinese higher education journals. Additionally, he has given more than ten invited lectures, or keynote or plenary presentations in Asia covering U.S. higher education or other higher education research topics. Through these endeavors, Dr. Hu has introduced U.S. higher education trends and experiences to postsecondary education scholars, administrators, and policy makers in Asia and promoted scholarly exchanges between U.S. and Asian higher education communities.

CONCLUSION

After reviewing Dr. Hu's experiences, the central role of preparation and guidance during his graduate school days becomes apparent. It is crucial to find out one's interests and specialties, and develop them. At the same time, building good interpersonal relationships is also important. On the one hand, it is an effective way of developing research skills; on the other hand, good relationships mean potentially powerful professional references. "Do good work, know good people, and have a good time" are the words Dr. Hu always said to himself and shared with his students. These words could be the embodiment of the "human resources" and "social capital" theories (Tonkaboni, Yousefy, & Keshtiaray, 2013). "One thing that is particularly worth mentioning is that building good interpersonal relationships based on mutual trust can be beneficial for one's whole life,"

Dr. Hu said. "I can still receive candid guidance and advice from my advisor and professors at Indiana University."

As a teacher who followed the pathway to a tenured full professorship, Dr. Hu said he has little trouble with two oft-discussed concerns by academics: the balance between work and family and the balance between teaching and research. Regarding work and family, his principle is "do not let your work interfere with your life." As Dr. Hu said, "it will be great if you have more time and energy to be devoted to work, but you do not have to be stressed out during normal life." The work itself is not the purpose of life, after all; having a high quality of life should be the aim. Dr. Hu is a very organized professor: he has a regular time on campus when he focuses on his researching and teaching. He also schedules time for his family, especially during semester breaks and sabbatical. As for the balance between teaching and research, Dr. Hu stated that teaching can increase knowledge and enlighten research, while research can enrich and improve teaching.

By all accounts, including peer reviews and citations of Dr. Hu's research, he has made significant and substantive contributions to the higher education knowledge base. His research has informed higher education policy and practice. The topical areas that Dr. Hu has focused on, such as college student engagement, financial aid programs, and developmental education reform, are highly relevant to the quality of American higher education and the overall well-being of the American society, now and in the future. Back to Dr. Hu's motto: "Do good work, know good people, and have a good time."

REFERENCES

Gutherie, K., Bertrand Jones, T., Osteen, L., and Hu, S. (2013). *Cultivating leader identity and capacity in students from diverse backgrounds.* San Francisco, CA: Jossey-Bass.

Hu, S. (2005). *Beyond grade inflation: Grading problems in higher education.* San Francisco, CA: Jossey-Bass.

Hu, S. (2008a). Do financial aid awards in college affect graduates' democratic values and civic engagement? *Journal of College and Character, 10*(1), 1–16.

Hu, S. (2008b). *Gates Millennium Scholars (GMS) program and college graduates' development of democratic values, civic engagement, leadership capacity, and career choice.* Washington, DC: Institute of Higher Education Policy.

Hu, S., Bertrand Jones, T., Brower, R. L., Park, T., Nix, A., Rahming, S., … Daniels, H. (2017). *Changes on the ground: Site visit report of the third year of developmental education reform in the Florida College System.* Tallahassee, FL: Center for Postsecondary Success. Retrieved from http://fsu.digital.flvc.org/islandora/object/fsu%3A492967

Hu, S., Kuh, G. D., & Gayles, J. G. (2007). Engaging undergraduate students in research activities: Are research universities doing a better job? *Innovative Higher Education, 32*(3), 167–177.

Hu, S., Kuh, G. D., & Li, S. (2008). The effects of engagement in inquiry-oriented activities on student learning and personal development. *Innovative Higher Education, 33*(2), 71–81.

Hu, S., & Li, S., eds. (2011). *Using typological approaches to understand college student experiences and outcomes.* San Francisco, CA: Jossey-Bass.

Hu, S., Park, T., Woods, C., Richard, K., Tandberg, D., & Bertrand Jones, T. (2016). *Probability of success: Evaluation of Florida's developmental education redesign based on cohorts of first-time-in-college students from 2009–10 to 2014–15.* Tallahassee, FL: Center for Postsecondary Success. Retrieved from http://centerforpostsecondarysuccess.org/wp-content/ uploads/2016/07/ StudentDataReport2016–1.pdf

Hu, S., Scheuch, K., & Gayles, J. (2009). The influences of faculty on undergraduate student participation in research and creative activities. *Innovative Higher Education, 34*(3), 173–183.

Hu, S., Scheuch, K., Schwartz, R., Gayles, J., & Li, S. (2008). *Reinventing undergraduate education: Engaging college students in research and creative activities.* San Francisco, CA: Jossey-Bass.

Hu, S., & Wolniak, G. (2010). Initial evidence of the influence of college student engagement on early career earnings. *Research in Higher Education, 51*(8), 750–766.

Hu, S., & Wolniak, G. (2013). College student engagement and early career earnings: Differences by gender, race/ethnicity, and academic preparation. *Review of Higher Education, 36,* 211–233.

Lederman, D. (2008, May 29). Unintended consequences of state merit-based aid. *Inside Higher Education.* Retrieved from https://www.insidehighered.com/news/2008/05/29/merit

Pascarella, E. T., & Terenzini, P. T. (2005). *How college affects students: A third decade of research* (volume 2). San Francisco, CA: Jossey-Bass.

St. John, E. P., & Hu, S. (2006). The impact of guarantees of financial aid on college enrollment: An evaluation of the Washington State Achievers Program. *Readings on Equal Education, 21,* 211–256.

St. John, E. P., & Hu, S. (2007). *School reform, scholarship guarantees, and college enrollment: A study of the Washington State Achievers program.* Seattle, WA: The Bill & Melinda Gates Foundation.

Tonkaboni, F., Yousefy, A., & Keshtiaray, N. (2013). Description and recognition the concept of social capital in higher education system. *International Education Studies, 6*(9), 40–50.

CHAPTER ELEVEN

Lucky to Be Alive

Ming Ming Chiu's Persistent, Creative Path Via Computer Science, Education, and Statistics

GAOWEI CHEN

At the precarious border between Chinatown and Little Italy in New York City, Ming Ming Chiu (please call him Ming), a poor, small boy (the shortest in his class) grew up surrounded by John Gotti's Mafia, the Ghost Shadows, and the Flying Dragons. In 6th grade, Ming was walking along Mott Street when three Ghost Shadows gang members approached him. One grabbed his jacket and told him to walk over to a doorway. Ming politely said, "No, thank you," pushed the gang member away, and ran through oncoming cars onto Canal Street. He zigzagged for several more blocks, boarded an uptown train, and was relieved to see the doors close with no gang members in sight. His childhood would include several more violent incidents. One day, his best friend disappeared; to avoid being recruited into the Flying Dragons, his best friend's entire family moved away. Another friend was killed in a heroin war between the Ghost Shadows and the Flying Dragons. His schoolmate was gang-raped in her apartment building. Daily newspaper stories about murders flowed from his dad at the dinner table, always ending with a plea to "Be careful." Fear was always nearby.

In this world, curiosity was dangerous, but Ming was curious about everything. As an infant, he put anything nearby into his mouth and unlocked gates, once crawling out on to a main road. Luckily for him, his parents fished out bones and toys from his throat, and a quick-thinking teenager tossed his bike onto the road to stop oncoming cars. His parents repeatedly told Ming these stories to deter his curiosity and keep him safe.

LEARNING

School was an oasis for Ming. He felt safe, and his teachers welcomed his curiosity. For example, his teachers often ended a lesson by asking if their students had any questions, which he interpreted broadly. After a lesson about sunlight, he asked, "If light can't escape a black hole, how do we know it's there?" While his classmates rolled their eyes, his teachers always tried to answer his questions. Encouraged by his teachers' responsiveness, Ming excelled in school academically.

But not in his parents' eyes. Ming was careless and, hence, rarely perfect (many 98s and 99s), so his parents criticized him for not studying hard enough. Perhaps if he were wiser, he would have understood that his parents knew little about the United States or its schools and only wanted him to do his best. In China, his mom and dad completed 4th grade and 6th grade, respectively, and they spoke little English. As early as the 1st grade, Ming began to interpret English and U.S. culture for them. The contradiction of his parents' criticism versus his interpretation responsibilities and his teachers' praise led him as an eight-year-old to trust his own judgment over that of his parents. At that time, his family wanted to buy a refrigerator, so he read the relevant *Consumer Reports* article and guided his parents toward his targeted model. Relying only on his own judgment however, he also tackled many unnecessary challenges and made many errors, such as turning white underwear pink by washing it with a red t-shirt in a hot wash cycle.

Through a little cleverness and a lot of luck, he survived his childhood (being born on the 7th day of the 11th month didn't hurt). By passing a test for gifted students, he entered Hunter College High School. His wonderful teachers asked him to write a new constitution for the United States, use imaginary numbers to solve electricity problems, and design art murals for three mathematics classroom walls. He was proud of his winning 3rd-place design, 4 reflected diamonds, and of how he and his friends carefully painted it on the third wall. Moreover, he enjoyed his varied discussions with his new friends, ranging from justifiable conditions for suicide to a classified ad in the school newspaper, "Oral sex prevents tooth decay."

While he appreciated his talented teachers and schoolmates, he adored his free train pass. After surviving his childhood—while embracing adult-like responsibilities—Ming felt emboldened to explore the metropolis (with appropriate defensive tactics such as walk fast, hide money, don't stare, and so on). His train pass let him traverse the city from the burning cars in Harlem to the glorious sopranos at Lincoln Center (only $2 for the Wednesday afternoon back row!). As his parents would not have approved, Ming and his sister self-imposed an 8:00 PM curfew to ensure that they returned home well before their parents did at 10:30 PM.

Ming thrived academically at Hunter, but he was still careless. Competing against gifted students, his imperfect tests, essays, and projects were costly; he never had the highest score in any course. Despite graduating near the top of his class, he won only one honorable mention in chemistry in six years. While initially disappointing, it also freed him to explore unusual projects without worrying about grades. Some were successful, such as explaining the possible paths of stellar evolution on a poster. Others were not, such as a story about a walking wall: Ming loves to tell how he managed to get a failing grade on this paper.

After high school, Ming continued his exploration of diverse topics. At Columbia University, he took an "Introduction to Computer Programming" course, which included assignments ranging from creating electronic address books to simulating lines at a supermarket. Enamored of the seemingly limitless possibilities in this new and growing field, Ming majored in Computer Science.

In the next semester, however, the second computer course "Software Design" was taught by the worst teacher Ming ever had. This professor not only lectured by reading from the textbook but also assigned an insanely difficult problem, namely create a word processor (like MS Word). When his classmates complained, the professor let them work in pairs, but only 6 students did so (including Ming; he was afraid of failing). No one created a word processor, but the three pairs created primitive line editors that had some functions and they each received an A+. Ming and his partner, Diana, shared ideas, but more importantly, they lifted one another's spirits, especially when they were anxious about the impossibility of completing the assignment. Knowing that they were committed to doing this together enabled them to continue making progress. This experience highlighted the value of collaboration for Ming and sparked his ongoing research on how people work together.

Of all his computer science courses, Ming liked his "Artificial Intelligence" course best. For the final project, he created a Chinese checkers computer program that incorporated all his relevant knowledge, strategies, and tactics. Unlike Ming, the Chinese checkers program did not make any mistakes, so he lost every game he played against it.

TEACHING

To pay for his college tuition, Ming tutored and taught at an alternative education program encompassing adult literacy, teenage apprenticeships and half-way house programs between jail and parole. Many elderly Blacks had attended inadequate schools as children and thus did not learn to read, so they embraced his guidance as he tutored them; they were, by far, his most enthusiastic students. When teacher aides, assistant teachers, or teachers were absent, he substituted for them, and was eventually promoted to teacher. Without proper teacher training though, Ming made many mistakes. He especially remembers a 20-year-old halfway house student who only read at a second-grade level. As the alternative education program only had middle school and high school educational materials, Ming tried various ideas, including reading aloud, borrowing children's books, and drawing sentence diagrams. However, his student did not learn much through any of these methods, became frustrated, and eventually left the program. Ming failed, and his student suffered. Later, to comfort novice teachers who were having difficulties, Ming would tell them this story, concluding that "no matter how badly you feel about your teaching, none of your students would rather go to jail than be in your class."

This failure drives Ming's constant teaching experimentation with different students, content, methods, and media. His students encompass every level: underprivileged preschoolers, gifted elementary school students, teenage Vietnamese gang members, Ivy League undergraduates, pre-service and in-service teachers, and mainland Chinese Ph.D. students. Ming has taught reading, writing, mathematics, geology, electrical circuits, computer science, education, psychology, and statistics. Adapting his teaching to the local culture, his tool kit includes mini-lectures, demonstrations, quiet reflection, student pairing-and-sharing, group problem solving, role-play, whole-class discussion, and videotape analysis. Moreover, his teaching media include traditional face-to-face classrooms, distance instruction via video cameras, Google Docs discussions, online courses, and hybrids of these. Overall, he generally fosters student analyses of their classroom activities to understand key ideas such as algebraic representation, and to develop important skills such as seeing and understanding others' perspectives. By having students collaborate and openly discuss their work, he aims to foster a community of learners. Working together, they are motivated to improve their understanding from multiple viewpoints (e.g., student and teacher), recognize more difficulties, and develop suitable adaptations to improve their learning (and teaching for pre-service and in-service teachers).

POST-GRADUATE RESEARCH

Ming's teaching failures fueled his interest in understanding how people learn and how teachers can foster their learning, so he earned a Master's in Education at Harvard. Combining computer science and education, he created an algebra learning environment based on the metaphor of a pair of twins each holding different boxes and coins to represent the same quantity on each side of an equation despite different variables and numbers.

In his Ph.D. program at the University of California at Berkeley, he continued his education studies under the guidance of Dr. Andy diSessa (advisor), Dr. George Lakoff, Dr. Alan Schoenfeld, and Dr. Rogers Hall. Although diSessa's expertise was in computational thinking and science learning, he encouraged his students to pursue their own interests, which ranged from gender identity to learning how to dive. Regardless of the topic, diSessa painted each of his students' papers red with criticisms and suggestions, pushing his students to consider their assumptions, other alternatives, and implications. Likewise, Lakoff's, Schoenfeld's, and Hall's respective areas of expertise in metaphors, mathematics education, and representation practices changed Ming's understanding of his dissertation topic, how students collaborate to solve mathematics problems using talk and metaphors during classroom lessons.

Ming benefited from not only his professors' voluminous feedback, but also from simple luck. In the Berkeley library, he saw a counseling journal article on a table. Curious, he looked at the open page and saw a multi-dimensional scheme for patients' stories (Stiles, 1978). Immediately recognizing the value of multiple dimensions, he eventually created a three-dimensional scheme (*evaluation* [agree, disagree, ignore], *knowledge* [new, old, unrelated], *invitation to participate* [question, command, statement]), which captures 27 different types of talk (27 = 3 × 3 × 3). Also, he saw that statistically analyzing turns of talk, rather than individuals, yields much larger sample sizes for statistical analyses (e.g., 500 turns vs. 2 students). Although he wanted to use statistics to model students' talk in his Ph.D. dissertation, the statistical method did not exist yet, so he settled for a qualitative dissertation.

ANALYZING TALK WITH STATISTICS

After graduating with his doctorate, Ming won a McDonnell Foundation post-doctoral fellowship at the University of California at Los Angeles (UCLA) under the formal and informal mentoring of Drs. Kris Gutiérrez and Noreen Webb. There, he spent most of his time talking with them and other scholars in linguistics and statistics about how to statistically analyze conversations. They told him about eight analytic difficulties, which Ming had to address before publishing his work. His early attempts failed, resulting in 16 consecutive manuscript rejections.

Fortunately, as a graduate student, he had published a separate study on geometry intuitions in a top mathematics education journal (Chiu, 1996), which persuaded The Chinese University of Hong Kong to hire him as an assistant professor. There, he had lunch with his Harvard econometrician friend, Dr. Lawrence Khoo, who had also moved to Hong Kong. Lunch at the Ritz-Carlton turned into dinner as they discussed the statistics issues and identified additional analytic challenges. After working together for five years, they invented "Dynamic Multilevel Analysis" (DMA, Chiu & Khoo, 2005a), which Ming further improved to become "Statistical Discourse Analysis" (SDA, Chiu & Lehmann-Willenbrock, 2016).

SDA identifies pivotal moments, tests complex hypotheses, and applies to small samples. SDA statistically identifies the critical moments in a conversation that radically change the interactions among speakers (e.g., insights, insults, topic shifts). SDA also simultaneously tests multiple hypotheses about factors at various levels that affect attributes of a speaker's talk across time; for example, after a disagreement by a girl in a mixed racial group at the beginning of a discussion, is the next speaker more likely to express a new idea than otherwise? Furthermore, SDA tests whether specific actions or sequences of them are related to broader outcomes. For example, are groups with disagreements followed by new ideas (*disagree → new idea* sequence) more likely than other groups to solve an algebra problem?

As SDA is computationally intensive, Ming designed an artificial intelligence program *Statistician* to run it. He hired research assistant, statistician, and computer programmer Yik Ting Choi to incorporate almost everything Ming knows about statistics into SDA. *Statistician* runs analyses and interprets the results. If the results meet the a priori satisfaction criteria, it produces a table suitable for a manuscript. If the results do not, *Statistician* re-writes itself to run further analyses until it meets the satisfaction criteria.

SDA can statistically address many research questions about talk, and *Statistician* can run analyses quickly; hence, Ming sought co-authors who might benefit from SDA and his other statistics skills (110 co-authors on publications so far). Ming has applied SDA to complex models of sequences of thinking and social processes by individuals and groups, ranging from preschoolers to adults in various countries. When pairs of U.S. preschoolers talk about books, their behaviors affect one another's subsequent behaviors (e.g., *agree → inference*; *specify reading purpose → express story information*) (see Christ, Chiu, & Wang, 2014). Among triads of Dutch third-grade students writing reports, sequences of *planning, low-level thinking*, or *evaluations* raised the likelihood of subsequent *high-level thinking* (Molenaar & Chiu, 2014). Canadian university student teams designing lessons online often engaged in the following sequence of thinking: *opinion → elaborate → theorize* (Chiu & Fujita, 2014).

Beyond students, Ming used SDA to analyze teachers and technicians. When a female U.S. teacher teaches a lesson and reflects on it, she often follows this sequence: *problem exploration → teaching adaptation → problem resolution* (Hayden & Chiu, 2015). After a professor *shares personal experiences* or *asks for critical thinking* or a classmate *recalls facts* or *thinks critically thinking*, a

U.S. in-service teacher is more likely to *recall facts* and *think critically* (Arya, Christ, & Chiu, 2014). During U.S. teachers' discussions of a video of their work, the following factors increase the *generation* or *application of teaching suggestions*: a *video of instruction* (rather than assessment), *sharing a teaching problem* (rather than a solution), and specific conversation turn attributes (type of *pedagogy*, aspects of *subject matter*, *sources of knowledge*) (see Arya, Christ, & Chiu, 2015). Among German technicians solving problems during team meetings, *solution-focused behaviors* and *past emotional positivity* increase subsequent *emotional positivity* but *problem-focused behavior* decreases it (Lehmann-Willenbrock, Chiu, Lei, & Kauffeld, 2017). As suggested by these studies, SDA analyses of conversations or sequences of thinking can increase our understanding of them and thereby encourage desirable behaviors/sequences and deter harmful ones.

CORRUPTION, BIG DATA, AND SEXUAL PREDATORS

Along the way, Ming discovered many collaborators who required different statistical analyses, so he invented new statistical methods and applied them to complex data sets. For example, between singing karaoke songs in Tokyo, Ming and his new friend Joeri Mol discussed how to detect corruption in the music industry. When record companies bribe radio stations to play specific songs (payola songs), their airplay and sales patterns differ from those of other songs. To detect this difference, Ming invented another statistical method, "Multilevel Diffusion Analysis" (MDA), which models how multiple songs, ideas, etc. spread through a population (Rossman, Chiu, & Mol, 2008).

As Ming's skills in statistics improved, he began analyzing larger and more complex data sets. He downloaded free, large-scale international data on the learning outcomes of half a million students in 65 countries, including the Program for International Student Assessment (PISA) and Progress in International Reading Literacy Study (PIRLS). Motivated by his experience of living in poverty as a child, he theorized that both rich and poor students in less equal schools (e.g., unequal educational resources) and in less equal countries (e.g., unequal family income) learn less overall. Using the PISA data, he empirically showed that these students indeed had lower reading, mathematics, and science test scores (Chiu & Khoo, 2005b). He further analyzed the PISA data to show evidence of microeconomic mechanisms of inequality, specifically fewer resources and inefficient allocation (also known as *economic rent* and *diminishing marginal returns*, respectively).

Using the PIRLS data, Ming showed that grouping similar students together within classrooms (*tracking*) or within schools (*streaming*) yield opposite effects on learning outcomes (Chiu, Chow & Joh, 2017). As streaming enables teachers to *customize their instruction* for similar students in an entire school, reading test scores are higher in school systems with more streaming. In contrast, teachers do not necessarily prepare multiple lesson plans to suit students in different sections of the same course, and reading test scores are lower in tracked classes. Indeed, mixing high- and low-achieving students together can increase opportunities for the former to *help* the latter, which might help both learn (helpers re-organize their knowledge and help recipients receive information). Meanwhile, mixing privileged and underprivileged students supports their learning from one another's *diverse* experiences. Also, greater differences in classmates' attitudes toward reading help students recognize their positive and negative consequences (*contrasting cases*) and pursue positive attitudes to learn more. Together, these results can help school principals design arrangements of students into classrooms to improve their overall learning at little cost.

Recently, Ming has begun examining the complex data of text messages to detect online sexual predators and thereby reduce crime. According to the Federal Bureau of Investigations, 750,000 adults seek sex with youths daily (Rodas, 2014), but less than 10% are arrested (U.S. Department of Justice, 2017). To address this problem, Ming invented a new way to detect how these predators attract children (*grooming*). For example, a predator targets unhappy children with few friends and poor family relationships by talking about their own unhappy experiences and encouraging them to reciprocate. By doing so, the predator engenders sufficient trust in his victims to meet with him. Ming invented a way to detect this grooming by combining automatic computer analyses of words in messages (*computational linguistics*) with SDA and *Statistician* (Chiu, Seigfried-Spellar & Ringenberg, 2018).

LEADERSHIP AND SERVICE

Ming joined the University at Buffalo's Department of Learning and Instruction as a professor, and later became its associate chair. There, he helped foster a culture of collaboration via birthday parties, flash research panels, best idea prizes, Google Docs discussions, and so on. In addition to building a stronger collaboration infrastructure (faculty expertise databases, one-stop information websites, communication tools, etc.), he cultivated relationships among colleagues to foster a community of scholars, co-authoring 14 publications with 11 faculty and 6 students in 5 years. Overall, his colleagues' average research productivity nearly tripled, rising from 0.5 to 1.4 publications per year from 2008 to 2014.

To raise the academic profile of University at Buffalo, he led its successful application for membership in the *International Society of the Learning Sciences'* Network of Academic Programs in the Learning Sciences (NAPLeS). In 2017, the University at Buffalo's Ph.D. program in Curriculum, Instruction and the Science of Learning (CISL) was one of only 33 programs in NAPLeS worldwide and was ranked as the fifth best online Ph.D. program in the United States (College Values Online, 2017).

Outside the United States, Ming has advised the Qatari and mainland Chinese governments on their education systems. The Qatar Ministry of Education and Higher Education invited Ming to analyze their student data and advise them on their education policy. Ming showed them that Qatari family influences (socio-economic status, parent attitudes, books at home, parent-child activities) on students' reading test scores were much stronger (192%) than those in European countries. Qatari preschoolers' many family resources help them develop greater literacy skills compared to many European preschoolers. However, after four years of school, Qatari students were 20% behind their European counterparts in reading, in part because many Qatari students believed that their teachers did not care about them. As a result, Ming advised Qatari education officials to invest in programs to improve young children's learning and the training of principals and teachers.

Ming currently serves on the Advisory Board for mainland China's Ministry of Education's *National Assessment of Primary and Secondary Schools*. After many meetings over meals, Ming persuaded the Ministry to re-design their overall testing strategy (from annual, isolated data fragments in each province) to an integrated database across provinces and across time linked to government information (e.g., demography, economy) at all levels (student, school, district, province). He also introduced ministry officials to new statistical analyses (multilevel cross-classification and multilevel growth models), and is gently suggesting integration of statistical analyses with computer algorithms to increase precision and efficiency.

Ming was the Charles R. Hicks Professor of Educational Psychology and Research Methodology in the College of Education at Purdue University from 2014 to 2017 and is currently Chair Professor of Analytics and Diversity at The Education University of Hong Kong (EdUHK; chair professors at EdUHK are essentially endowed professors). Supported by 34 grants ($8.7 million), he has disseminated his research through 178 publications (100 journal articles), 3 television broadcasts, 17 radio broadcasts, and 148 news articles in 21 countries. In addition to his research, he also runs Education Film Night, Publication Problem

Solving Circles (small groups of faculty who answer one another's research questions), and is creating and merging databases to support data-driven decision-making at EdUHK.

CODA

When Ming nurtured his own students, he followed many of his advisor's practices. He let his students, like me, choose our research goals and tried to accelerate us along our chosen paths. Born in China, I had gone to The Chinese University of Hong Kong (CUHK) to do my Ph.D. and was Ming's first doctoral student.

For my thesis, I studied how people in public online forums in China discussed and solved mathematics problems, especially how they created new ideas to do so. I expected that many people would be using online forums to learn in the future, so I thought this would be an important issue. Specifically, I considered how feelings, displayed personal information (e.g., username, avatar), evaluations, elicitations, and knowledge content affected subsequent responses. It was a broad and challenging topic for me, because there was nothing like it in the literature at the time: no theory of online behaviors and emotions, no way of measuring emotions online, and no analysis of parallel online messages.

When I delineated these problems, Ming smiled confidently and said, "If there is no existing theory or methodology, let's create them." We explicated a new theoretical model of how online behaviors and emotions differ from face-to-face behaviors and emotions. Furthermore, we enhanced dynamic multilevel analysis to analyze online messages. I designed and created a computer program to organize and code online discussion data to reflect the complex tree of relations among messages in parallel streams. I used this methodology to identify critical events that radically changed online interactions and tested whether attributes of recent messages affected the nature of the current message. Our work yielded three journal publications and a press conference to disseminate the study to the public. At the press conference, photographers took our picture, which appeared in several newspapers in Hong Kong and China (see Figure 11.1).

When my mom saw the newspaper photo, she said that was the proudest moment of her life. When my dad called me and told me that, my eyes teared, and a voice from the bottom of my heart said, "Thank you, Ming, for encouraging and supporting me to go forward with courage." After I won the CUHK's best postgraduate research award, Ming encouraged me to search broadly for jobs, contacting his friends and acquaintances, including ones at the University of Pittsburgh and The University of Hong Kong, both of which eventually extended offers to me at the same time. I am now an Associate Professor in the Faculty of Education at the University of Hong Kong.

Figure 11.1. Photo from Press Conference. Ming Ming Chiu (left), Gaowei Chen (right).
Source: Copyright ©2018 *Hong Kong Economic Times*. All rights reserved. Reprinted with permission.

REFERENCES

Arya, P., Christ, T., & Chiu, M. M. (2014). Facilitation and teacher behaviors: An analysis of literacy teachers' video-case discussions. *Journal of Teacher Education, 65*(2), 111–127.

Arya, P., Christ, T., & Chiu, M. M. (2015). Links between characteristics of collaborative peer video analysis events and literacy teachers' outcomes. *Journal of Technology and Teacher Education, 23*(2), 159–183.

Chiu, M. M. (1996). Exploring the origins, uses and interactions of student intuitions: Comparing the lengths of paths. *Journal for Research in Mathematics Education, 27*(4), 478–504.

Chiu, M. M., Chow, B. W. Y., & Joh, S. W. (2017). Streaming, tracking and reading achievement: A multilevel analysis of students in 40 countries. *Journal of Educational Psychology*.

Chiu, M. M., & Fujita, N. (2014). Statistical discourse analysis: A method for modelling online discussion processes. *Journal of Learning Analytics, 1*(3), 61–83.

Chiu, M. M., & Khoo, L. (2005a). A new method for analyzing sequential processes: Dynamic multi-level analysis. *Small Group Research, 36*, 600–631.

Chiu, M. M., & Khoo, L. (2005b). Effects of resources, inequality, and privilege bias on achievement. *American Educational Research Journal, 42*, 575–603.

Chiu, M. M., & Lehmann-Willenbrock, N. (2016). Statistical discourse analysis: Modeling sequences of individual behaviors during group interactions across time. *Group Dynamics: Theory, Research, and Practice, 20*(3), 242–258.

Chiu, M. M., Seigfried-Spellar, K. C., & Ringenberg, T. R. (2018). Detecting contact vs. fantasy child sex offenders in online chats: Statistical discourse analysis of self-disclosure and emotion words. *Child Abuse & Neglect, 81*, 128–138.

Christ, T., Chiu, M. M., & Wang, X. C. (2014). Preschoolers' engagement with reading behaviours: A statistical discourse analysis of peer buddy-reading interactions. *Journal of Research in Reading, 37*(4), 375–408.

College Values Online. (2017). *Highly ranked online PhDs*. Retrieved from http://ed.buffalo.edu/online/home/college-value-ranking.html

Hayden, H. E., & Chiu, M. M. (2015). Reflective teaching via a problem exploration-teaching adaptations-resolution cycle: A mixed methods study of pre-service teachers' reflective notes. *Journal of Mixed Methods Research, 9*(2), 133–153.

Lehmann-Willenbrock, N., Chiu, M. M., Lei, Z., & Kauffeld, S. (2017). Understanding positivity within dynamic team interactions: A statistical discourse analysis. *Group & Organization Management, 42*(1), 39–78.

Molenaar, I., & Chiu, M. M. (2014). Dissecting sequences of regulation and cognition: Statistical discourse analysis of primary school children's collaborative learning. *Metacognition and Learning, 9*, 137–160.

Rodas, E. (2014). *The multi-facets of cyber-sex trafficking: A call for action and reform from society.* Unpublished manuscript.

Rossman, G., Chiu, M. M., & Mol, J. (2008). Modeling diffusion of multiple innovations via multilevel diffusion curves: Payola in pop music radio. *Sociological Methodology, 38*(1), 201–230.

Stiles, W. B. (1978). Verbal response modes and dimensions of interpersonal roles: A method of discourse analysis. *Journal of Personality and Social Psychology, 36*(7), 693–703.

U.S. Department of Justice. (2017, December 14). *Violent crime victimization*. Retrieved from https://www.ojjdp.gov/ojstatbb/victims/faqs.asp

CHAPTER TWELVE

Journey to Excellence

Professor Hua-Hua Chang's Success through Passion and Dedication

CHANJIN ZHENG

INTRODUCTION

Dr. Hua-Hua Chang is the Charles R. Hicks Chair Professor of Educational Measurement and Research Methodology at Purdue University and a professor emeritus at the University of Illinois at Urbana-Champaign (UIUC). He also holds honorary professorships at multiple universities in mainland China and Taiwan. He is one of the most influential scholars in the field of educational measurement today. His achievements in the field of testing are perhaps best evidenced by the fact that he received the 2017 E.F. Lindquist Award, one of the most prestigious awards for outstanding applied or theoretical research in the field of testing and measurement, awarded by the American Educational Research Association (AERA) and ACT, Inc. The award committee wrote: *"What sets Dr. Chang apart from other researchers in the field is the originality and creativity of his work. The development of computerized adaptive testing would be nowhere near what it is today without his contributions."* He has delivered keynote presentations in more than a dozen countries, and he has worked with schools, international educational organizations, and governments all over the world. His writings, and there are lot of them—80 refereed journal papers, one book and numerous book chapters—are read around the globe.

Equipped with rigorous statistical training, driven by a passion for scientific truth, and through relentless dedicated efforts, Dr. Chang embarked on his journey to excellence as a scientist in the field of educational testing by resolving one technical issue after another, and as an educator by nurturing a new generation of scholars and lecturing to a general audience. He is a fellow of both the American Educational Research Association and the American Statistical Association. From 2012 to 2013, Dr. Chang served as president of the Psychometric Society.

EARLY YEARS

Dr. Chang was born in Shanghai, China, in 1953. He did not have the opportunity to finish junior high because of the Cultural Revolution. In 1970, along with millions of urban teenagers, he was sent to the countryside as a farm worker. He worked on the farms for seven years and almost completed his high school education by self-study. He obtained a diploma in Mathematics from the East China Normal University in 1980 and a Ph.D. in Statistics from the University of Illinois at Urbana-Champaign (UIUC) in 1992. Dr. Chang attributed his academic success to *diversity, equity, and inclusion* as indicated in a recent diversity statement:

> "I came to the University of Illinois from China in December 1984 as a student with only $60 in my pocket, and so many nice people touched my life and made me feel welcome! I felt strongly that the University at that time provided a platform to students with different backgrounds … My personal experience constantly reminds me of the importance of diversity, equity, and inclusion. As a beneficiary myself, many of my research activities are about promoting diversity and equity."

After earning his Ph.D. in Statistics from UIUC in 1992, Dr. Chang joined the testing industry, where he worked for nine years before moving to academia in 2001. From 1992 to 1999, he was a research scientist at Educational Testing Service (ETS), Princeton, NJ, where he directed and co-directed statistical analyses of several large-scale projects for the National Assessment of Educational Process (NAEP), also known as The Nation's Report Card. NAEP is the only assessment that measures what U.S. students know and can do in various subjects. From 1999 to 2001, Dr. Chang served as a Senior Psychometrician and Director of Computerized Testing Research at the National Board of Medical Examiners (NBME), Philadelphia, PA, where he worked extensively on various research projects for the United States Medical Licensing Examination (USMLE). The USMLE assesses a physician's ability and skills, a process that is essential to ensure safe and effective patient care.

Working for nine years in the testing industry was crucial to Dr. Chang's development, since most of his work—theoretical and applied alike—is to tackle hard-to-solve problems in the field of educational testing. Working at various testing companies proved to be an eye opener for Dr. Chang, who benefited from his exposure to and experience with a wide range of complications associated with implementing large-scale assessment in the real world. Dr. Change views every challenge arising from testing practices as an opportunity to push scientific investigation and create invaluable knowledge for humankind.

DIF: THE STARTING POINT

In his early career as a scientist, Dr. Chang grappled with a politically loaded topic—test fairness. Educational testing carries important consequences at the personal, institutional, and societal level. The social and legal impacts of testing push the rigor of testing development and implementation. One critical requirement of a test is its fairness, which can be—at least partially—ensured by various statistical techniques. The out-of-court settlement of the case *Golden Rule Life Insurance Company v. John E. Washburn* (1984), was an important catalyst for test fairness research at ETS. The case centered around an agent licensure test required for agent candidates by the Golden Rule Life Insurance Company, a test for which the passing rate of Blacks was 25% below that of Whites (Bandalos, 2018, p. 511). The plaintiffs, including several Black individuals, contended they were harmed by bias in the examination, and sought damages and fees from ETS and the director of the Illinois Department of Insurance on the grounds that the examination was not truly job-related and unfairly discriminated against African Americans. A significant result of the settlement in this case was the stipulation that "if a test resulted in differences in the rates of correct responses between minority and majority candidates, the items with the smallest such differences should be used" (Bandalos, 2018, p. 511).

Through ingenious use of statistical methods combined with expert review, ETS aimed to develop tests that are fair regardless of examinees' gender, race/ethnicity, etc. With two colleagues, Dr. Chang developed the Poly-SIBTEST (Chang, Mazzeo, & Roussos, 1996), a non-parametric hypothesis testing statistic and estimation procedure for detecting item bias, also known as differential item functioning (DIF). The Poly-SIBTEST detects test score differences possibly caused by race/ethnicity or gender differences rather than ability differences. This procedure was accepted as a primary item/test bias screening procedure for NAEP data analyses at ETS. In fact, it has become one of the most popular item-bias detection procedures worldwide. From the start, Dr. Chang's work was always to ensure the highest quality of testing and to offer the best experience possible for test-takers.

CAT: THE PRACTICAL CHALLENGES

Dr. Chang's most influential contribution to the world of testing is his theoretical and empirical advancement in the field of Computerized Adaptive Testing (CAT). CAT, also known as tailored testing, is a method for administering tests that adapt to the examinee's ability level. The most important component in CAT is the item selection strategy for sequentially selecting the next item based on answers to previous items. Some of his most well-known work includes the studies he collaborated on with Dr. Zhiliang Ying concerning item selection in CAT.

Dr. Chang started to work on this topic soon after his arrival at ETS in 1992 which coincided with the launch of the CAT version of the Graduate Record Examination (GRE-CAT) by ETS. The traditional method, the Fisher information strategy, suggested choosing an item that is close to the examinee's estimated proficiency and with high discrimination (the power of an item to tell the difference between two students). After several years of conducting a series of studies, Chang and Ying (1999) identified and summarized two flaws with that approach. First, sharply discriminating items would always be chosen first, and consequently, many high-quality, albeit less discriminating, items turned out to be rarely used. Cost of item development averages more than $1,000 per item; therefore, this tendency was wasteful and moreover, weakened the security of a given exam because consequently, it was easier to cheat.

Chang and Ying recognized that this weakness was having a profound negative effect on the testing industry which explained and even predicted the unfortunate happenings of the GRE-CAT. When ETS launched GRE-CAT employing the Fisher information strategy in 1992, the test prep company Kaplan detected the loophole of the CAT system by sending out a team of professional test-takers. The test-takers were able to exhaust the GRE item bank quickly, since highly discriminating items are always preferred by the algorithm. Kaplan and others raised questions about the security of the GRE-CAT because, given the test's continuous nature, test-takers could pass on to subsequent examinees the questions that were asked. While ETS initially assured that the examination was secure because "the GRE program has chosen to use many pools of questions simultaneously," subsequent events proved that this assurance was ill-founded (See Davey & Nering, 2002).

Second, at the same time, Chang and Ying demonstrated that the Fisher information strategy is not appropriate at earlier stages of CAT testing because the ability of the examinee may not be accurately estimated when based on only a few items. In turn, when the examinee's proficiency was not accurately estimated, the algorithm selected highly discriminating questions in an ability range that may be far from the examinee's true ability.

The second problem also bears important consequences for the testing industry. For instance, as a result of this flaw in the algorithm and predicted in Dr. Chang's earlier papers on this issue, from 2000 to 2002 the GRE and GMAT incorrectly scored several thousand test-takers, thereby affecting their chances of acceptance to the schools to which they were applying (Carlson, 2000; Merritt, 2003). Supported by the NSF, Dr. Chang collaborated with Dr. Zhiliang Ying and facilitated a remedy to the Fisher information strategy (e.g., see Chang & Ying, 2008). In order to disseminate their research findings quickly, Dr. Chang initiated a visit to ETS in 2003 and made a presentation there. As a result, both the GRE and the GMAT redesigned the corresponding item selection algorithms prior to 2006.

Besides his insight into the problems of the old CAT strategy which was proved to be correct by a series of incidents involving the ETS CAT program at later time, Dr. Chang also offered some solutions to these problems which had not been adopted in the operational CAT program yet, but approved by some prestigious members of the research community. Initially, in order to solve the first problem, Chang and Ying proposed a framework that employed Kullback-Leibler (KL) information at the beginning of the test, and Fisher information later in the test. This approach had immediate pay-off—it not only improved the efficiency of ability estimation, but also promoted the utilization of previously unused items. His theoretical work on the KL information for item selection in CAT has been acclaimed by many statisticians and psychometricians. In 1995, Dr. Chang received a letter from Erich Leo Lehmann (1917–2009), a prominent American statistician, with a list of positive comments and specific suggestions on a preprint (see Chang & Ying, 1996).

In order to provide a simple and user-friendly procedure for practitioners, Chang and Ying (1999) and Chang, Qian, and Ying (2001) further developed an alpha-stratified method that imitates the KL method but without heavy computing. Items in a pool are stratified in an ascending order of item discrimination. Less discriminating items became valuable at the beginning of a test and would be effectively utilized, and highly discriminating items were favored later in the test, when ability was estimated more accurately. The alpha-stratified method provided a simple, powerful, and ingenious solution that utilized information over a plausible distribution of proficiency and solved both problems at once. The 1999 paper has generated a great number of follow-up studies by hundreds of authors and has literally turned CAT item selection on its direction, significantly improving efficiency, item pool usage, and test security.

CAT: THE MATHEMATICAL UNDERPINNINGS

In addition to the important applied problems in CAT, the mathematical problem of item response theory (IRT)/CAT is another theme running through Dr. Chang's career. Dr. Chang's nine years of experience in the testing industry has been crucial to his career, as is evidenced by the grounding of his theoretical and empirical solutions to various practical problems arising in the field of psychometrics. In the early years of his career, Dr. Chang proved asymptotic posterior normality of the latent ability under item response theory models (Chang, 1996; Chang & Stout, 1993). This research provided essential statistical theory for computational methods and score-reporting conventions in test theory. Prior to this finding, Paul Holland (1990) indicated that the establishment of the asymptotic posterior normality *"would appear to be an interesting area for further research"* for latent variable distributions. As a by-product, the weak and strong consistencies for maximum likelihood estimate (MLE) of examinee ability were also established. In both of Chang's papers on this topic, the sufficient conditions for MLE convergence were thoroughly discussed, which later helped Dr. Chang's endeavors to work on a large sample theory for adaptive testing.

Though CAT has become a popular model in large scale assessment since the 1990s, some important large sample properties have historically not been well studied. The challenge for establishing a large sample theory for CAT lies in its sequential nature, that is, the selection of the next item is based on the examinee's responses to the items previously administered, and thus, many standard tools created for independent variables, such as the central limit theorem and law of large numbers, cannot be applied. Chang and Ying (2009) found that CAT settings are well connected to martingale. To put it simply, martingale describes how the current values of random variables can have nothing to do with their previous states, with some assumptions and restrictions. By using the martingale local convergence theorem and martingale central limit theorem, they showed that the sequentially estimated ability under the maximum information design is consistent and asymptotically normal for the Rasch model. For the two- and three-parameter logistic models, the asymptotic properties hold if some minor regularity conditions are met, such as, the discrimination parameters must be bounded. Chang and Ying (2009) also illustrated that relaxing the boundary constraint may lead to divergence. As a result, an asymptotic theory for sequential maximum likelihood estimates of latent trait in CAT (CAT-MLE) was established about four decades after its inception.

To most educational researchers, martingale may sound interesting but too theoretical. Dr. Chang wrote in his presidential address at the 2013 International Meeting of the Psychometric Society (Chang, 2015) that when he studied martingale as a student many years ago, he never thought that one day he would use martingale to solve big problems himself in educational research. However, the asymptotic theory for CAT-MLE later produced a number of interesting and important solutions in CAT implementations. For instance, one notable application is to develop techniques for item review in CAT that allow examinees to change their answers during a CAT administration. Most CAT programs do not allow examinees to review and change their responses because it was believed that would seriously decrease the efficiency of measurement, and make the test vulnerable to manipulation via test-taking strategies. However, some researchers have shown that allowing examinees to change their responses can help reduce anxiety and stress levels during testing. The issue of anxiety and stress during testing has become a central concern for both examinees and testing companies. Dr. Chang and colleagues provided rigorous statistical evidence that, in plain words, allowing revision reduces measurement error and hence increases efficiency (Wang, Fellouris, & Chang, 2017).

CAT: LEARNING AND BEYOND

Dr. Chang is a visionary. He is an enthusiastic advocate of CAT for learning in addition to the traditional CAT applications such as high-stakes testing, K–12 accountability assessment, quality of life measurement, survey research, etc. He believes that CAT and educational measurement in general can be used to *serve* students instead of just evaluating them. And he is also fully aware that it is the testing community itself that must take ownership of this possibility and develop necessary techniques to deliver this promise.

In the aforementioned 2013 presidential address at the International Meeting of the Psychometric Society (Chang, 2015), Dr. Chang predicted CAT will help learning, both in class and online, while he reviewed technical developments in CAT over the previous 20 years. He remarked on the potential of cognitive diagnosis models (CD) in their ability to provide detailed information about students' strengths and weaknesses and the advantages of their implementation with CAT (McGlohen & Chang, 2008). However, building an item selection algorithm from original unidimensional latent variable to multidimensional latent is not simple.

Dr. Chang's confidence in CAT to help learning stems from segments of his own research. As early as 2004, thanks to Dr. Chang and two collaborators working on KL information and Shannon entropy, a set of novel item selection algorithms for CD-CAT made their debut (Xu, Chang, & Douglas, April 2004). Since then, hundreds of further extensions concerning CD-CAT have been published.

In addition to developing various algorithms and models, Dr. Chang was determined to put learning-oriented CAT applications into educational practice from which thousands of students would benefit, which inspired two specific projects. In 2011, Dr. Chang served as a lead consultant on building a cognitive diagnostic computerized adaptive testing (CD-CAT) system in Dalian, China, to assess whether students' mastery levels on the cognitive skills being taught in class can be efficiently classified (Liu et al., 2013). With 2000 PCs connected via the Internet and about 30,000 students participating, Dr. Chang's project has been considered the world's largest-scale CD-CAT assessment. A validation study, which compared the diagnoses between computers and teachers, demonstrated a high degree of consistency.

From 2014 to 2018, Dr. Chang served as a co-PI on an NSF grant with the objective to use CD-CAT to reduce dropout rate in a large undergraduate STEM class, Physics 211, at the University of Illinois at Urbana-Champaign (UIUC). He collaborated with two physics professors and developed a CD-CAT system. Their study showed that students who used the system and received help with the computer-generated diagnostic reports did significantly better on the final examination than those who did not (see Morphew et al., 2018).

Dr. Chang has taken more bold moves and his current interest in adaptive testing has expanded into adaptive learning, an unknown frontline in the field of testing that has rarely been explored. The increasing popularity of online learning and the growing emphasis of *inclusion* in education have greatly increased access to education, but new challenges arise as the student body becomes more diverse—students with different levels of background knowledge, interests, resources, and learning styles may end up in the same class. Additionally, when education moves from in-person to online, especially during the COVID-19 pandemic, the learning environment may become less controllable as teachers cannot interact face-to-face with students. Methods to reliably and unobtrusively pick up here measure students' skills, knowledge acquisition, and other learning-related traits are thus strongly desired, so that educators can monitor students' progress and reactions in real time, and personalize instructional content accordingly. The availability of testing techniques to accurately measure and profile each examinee and pinpoint their strengths and weaknesses has made it possible for psychometrics to inform personalized online learning. For example, by assessing the skill mastery profile of a student using a cognitive diagnosis, personalized instructional materials that target one or more unmastered skill can subsequently be selected for the student (see Zhang & Chang, 2016).

Dr. Chang and his colleagues believe that the landscape of today's teaching and learning can be transformed by the integration of cutting-edge statistical research and measurement theory. Dr. Chang and his colleagues/students are actively engaged in this line of research (see Chang, Wang, & Zhang, 2021).

During his term as Editor-in-Chief of *Applied Psychological Measurement*, two special issues focused on statistical methods that enhance student learning were published.

AS A CONSULTANT

While working in academia as a professor, Dr. Chang continued his research in psychometrics and provided consultation to the testing industry, government agencies, and international organizations.

In the early 2000s, when examinations in the U.S. were moving from paper and pencil to computerized adaptive testing (CAT), many challenging technical issues emerged. Dr. Chang made important contributions during this transition by providing statistically-sound solutions to numerous hard-to-solve problems. He proposed an array of new algorithms for item selection, test security screening, and constraint management (e.g., see Chang, 2015). His research helped the industry fine-tune existing methodologies to improve reliability and efficiency of CAT.

Dr. Chang has also served on technical advisory committees and as an external consultant to licensure testing. In 2004 and 2014, Dr. Chang helped the National Board of Osteopathic Medical Examiners (Chicago, IL) design and refine an automated test assembly system. The system has been working smoothly since 2005 for generating parallel forms for the computer-based licensure examinations for U.S. osteopathic physicians.

From 2010 to 2012, Dr. Chang helped UNESCO (Paris, France) design a framework to assess Media and Information Literacy (MIL) worldwide. The statistical measurement models and cost-effective assessment delivery system Dr. Chang proposed was accepted as UNESCO's recommendation for assessing MIL Country Readiness and Competencies (UNESCO, 2013).

AS AN EDUCATOR

Dr. Chang has made significant contributions to the teaching of psychometrics and statistics at universities. From 2001 to 2005 at the University of Texas at Austin (UT Austin), he taught three campus-wide statistics service courses: Introduction to Statistics, Correlation & Regression, and Multivariate Analysis (note that UT did not have a statistics department during that period.) Also, he taught two advanced psychometrics courses: Measurement & Evaluation, and Item Response Theory. From 2005 to 2018 at UIUC, he taught Theories of Measurement I & II, Measurement & Test Development Laboratory, Computerized Adaptive Testing, and Hierarchical Linear Models. The audience for these classes ranged from senior undergraduates to advanced graduate students in quantitative methods and statistics. These courses are cross-listed in three departments: Psychology, Educational Psychology, and Statistics. Since Dr. Chang joined Purdue University in August 2018, he has taught four different measurement courses ranging from introductory to advanced.

Teaching quantitative classes is challenging and instructors tend to receive lower ratings on course evaluations. However, Dr. Chang's broad knowledge, rich experience, and expertise across fields made these classes both informative and interesting to students. He took every opportunity to emphasize the importance and relevance of statistical training. Through his classroom teaching, many students were inspired. For example, at the 2017 Convocation of the College of Education at UIUC, Dr. Gabriel Merrin, a recipient of the 2017 Outstanding Student Medal, told the audience in his commencement speech that Dr. Chang's advice in one class motivated him all those years and he asked the audience to remember "Professor Chang's words of wisdom." Dr. Chang was named to UIUC's list of "Teachers Ranked as Excellent by Their Students" for ten consecutive years, from 2008 to 2018. He was the recipient of the 2016 Award for Outstanding Graduate Teaching at the College of Education at UIUC.

Dr. Chang has devoted a significant amount of time to helping his students identify innovative statistical solutions to problems in psychometrics. Many of his advisees have published first-authored manuscripts in top-tier journals before their graduation. Here are just two examples: 1) In large-scale testing, some item parameters may change values across different test administrations and thereby pose a threat to the fairness and validity of test score interpretation. Detecting item parameter drift has always been a hot research topic and various methods have already been proposed. Guo, Zheng, and Chang (2015) introduced a totally new approach known as stepwise detection. Analogous to stepwise deduction in linear regression, the new procedure automatically detects parameter drift iteratively based on test characteristic curves without prespecifying item sets nor any critical values. 2) Item response times (RTs) collected from online testing represent an underutilized type of information about both items and examinees. Current statistical models for RTs only focus on parametric models, which have the advantage of conciseness, but may suffer from reduced flexibility to fit real data. Wang, Fan, Chang, and Douglas (2013) proposed a semiparametric approach, the Cox proportional hazards model, with a latent speed covariate to model the RTs. The new approach combines the flexibility of nonparametric modeling and the brevity and interpretability of parametric modeling.

As a result of his teaching and mentoring, Dr. Chang has nurtured numerous successful quantitative researchers and top-quality psychometricians and statisticians. Since 2003, Dr. Chang has advised and co-advised more than 30

Ph.D. students and served on more than 70 doctoral thesis committees. Many of his direct advisees found faculty positions at top-tier universities as newly minted Ph.Ds., including Arizona State University, Beijing Normal University, East China Normal University, UIUC, University of Minnesota, University of Notre Dame, and UT Austin. Others have become data scientists, psychometricians, and statisticians at leading testing companies, government institutions, and research organizations in the U.S., mainland China, South Korea, Taiwan, and Singapore.

Dr. Chang has devoted enormous effort to disseminate knowledge and information in measurement and statistics worldwide. He twice served as Fulbright Specialist and conducted numerous psychometric workshops in Colombia in 2019 and Australia in 2005. Dr. Chang was selected twice as the International Keynote Speaker by the 11th (1995) and 25th (2009) Dutch Item Response Theory Workshops. In 2013, Dr. Chang was named Chang-Jiang Scholar Chair Professor by the Ministry of Education of China. In 2014, Dr. Chang was honored as the Robert Bohrer Lecturer by UIUC. Dr. Chang has made more than 130 invited presentations and conduced various workshops with contents related to statistics and measurement in the U.S., Australia, Brazil, Canada, mainland China, Colombia, Japan, Norway, Puerto Rico, Singapore, Taiwan, Thailand, the Netherlands, and the United Kingdom.

CLOSING

Professor Chang is a scholar with passion and dedication. His 30-year career, spanning from the testing industry to academia, is exemplary and demonstrates how a scholar who bears a great resemblance to a scientist and engineer can make a huge impact on the field of education. With clear and focused goals in his scientific pursuits, Dr. Chang made dedicated efforts in developing ingenious solutions to practical challenges whose effects ripple from testing to education. When you put his studies and his practices together, you will see how the future of education, such as the splendid vision of personalized learning, can be engineered by the magic of statistics, computer science, and big data.

Dr. Chang is a person of big heart. His willingness to have dialogs with and provide opportunities for students, young testing professionals, and professors is another precious trait of his. I really love to meet with him, because every time I learn something or receive help from him. Dr. Chang is also a person of charisma due to his achievements, rich experiences in both industry and academia, and his kindness. At academic occasions, he is always the center of attention. One perk of being his student are the numerous invitations to dinners and beer drinking with Dr. Chang and his friends, occasions during which I have met many interesting professionals from the testing industry.

Dr. Chang provides me the inspiration, the passion, and the confidence that I need to dedicate myself to my academic career. It is an honor and privilege for me to write a book chapter about him for this volume. He made me understand what it takes to be a true education scholar and leader. The passion he holds for his studies, the ingenuity he has in solving real-world problems, and the dedication he has to his scientific career will always guide me through my life.

REFERENCES

Bandalos, D. (2018). *Measurement theory applications for the social sciences.* New York, NY: The Free Press.

Carlson, S. (2000). ETS finds flaws in the way online GRE rates some students. *Chronicle of Higher Education, 47*(8), A47.

Chang, H.-H. (1996). The asymptotic posterior normality of the latent trait for polytomous IRT models. *Psychometrika, 61*(3), 445–453.

Chang, H.-H. (2015). Psychometrics behind computerized adaptive testing. *Psychometrika, 80*(1), 1–20.

Chang, H. H., & Roussos, M. L. (1996). Detecting DIF for polytomously scored items: An adaptation of the sibtest procedure. *Journal of Educational Measurement, 33*(3), 333–353.

Chang, H.-H., Qian, J., & Ying, Z. (2001). a-Stratified multistage computerized adaptive testing with b blocking. *Applied Psychological Measurement, 25*(4), 333–341.

Chang, H.-H., & Stout, W. (1993). The asymptotic posterior normality of the latent trait in an IRT model. *Psychometrika, 58*(1), 37–52, 77.

Chang, H.-H., Wang, C., & Zhang, S. (2021). Statistical applications in educational measurement. *Annual Review of Statistics and Its Application, 8*, 439–461.

Chang, H.-H., & Ying, Z. (1996). A global information approach to computerized adaptive testing. *Applied Psychological Measurement, 20*(3), 213–229.

Chang, H.-H., & Ying, Z. (1999). A-stratified multistage computerized adaptive testing. *Applied Psychological Measurement, 23*(3), 211–222.

Chang, H.-H., Ying, Z. (2008). To weight or not to weight? Balancing influence of initial items in adaptive testing. *Psychometrika, 73*, 441.

Chang, H.-H., & Ying, Z. (2009). Nonlinear sequential designs for logistic item response theory models with applications to computerized adaptive tests. *The Annals of Statistics, 37*(3), 1466–1488.

Davey, T., & Nering, M. (2002). Controlling item exposure and maintaining item security. In C. N. Mills, M. Potenza, J. J. Fremer, & W. C. Ward (Eds.), *Compute based testing: Building the foundation for future assessments* (pp. 165–191). Mahwah, NJ: Lawrence Erlbaum.

Guo, R., Zheng, Y., & Chang, H. H. (2015). A stepwise test characteristic curve method to detect item parameter drift. *Journal of Educational Measurement, 52*(3), 280–300.

Holland, P. W. (1990). The Dutch identity: A new tool for the study of item response theory model. *Psychometrika, 55*, 577–601.

Liu, H. Y., You, X. F., Wang, W. Y., Ding, S. L., & Chang, H. H. (2013). The development of computerized adaptive testing with cognitive diagnosis for an english achievement test in china. *Journal of Classification*, *30*(2), 152–172.

McGlohen, M., & Chang, H.-H. (2008). Combining computer adaptive testing technology with cognitively diagnostic assessment. *Behavior Research Methods* 40, 808–821.

Merritt, J. (2003). Why the folks at ETS flunked the course—a tech-savvy service will soon be giving B-school applicants their GMATs. *Business Week*, December 29, 2003.

Morphew, J., Mestre, J., Kang, H., Chang, H.-H., & Fabry, G. (2018). Using computer adaptive testing to assess physics proficiency and improve exam performance. *Physical Review Physics Education Research*. DOI: https://doi.org/10.1103/PhysRevPhysEducRes.14.010127

UNESCO. (2013). *Global media and information literacy assessment framework: Country readiness and competencies.* United Nations Educational, Scientific and Cultural Organization (UNESCO). 7, place de Fontenoy, 75352 Paris 07 SP, Paris, France.

Wang, C., Fan, Z,. Chang, H.-H., & Douglas, J.A. (2013). A semiparametric model for jointly analyzing response times and accuracy in computerized testing. *Journal of Educational and Behavioral Statistics*, *38*(4), 381–417.

Wang, S., Fellouris, G., & Chang, H.-H. (2017). Computerized adaptive testing that allows for response revision: Design and asymptotic theory. *Statistica Sinica* (27), 1987–2010.

Xu, X., Chang, H., & Douglas, J. (April 2003). *A simulation study to compare CAT strategies for cognitive diagnoses.* Paper presented at the annual meeting of the National Council on Measurement in Education, Chicago.

Zhang, S., & Chang, H.-H. (2016). From smart testing to smart learning: How testing technology can assist the new generation of education. *International Journal of Smart Technology and Learning*, *1*(1), 67–92.

CHAPTER THIRTEEN

A Wandering Moon and the (Summer) Class That Changed My Life

BRANDON O. HENSLEY

Wandering moon smiling

a faintly ironical smile

at this

brilliant, dew-moistened

summer morning …

a wanderer's smile …

sky-blue …

Where would they carry me?[1]

It may seem an exaggeration, or a curious statement at the least, to say that "summer school" changed my life. It wasn't in elementary school, middle school, or even high school. I wasn't there for remedial, or disciplinary, or extrinsic motivations. In fact, I'd broken away from my doctoral cohort's track of classes to take this one class.

It was the summer of 2014, and the class was Cultural Foundations of Education. The professor was Dr. Nicholas Hartlep. I wandered into this class; not literally, but figuratively as I had jaunted off the prescribed path of coursework for my doctoral cohort in Education, deciding that three stats classes were enough. My department, Educational Administration and Foundations, leaned quantitative, so course offerings for foundations courses were limited—*cultural* foundations even more so.

Let me back up—I had seen Dr. Hartlep once before our fateful summer. In the Spring semester of 2014, I attended an electrifying book talk that Dr. Hartlep gave on our campus regarding his research demystifying the model minority stereotype (Hartlep, 2013). I say that the talk was electric because the energy and passion he emanated (re)activated critical race concerns I had around whiteness that I wasn't able to explore in my Ph.D. coursework. Witnessing his direct engagement with the audience and the raw dynamism he exhibited as a scholar and speaker, I knew that I wanted to know more about Dr. Hartlep. I knew that Dr. Hartlep's concern for the perpetuation of the model minority stereotype (MMS) came from a personal place; I just didn't know how personal yet.

When I state that it's curious to suggest a summer class would be life-changing, that statement is within the confines of the U.S. dominant narrative around summer schooling. The dominant narrative around summer school in the United States is that it is a joyless experience laden with busy work, something the unfortunate summer student must endure and find a way to make the most of (Cooper, Charlton, Valentine, Muhlenbruck, & Borman, 2000) despite the temptations of summer beyond the classroom doors.

Myths of summer school pervade Western pop culture in movies, television, music, and the language around summer schooling. In postsecondary education, the images of summer school persist—that it's mainly for remedial students or people that need to retake classes; that summer schooling is an easier, more laid-back, laissez faire type of education than during the Fall or Spring semesters; that summer schooling is pointless, or often misses the point of student learning in hyper-condensed four-, six-, and eight-week sessions.

What I encountered was not summer schooling. My summer *education* in 2014 was transformative and shattered the popular mythos of the summer class, in part because of the vulnerable, brave bond we all forged, together, as equal co-creators of the classroom experience and what we became willing to explore. We were willing to take risks in the pursuit of a pluralistic truth. On the first day, we all sat in a circle and Dr. Hartlep introduced himself by saying he was going to learn as much from us as we would from him. Parker Palmer (1998) writes,

> As we gather around the subject in the community of truth, it is not only we who correct each other's attempts at knowing, rejecting blurry observations and false interpretations. The subject itself corrects us, resisting our false framings with the strength of its own identity, refusing to be reduced to our self-certain ways of naming in otherness … the transcendent subject always stands ready to take us by surprise, calling us into new observations, interpretations, and namings and into the mystery that can never fully be named. (p. 106)

Dr. Hartlep approached the first day as an opportunity for students to form a compact as a group, rather than as an opportunity to drill the syllabus into us and ensconce familiar professor-student power relations. For some, the uncertainty and organic nature of the class was difficult, but when we met those summer weeks we coalesced around that ambiguity and it allowed us to grapple with very difficult subjects that may not have been discussed as deeply through traditional class discussions (where the teacher often calls on students to recite what they know from the reading).

As a class we dove into *Unhooking from Whiteness*, an edited anthology which critically explored whiteness as a system of oppression and inequality (Hayes & Hartlep, 2013). Instead of pontificating his own evaluations and interpretations (as one of the authors and co-editors of the book), Professor Hartlep leaned back as we leaned forward, not leading the discussion toward worksheet busyness or arbitrary group-discussion activity or swaying us toward what *he felt* the chapter authors were saying. I felt like a co-learner, a co-creator of the emerging understandings we were generating as a group of scholars practicing vulnerable discussions around race, economic class, privilege, and power relations with an ethic of care. Out of these discussions, the first volume of *Critical Storytelling in Uncritical Times* (Hartlep & Hensley, 2015) was born. My chapter explored adjunct faculty working conditions; my peers in the class investigated racial microaggressions, marginalization of undocumented immigrants, and other topics of critical societal import. *Critical Storytelling* has since grown into an international book series with five editions in print and more to come.

But it was what I learned about Dr. Hartlep *outside* the class, on my own time, that made as big an impact on my education and how I see whiteness practiced in institutions of higher education. His struggle in an exclusionary institution was closer to home than I thought when seeing his book talk or experiencing his mindful, energetic, inclusionary practices as a professor. That is because at the very institution (and academic unit and department) where we had our transformative experience, Dr. Hartlep was experiencing Racial Battle Fatigue (RBF) from microaggressions enacted by his colleagues and larger systemic barriers at the predominantly white institution (PWI) for including, retaining, and promoting minority junior faculty members (Hartlep, 2015). As I learned more about Dr. Hartlep's lived experiences through his research and writing, my heart ached at the mistreatment and prejudice (through assumptions, racist comments, and other microaggressions) he'd received as a budding Asian American scholar and professor—battling RBF all the while.

It occurred to me, in a way that has changed the trajectory of my critical outlook, that my whiteness imbues me with privileges including the likelihood that I will never be treated as Dr. Hartlep was at a PWI. His success on both fronts—prolific critical researcher and enlivened, empathic teacher—is indicative of STAR teachers, about which Hartlep has also written extensively (Hill-Jackson, Hartlep, & Stafford, 2019). But to call Dr. Hartlep a student-centered educator who exhibits all seven dispositions of a STAR teacher would still be an incomplete assessment. The slights, racial battle fatigue, and disparate treatment he has experienced at many PWIs as a transracial adoptee from South Korea make Dr. Hartlep's ascent to the endowed position of Robert C. Billings Chair in Education at Berea College all the more remarkable, but apposite given Berea's commitment to its students and social justice/equity issues.

Cultural Foundations of Education in Summer 2014 was not a typical, or stereotypical, or even archetypal summer class. I was called, encouraged into being, more so than was the case for most of my education, graduate or otherwise. Summer of 2014 we practiced freedom in the classroom (Freire, 2000), vulnerability in the liminal spaces in-between, and an ethic of care and listening that contributed to a finding of voices in a book volume and many critical conversations and collaborations since. I was encouraged to wander that summer, and it has made all the difference in coming into my own criticality and potential as a teacher, editor, and listener.

This book pays homage to Asian American Education professors who are "endowed" or "distinguished." Shockingly, in my 12+ years as a college student (and also as an instructor at three different universities) I've only encountered one Asian American professor vested with such titles—Dr. Hartlep, whose class I was only lucky to have wandered in to at the "last second," in my final semesters as a doctoral student. I am fortunate to have experienced Hartlep's pedagogy of personhood, and cannot help but feel that students are missing out from the paucity of Asian American scholars who are institutionally valued (e.g. elevated to "distinguished" status at U.S. colleges and universities) or who are on an intentional, institutionally-sanctioned path to such credit and respect.

As I write this in 2020, Nicholas D. Hartlep's work continues, he continues to be recognized for his prolific writing and STAR teaching, and he is highly valued, rightfully so, at his institution. How many Asian American professors in U.S. colleges are denied the distinction and recognition they so rightfully deserve?

NOTE

1 Poem adapted from "Summer Song" by William Carlos Williams (1917).

REFERENCES

Cooper, H., Charlton, K., Valentine, J. C., Muhlenbruck, L., & Borman, G. D. (2000). Making the most of summer school: A meta-analytic and narrative review. *Monographs of the Society for Research in Child Development*, *65*(1), 1–127.

Freire, P. (2000). *Pedagogy of the oppressed*. New York: Continuum. (Original work published 1970).

Hartlep, N. D. (2013). *The model minority stereotype: Demystifying Asian American success*. Charlotte, NC: Information Age Publishing.

Hartlep, N. D. (2015). An adopted Korean speaks out about his racialized experiences as a faculty member at a predominantly white institution. In K. J. Fasching-Varner, K. A. Albert, R. W. Mitchell, & C. M. Allen (Eds.), *Racial battle fatigue in higher education* (pp. 115–122). Lanham, MD: Rowman & Littlefield.

Hartlep, N. D., & Hensley, B. O. (Eds.). (2015). *Critical storytelling in uncritical times: Stories disclosed in a Cultural Foundations of Education Course*. Rotterdam, The Netherlands: Sense Publishers.

Hayes, C., & Hartlep, N. D. (2013). *Unhooking from whiteness: The key to dismantling racism in the United States*. Rotterdam, The Netherlands: Sense Publishers.

Hill-Jackson, V., Hartlep, N. D., & Stafford, D. (2019). *What makes a Star teacher: 7 dispositions that support student learning*. Alexandria, VA: ASCD.

Palmer, P. J. (1998). *The courage to teach*. San Francisco: Jossey-Bass, Inc.

Williams, W. C. (1917). Summer song. Retrieved from https://poets.org/poem/summer-song

CHAPTER FOURTEEN

Transformative Vision

A 21st Century American Dream[1]

BETHANY D. MERILLAT

It is a question that Dr. Nicholas Hartlep, among other Asian American scholars in the field of Education, has persistently addressed in academia. To know the answer would beget a solution not only to crime, poverty, homelessness, and drug addiction, but to the ultimate and deepest desire of everyone who seeks to do more, who pursue the "American" dream, and who chase fulfillment in life.

But, perhaps, the answer is in the question, burning brightly for all to see in those individuals who have made exceptional contributions in their professional roles: those who have risen above the odds, triumphed despite hardship, and persevered in spite of the status quo. William Frederick Halsey said that, "There are no great people in this world, only great challenges which ordinary people rise to meet." Dr. Justin Perry's story is a testament to this truth. Rather than ask, "Why do some succeed in life when others fail?" we should instead ask, "What gives strength to ordinary people to rise?"

Lessons from Dr. Perry and those of others who have succeeded like him, hold the key to unfurling the potential within us, as well as each and every child to succeed and thrive. Scientific research is often an institutionalization of innate knowledge collective to cultures and societies. In this respect, Voltaire noted we should judge a man by his questions "… rather than by his answers."

For Dr. Perry, it's the questions he has asked throughout his career, and continues to ask, which have guided his path and helped lead the world of education closer to the answers it seeks.

I first met Dr. Perry at a pivotal time in my own career. I had just finished my master's degree in Experimental Psychology and had been accepted into and taken two years' worth of classes in a clinical psychology program as well. One aspect of my work that had always been frustrating to me was the gap between research and practice. There seemed to be so many amazing advancements taking place both in clinical and experimental psychology, yet a profound lack of real-world acceptance and thus application of those findings.

Yet, despite all of this, I knew there were researchers who were making a difference, and the key to me seemed to be effective education. I had always wanted to give back to Cleveland, Ohio, my hometown, and was intrigued by Cleveland State University's novel Master of Urban Secondary Teaching (MUST) program. Through the program, students passionate about igniting change and serving as catalysts for growth and development in some of Cleveland's worst schools were thrust into a whirlwind teaching program in which they earned their master's and teaching license in a year and a half.

The program seemed like the perfect opportunity for me to further develop and refine my research skills and learn more about how to bridge the research-practice void, and yet the biggest barrier to me was finances. Having been in graduate school over four years, the cost of the program, while still modest compared to other degrees, was significant.

It was about that time that Diane Corrigan, the director of the program, put me in contact with Dr. Justin Perry. He was looking for a student to assist him in his research with a background in quantitative statistics, and I jumped at the opportunity. I still remember the first time we met, for what would be one of the most unique interviews I had ever experienced.

His passion for educational research was contagious. Despite having published and conducted research exclusively in the field of psychology, I left the meeting with my mind racing, filled with thoughts of research projects and opportunities for interventions. From the moment we met I knew that this was not just a job for him—it was a quest, fueled by a candid, burning desire to help others succeed.

Unlike many in academia that I had met in the past, he seemed entirely unconcerned with his title, accomplishments, or the prestige he had obtained through his prolific academic career. From that first day, and in the months and years to come, he made me feel like a colleague, a collaborator, someone who valued my ideas and considered them with the same weight as those of a colleague's.

In the world of academia, where those with advanced degrees may tend to disdain those without them and enjoy flaunting around their titles, Dr. Perry was just the opposite. He was frank, down to earth, and so humble that, until I began to write this chapter, I was almost completely unaware of just how much he has done and continues to do.

His guiding hand and mentorship that year in the MUST program, and in the years that followed, resulted in the single largest period of growth and development for me as a researcher, educator, and young professional. The similarities in our backgrounds aside, Dr. Perry taught me to see the value in others beyond what a piece of paper says about them.

He reframed what success looked like to me, or more accurately, he dispelled the myth of what society told me success should be. As I watched his interactions with students, faculty, and children, and pondered his own collaborative nature with me and his colleagues, I saw a seamless thread: equality. Everyone's thoughts had value, from the smallest child to the most distinguished faculty. And Dr. Perry did not just pretend to listen, as if to keep up appearances as so many do, but he considered the words of every person as holding equal weight and magnitude.

As a student who had been bent upon obtaining a Ph.D. since day one, I realized how starkly different his pattern of interacting with the world was compared to mine—and that made me want to change. He modeled behavior that not only made me feel respected and valued but ignited within me a burning desire to see the world as he did and change my behavior to imitate his.

THE BEGINNING

So how did Dr. Justin Perry get to where he is today? The current Dean of the University of Missouri—Kansas City's School of Education and Ewing Marion Kauffman/Missouri Endowed Chair's road to success was not the "yellow-brick road" lined path that many American children have laid out for them.

Born in Pusan, Korea, Dr. Perry was adopted as an infant in the state of Washington. His younger sister was also adopted (from Mexico). His adoptive father, a physician, was working in a small rural area outside Seattle at the time while paying off his loans from medical school. They moved to Seattle, Washington, a few years later where he spent most of his childhood. His family moved to the state of Georgia (USA) when he was a teenager, which is where he graduated from high school.

Dr. Perry's early years were similar in many ways to the experience of other children growing up in America. He was raised by two loving, hardworking parents in a traditional nuclear family who made sacrifices to help him and his sister succeed. However, unlike many children, he and his sister had an added burden to bear.

Not only did he and his sister differ greatly in physical appearance from one another, they also did not resemble their parents at all. While adoption has become increasingly accepted and normalized over the past three decades, those outside of the adoptive circle often fail to comprehend the challenges and internal struggles faced by transracial adoptees as they strive to carve out their own unique path to identity in adulthood.

The challenge is even greater, to a degree, for transracial Korean adoptees. Despite being one of the largest groups of adoptees in the U.S., a study by McGinnis (2007) estimates that one out of every ten Korean Americans is an adoptee, a trend that continues today, with over 20,800 transracial Korean adoptions occurring between 1999 and 2018 (U.S. State Department Bureau of Consular Affairs, 2018). Research has found that these individuals struggle with the dual hurdle of pursuing higher education while trying to carve out and define their identity (Dickinson, 2019).

Adoptees, and in particular those who are transnationally adopted, tend to have higher rates of maladjustment issues such as unemployment, and alcohol and drug use, when compared to their non-adopted peers, as well as higher rates of suicide ideation and attempts (Keyes, Malone, Sharma, Iacono, & McGue, 2013). A study by Hjern, Lindblad, and Vinnerljung (2002) also found that transnational adopted individuals from Asia and Latin America had similar or higher levels of mental distress than other non-adopted immigrant adolescents from the same regions.

While these struggles form a barrier for many young adoptees seeking to find a way to relate to the world, and stamp out their own mark upon it, they served as a catalyst for Justin. His experience was never easy, but he believes his capacity for empathy, perspective taking, and his ability to form deep, meaningful connections with others, is directly related to the experience he had as a transracial adoptee growing up in the U.S. He chose to embrace his dual heritage and found a way to thrive.

And thrive he did, taking advantage of every opportunity afforded him. From skiing and tennis, to track, basketball, and cross country running, Justin did it all. A standout in soccer and swimming with a deep fondness for world literature, Justin was fascinated with understanding the different ways people lived and found meaning across the globe.

His parents' passion for mission work and strong moral compass also imbued him with a deep desire to help others, emphasizing the importance and value of public service. From summer escapes to South Carolina with his family, to the interactions he experienced at an early age through his parents' work, he had the opportunity to be exposed to a wide range of regions and cultures. His involvement in, and observations of, his parents' work lives and experiences at home left Justin with a unique frame of reference on the world.

While the eclectic and diverse culture and demographic composition of Seattle certainly had a significant impact on his world view, Justin also credits his parents for opening their home to foreign exchange students. Having the opportunity to live with and learn from students from all over the world—from Finland and Japan, to Hungary and Mexico—inspired in him a deeper appreciation for other cultures. His openness to new experiences, interest in the human condition, and pursuit of altruistic, service-oriented causes can be traced back to these early developmental experiences.

What is most unique about Justin, however, is how he has managed to merge these varied life experiences into a cohesive narrative which both connected him to the world and empowered him with the skill set to change it. Gaining inner resilience, self-esteem, and character from the natural vicissitudes of his life experiences, Justin's path unraveled before him not as the way of least resistance, but rather, as something forged through the metal of personal challenge and adversity.

A HIGHER ROAD: COUNSELING AND ACADEMIA

When asked how his chosen career path came about, Justin points indirectly to his experience as an adoptee, especially through the lens of a child dealing with developmental tasks under the spotlight of stereotypes and racism as a visible Asian male. In particular, he points toward trying to reconcile who he was with regard to his racial and ethnic identity. In his own words, "The questions of why I was adopted, how 'Asian' I was, how 'White' I was, which culture I belonged to, and so forth, always were suspended in the back of my mind as a child."

His family's move from Washington state to Atlanta, Georgia, however, set in motion a series of events that guided his career path to where he is today—something he believes would never have happened had they stayed in Seattle. In Georgia, he experienced counseling for the first time as a client—something that, combined with his dad's encouragement to become a psychologist and his own experience in childhood, sparked within him a deep interest in the field.

After high school, Justin attended Tulane University where he obtained a bachelor's in Psychology, along with a minor in English, which included a year spent abroad at the University of Sussex in Brighton, England. Through the help of outstanding mentors along the way, and in particular one Dr. Melanie McGrath at Tulane, Justin began to pursue in earnest a way to give back to the world.

In much the same way that his father cared for patients' physical ailments, Justin was eager to care for their emotional and psychological ones. He credits Dr. McGrath's investment in him through her research lab, including mentorship for his honors thesis, as not only helping him get into graduate school, but giving him a vision for what he could do, and what he could become—both as a professional clinician and academic.

Yet, as with any great story, the path to success is never easy, and Justin's own journey was no different. Like many students, he struggled to balance classes, life, and graduate responsibilities, while making ends meet on a ramen noodles budget. Nevertheless, Justin persevered and underwent a period of tremendous intellectual, personal, emotional, and social growth. With Dr. McGrath's help, he applied and was accepted into the mental health counseling program at Boston College, ultimately graduating with his Ph.D. in Counseling Psychology in 2006.

During this eight-year period of training to become a clinician, Justin wrestled with which path to take. While he loved working with and seeing clients, he was also fascinated with and saw the value in research; he sought a way to merge the two into a cohesive career.

With the help of a colorful group of peers, friends, family, mentors, and supervisors who played an integral role in his development, Justin was imbued with the wisdom, motivation, and guidance he needed to find a way to carve out a path that was ideally suited to his strengths and background. He claims no credit for his success, but rather points to those who supported him along his path.

Professors Jim Mahalik, Janet Helms, and David Blustein not only ignited within him the drive to succeed and grow, but also created opportunities for him to pursue, while offering advice and comfort in tough, uncertain times. Two of his clinical supervisors, Dr. Gary Pfeifer and Dr. Mariko Sakurai, shaped him both as a budding therapist and a young man. When asked how he got where he is today, Justin casts the spotlight on the amazing procession of individuals who stepped up to mentor, support, and shepherd him forward.

Yet his mentors did not reside solely in academia or the clinical realm. Between his academic and clinical training, Justin also became involved with work in the Boston Public School system. This body of work sparked a flood of creativity within Justin, and he threw himself into developing innovative, out-of-the-box ways to translate his training as a clinician and researcher into meaningful interventions and policies in the schools.

His perseverance and dedication to these children did not go unnoticed, and before his time in Boston had ended, he was honored with an AERA Dissertation Award. These experiences not only helped him grow but set the stage for his transition to the Cleveland Public School System where he would implement his bold, research-based interventions with continued success.

Most importantly, however, his time in Boston led him to clearly see and understand the inexorable link between mental health and change at both the individual and social level. His mentor Dr. David Blustein was highly instrumental in helping Justin amass his myriad collections of education and experience into one package—inspiring Justin to find ways to bring clinical and academic work into synchrony with K–12 and higher education.

After graduating with his Ph.D., he was hired by Cleveland State University (CSU), an institution which quickly realized his value and promoted him swiftly through the ranks. Beginning as an Assistant Professor in 2006 at CSU's College of Education and Human Services, Department of Counseling, Administration and Adult Learning, by 2011 he was promoted to Associate Professor with tenure. While at CSU, he made a significant impact on the University through teaching, mentorship, research, and service, where he was a faculty member in the Counselor Education and Counseling Psychology programs.

His incredible work and momentum did not go unnoticed, and he was eventually selected as Dean of the School of Education and Ewing Marion Kauffman/Missouri Endowed Chair at the University of Missouri—Kansas City (UMKC) in 2016, where he has continued to excel as he did at CSU.

Despite his relatively young career, he managed to submit over 75 grants within a short 10-year period. The vast majority of this grant activity was in his role as the Director of the Center for Urban Education at CSU. Under his leadership, the Center worked with dozens of faculty at CSU, as well as many other constituents in the K–12 and higher education sector, on a wide range of community based projects (27 in total), including interdisciplinary grants awarded by the National Science Foundation (NSF), National Institutes of Health (NIH), U.S. Department of Education, Health Resources and Services Administration (HRSA), Ohio Department of Education, and The Cleveland Foundation.

So far in his career, Justin has published 32 journal articles and 14 book chapters. He's also served on the editorial board of the *Journal of Career Development* and served as an ad hoc reviewer for more than 12 different journals.

Justin's significant accomplishments, despite him still being rather young in comparison to his peers, have not gone unnoticed. He has been the recipient of multiple awards, including the Distinguished Faculty Award in Research from CSU in 2013, the Early Career Professional Award from the Society for Vocational Psychology in 2012, and an Institute of Education Sciences (IES) federal grant award as PI in 2010. Despite these accomplishments, Justin has always remained humble, and approaches his work, research, and life with a deep care and concern for others.

THE FLUIDITY OF WORK AND LIFE IN BALANCE

While many might look at Justin's impressive list of accomplishments and wonder how he has managed to juggle it all, the reverse, rather, seems true. His uncanny ability to effortlessly integrate an abundance of activities and commitments became evident in his early childhood and adolescent years and is a hallmark characteristic of his personality—one that has not only opened doors but allowed for an incredible amount of productivity in short span of time.

It can be challenging for anyone to thrive under the rigors of academia, the drive for publication, and the relentless need to apply for and manage grants. Yet Justin has found a way to do all of that, and more—giving back to the community and making huge strides in advancements across the interrelated fields of education and psychology. More impressive, I would argue, is that he never seems rushed or harried.

Students (like myself) who find themselves in Justin's office always leave feeling like the most important person in the world. No matter his depth of education, stack of awards or fancy titles, Justin not only listens to every person like their ideas and thoughts matter—he invites everyone as a collaborator into his space. Perhaps that is why he has made so many great strides.

While I have found that others with advanced degrees and important roles tend to downplay the ideas and contributions of those beneath them in academia, Justin treats everyone as an equal, and celebrates, investigates, and champions their ideas.

Justin will admit that his progress has not come without sacrifice and long hours. Perhaps the reason he is so content, then, is because he does not place a huge emphasis on the worldly pursuits so many people chase to find fulfillment in life. Simple things like going for walks, attending sporting events, watching movies, and spending quality time with friends and family bring him gratification, contentment, and happiness.

Calling himself "your typical average Joe," Justin's free time is spent participating in pick-up soccer matches (or at the gym), listening to music, reading works of fiction, and watching the History Channel, perhaps with a nice cup of coffee. An avid tennis and football fan, his joy comes from simple things, not from lofty, materialistic pursuits.

SOME Q & A

When I sat down to write this chapter and interview Dr. Perry, I gained a deeper appreciation both for his accomplishments, as well as for his role in shaping my life and career trajectory. His impact seems exponential, and I mean this in the most literal sense of the term. His mentorship of one person, leads them to impact four, and that then goes up to 16 and beyond (you see my point).

Because not everyone can have the opportunity to sit across the table from Justin, I wanted to leave you with a few thoughtful responses that he gave me during our interview. I hope his words leave you with a deeper picture of this amazing man and inspire you to make a difference in your own way.

Bethany: When considering all you have accomplished; did you ever picture yourself where you are today?

Justin: I remember it like it was yesterday when my fourth-grade teacher, Mrs. Breckenridge, said that I would become a researcher. I had no idea what a researcher was, but from that day on it was forever chiseled in my brain as a destiny that would, upon a day, fully reveal itself—all because she took a moment to tell me something that she thought I was good at. Nobody tells a nine-year-old that sort of message, I suppose, but it worked. I dedicated my dissertation defense to her. The journey of becoming a licensed psychologist and working with so many people in the field has been a joy that I will never forget. Yet, it was my penchant and my natural talents as a researcher, scholar, writer, and academic at heart that ultimately got me to where I am today.

Bethany: What career accomplishments are you most proud of?

Justin: This might sound a little strange, but it's very true. The greatest accomplishment in my career that I am most proud of are all of the small, unknown, but never forgotten moments when I would, seemingly out of the blue, receive a letter, card, phone call, or an e-mail from a former student, colleague, patient, or client who simply wanted to tell me how they were doing, and how I changed their life in some way for the better. Those are the moments that make it all worth it, in my view.

Bethany: What accomplishments outside of academia are you most proud of?

Justin: I am very proud of the pro bono work I have done in the non-profit sector. In particular, my service on the Board of Directors at Esperanza, Inc., was deeply gratifying. The mission of this organization aligned with my professional interests; more than that, it helped me appreciate how change actually occurs at grassroots, community-based level. This kind of change, I can assure you, does not emanate from the ivory towers of universities and requires a long-term, frustrating, messy process. I was on the Board for nine consecutive years while I was in Cleveland. I made a lot of good friends along the way. It was a great ride.

Bethany: How have your interactions with the students you mentored (like me) impacted your growth and development?

Justin: The one great advantage of working in academia is the privilege of being inspired by those you seek to educate and inspire yourself. I can recall many experiences that impacted me. There is one, in particular, that I can briefly mention. There was a student who came back to get his master's degree as a career-changer, probably between the age of 40 and 50. He had been through a lot of ups and downs and had to deal with chronic health concerns. The first day he came to my office, he looked absolutely bewildered, befuddled, and lost—from where to buy books to how to take notes to getting around on campus. Our first conversation started out with the use of a notepad and a pencil. Well, it turned out that over time he became one of my most inspiring students. He earned a very high GPA by the end of his degree and landed a job at a local mental health organization. The amount of pride he got out of these accomplishments was palpable. This was a person who had not been in higher education for decades, and who found himself trying to acquire an entirely different set of skills and knowledge as he started to turn his life around. To this day, we remain in touch. He wasn't a superstar doctoral student who came up with the next brilliant idea in the field. But he was someone who made me feel every day the importance of why I do what I do. We don't do it to serve ourselves. In the end, we do it because we want to see students succeed, and we are just as fallible as they are.

Bethany: What is your advice for others who would like to follow in your footsteps?

Justin: I went down a very unusual path that most people from my discipline or profession rarely ever take. So, my advice has to be quite generic in nature, which is perhaps the best form of advice. No matter what background you come from, and regardless of the stage in your career, finding true success simply doesn't come without taking risks, sometimes rather big risks. Now, in the fairly sheltered world of academia, it is much easier to simply take the road that is known and lead a satisfying, predictable, secure career. Most people teach the same courses they always teach, do essentially the same research they always do, serve on the same committees, and so on, until it's time to retire with a nice pension. That's a very appealing lifestyle, and with very little risk. But without taking risks, it's very hard to break outside of the pack and realize your full potential, let alone create opportunities to genuinely grow as a person. So when the time comes to take that leap—if that is what you choose to do—remember that had it not been for the privileges that you enjoy, simply by virtue of being employed as an academic, you would not be in a position to take such a risk. It's important to keep a deep sense of humility and not let the lure of laurels, prestige, and status get to your head.

CONCLUSION

I hope these short interludes have served as a summary and testament to both the humility, and vast capacity for love, that Justin embodies with his life and work. It has been an honor not just to work with him, but for the chance to show others this amazing man and give them a glimpse into his own life and the path that led to where he is today.

What sets Justin apart and fuels his rapidly progressing trajectory to success is his burning passion to help others and consistent emphasis on placing the needs of others above his own. Jonathan Swift is credited with stating that, "Vision is the art of seeing what is invisible to others," and I believe that Justin's successes are a direct function of his ability to see what we all miss. The lessons we can learn from every person that we meet.

Justin's unparalleled perception and ability to catch and draw out the potential in others and fill them with so much passion and drive that they catch his momentum, thereby propelling others into success, is a rare quality not often found in today's world.

Justin is a remarkable man because he has never focused on awards or achievement. Rather, he has received praise and recognition because he treats every person, every job, every challenge with immense respect, care, and concern. The snowball effect of his trail of good work will continue to impact this generation and beyond. I can't wait to see what's next on his horizon.

NOTE

1 Since writing this chapter, Dr. Justin Perry is now the Dean of the Harriet L. Wilkes Honors College at Florida Atlantic University.

REFERENCES

Dickinson, A. Y. J. K. (2019). *Determining and addressing the needs of transracial Korean adoptees in higher education.* https://scholarworks.uni.edu/hpt/371

Hjern, A., Lindblad, F., & Vinnerljung, B. (2002). Suicide, psychiatric illness, and social maladjustment in intercountry adoptees in Sweden: A cohort study. *The Lancet, 360*(9331), 443–448.

Keyes, M. A., Malone, S. M., Sharma, A., Iacono, W. G., & McGue, M. (2013). Risk of suicide attempt in adopted and nonadopted offspring. *Pediatrics, 132*(4), 639–646.

McGinnis, H. A. (2007). From the ashes of war: Lessons from 50 years of Korean international adoption. *Handbook of adoption: Implications for researchers, practitioners, and families* (pp. 160–170). Thousand Oaks, CA: SAGE Publications.

U.S. State Department Bureau of Consular Affairs. (2018). Adoption Statistics. Retrieved from https://travel.state.gov/content/travel/en/IntercountryAdoption/adopt_ref/adoption-statistics.html

CHAPTER FIFTEEN

Adaptability, Collaboration, Mentorship, and Impact

Lessons Learned by a Leading Asian American Scholar

SHENG-LUN CHENG AND VANESSA W. VONGKULLUKSN

AN EARLY CAREER FACULTY MEMBER AT MISSISSIPPI STATE UNIVERSITY

Dr. Kui Xie graduated from the University of Oklahoma in 2006 with a Ph.D. in Instructional Psychology and Technology. He became an assistant professor in the Department of Instructional Systems and Workforce Development at Mississippi State University in Fall 2006. During his time at Mississippi State, Dr. Xie began a research program that situated the concept of engagement in online learning and identified objective indicators of various forms of engagement in the online environment. In doing so, he narrowed his research context to a specific activity that is widely used in online learning—asynchronous online discussion (AOD). For example, in Xie, DeBacker, and Ferguson (2006) and Xie, Durrington, and Yen (2011), he used the number of messages posted in an AOD system as an indicator of learning engagement. Ke and Xie (2009)and Xie and Ke (2011) focused on the textual information of AODs and performed content analyses to examine students' engagement in AODs. He created an *online learning interaction model* to guide the content analysis. The model conceptualized that learning engagement in AODs is manifested through two major dimensions—*social* and *cognitive engagement.* Learning in AODs is achieved based upon social interactions and through iterations of *internalization* (where students read and integrate shared information through assimilation and accommodation processes) and *externalization* (where students synthesize the collaborative constructed ideas and elaborate them through information sharing). Overall, his research has provided concrete and specific evidence on the behavioral, social, and cognitive dimensions of students' engagement in online learning.

In our interview with Dr. Xie, he expressed that he accomplished these major research goals while overcoming some significant hurdles in his years as an early career scholar. As a research-intensive R1 university, Mississippi provided professional development and infrastructure to support an active research agenda for faculty members. However, Dr. Xie had a 2:3 teaching load which took up a significant portion of his time. He reflected that like any other new faculty member, he taught a variety of new courses for which he had to rapidly prepare. He taught a diverse group of classes covering topics from human cognition and instructional design to graphic design and computer repair. In his reflection, Dr. Xie expressed that faculty members should divide time between teaching and research activities, making sure that research work also goes forward even with teaching commitments.

Another area of time commitment was grant writing. Dr. Xie expressed that he spent a significant amount of time developing and writing grant proposals in his early years. Although he was successful in securing some university seed grants, he found it hard to tap into external grant funding despite spending much time and effort. Looking back, Dr. Xie would advise early career faculty to collaborate with more senior scholars and to share the Primary Investigator (PI) status. He reflected that "if I were to do it all over again, I would strategically position myself as a co-PI and let the senior [scholar] who has the resources and experience lead the project even if I wrote the grant [and] even if I had the original idea." Collaborating with more senior scholars may be a good way to learn the ropes in terms of what funding agencies are looking for, alleviate time spent on grant writing, and provide funding agencies with the confidence that the grant can be carried out with necessary expertise.

On a more personal note, Dr. Xie also expressed that it was difficult to live in a small town without amenities tailored towards Asian Americans, such as Asian restaurants or grocery stores. He felt a degree of challenge in assimilating to a small-town lifestyle. His strategy was to "build collaboration network ... with [his] cohort of new faculty." He worked with new faculty in diverse fields, from computer science to agriculture. He also worked intensively with colleagues from graduate school and professional conferences. This led to collaborative research partnerships as well as a social and professional network from which to draw strength. His strategy evidently worked, as he produced 13 publications in peer-reviewed and highly ranked scholarly journals during this time despite other professional commitments.

A NEWLY TENURED PROFESSOR AT THE OHIO STATE UNIVERSITY

Dr. Kui Xie was promoted to associate professor at Mississippi State University in 2012 and then moved to The Ohio State University (OSU) as an assistant professor. During this time, he began to examine the sociocultural aspects of engagement in digital learning. For example, Xie, Lu, Cheng, and Izmirli (2017)and Xie, Miller, and Allison (2013) examined the phenomena of social conflict in online collaborative learning. In these studies, he developed a *Social Conflict Evolution Model* that represents the developmental processes of social conflict among students in online collaborative learning activities. In addition, Xie, Hensley, Law, and Sun (2019) and Xie, Yu, and Bradshaw (2014) examined the effects of social roles on student engagement. They focus on how individuals assuming different roles (e.g., leader and follower) in groups would engage differently and apply different learning strategies.

Dr. Xie's work at OSU also leverages affordances of new data sources and new research methodologies for digital learning research. He made great strides in building mechanisms to track students' learning engagement and developing analytical methods to explain learning phenomena exhibited in these objective data. His recent works applied machine learning techniques (e.g., text mining) and social network analysis in developing an algorithm to detect team leadership from online interaction data (Xie, Di Tosto, Lu, & Cho, 2018). Another methodological innovation he pioneered was the *ESM-Mobile* application that applied *experience sampling method* to collect students' self-report data in the moment and in the context of learning (Xie, Heddy, & Greene, 2019; Xie, Heddy, & Vongkulluksn, 2019). These projects bring new innovations to the traditions of educational research by collecting data with more objectivity and accuracy, and less methodological bias. These newer approaches also involve intensive fine-grained longitudinal data, allowing his research to apply various analytical methods and detect nuances in human learning.

He accomplished much of these significant research contributions as the learning technologies program at OSU was still expanding. There was only Dr. Xie and another faculty member to run the entire program in his first few years at OSU. Moreover, only a handful of students were enrolled in the program at that time. As a result, there were few opportunities for faculty members to collaborate with students on research projects. However, Dr. Xie was not discouraged by the situation. "Actually, a small program is not really a problem. You can quickly build your reputation and have the opportunity to expand your program," he stated. The Ohio State University has a great infrastructure and provides new faculty members with various resources and supports to ensure their success.

After staying at Mississippi State University for six years, Dr. Xie knew that he needed to have strategies in place as he transitioned to OSU. In his first semester there, Dr. Xie focused on setting up personal networks. He met many faculty members across campus from his own and other departments such as computer science and psychology. Through these meetings, people got to know his expertise and teamwork skills. Dr. Xie was able to work with collaborators on writing several grant proposals.

In 2014, his strategy paid off. Two of Dr. Xie's grant proposals were funded by the Ohio Department of Education. *Evaluating Digital Content for Instructional and Teaching Excellence (EDCITE)* received approximately 8.3 million dollars to implement a digital content evaluation system to help schools move from print to digital classroom materials and increase personalized learning. Comprehensive evaluation methods and a web-based system were also developed along with professional development to help teachers learn how to review digital resources and determine the most suitable and cost-efficient programs for their districts. *College Ready Ohio (CRO)* received approximately 13.5 million dollars to expand access to college-level courses to high school students across the states via mobile learning, open digital sources, and College Credit Plus opportunities. By studying both online and in-person learning formats, the project examined how K–12 teachers and students may best adapt to new teaching and learning strategies. Dr. Xie was in charge of researching and evaluating the longitudinal impact of these projects on school districts across six years. These evaluation efforts emphasized district-wide cost reduction and resource sharing, teacher technology integration, and student motivation, engagement, and achievement.

In 2014, Dr. Xie received tenure and was promoted to associate professor at The Ohio State University. He established his own research group: The Research Laboratory for Digital Learning (dl.ehe.osu.edu). With resources from the University and newly funded grants, Dr. Xie was able to attract talents around the country and overseas, including doctoral students, postdoctoral researchers (Dr. Min Kyu Kim, currently Assistant Professor at Georgia State University), and international visiting scholars. Apart from monetary support, EDCITE and CRO also had a significant impact on how Dr. Xie approached educational research. He shifted his research focus from small-scale studies on online learning to district-wide school-based research and intervention work, such as teacher professional development. Both projects provided Dr. Xie and members at the Research Laboratory for Digital Learning (RLDL) with great opportunities to build a close connection with local schools. RLDL brings digital learning research and innovation from the laboratory to K–12 classrooms to transform the education system across the state of Ohio.

In 2015, Dr. Xie collaborated with experts in early childhood research, and, as a co-investigator, secured another large-scale project, *Read It Again—Mobile,*

Technology-Supported Language & Literacy Intervention for Preschoolers At-Risk (RIA-Mobile), with an approximately 1.5 million dollars investment from the U.S. Department of Education Institute for Education Sciences (IES). In 2015, Dr. Xie was awarded the Ted and Lois Cyphert Distinguished Professorship by the College of Education and Human Ecology at The Ohio State University to recognize his tremendous effort in teaching, research, and service. He becomes the only Asian American who is holding an endowed professorship in the College.

LEADING UP TO FULL PROFESSOR

In 2017, The Research Laboratory for Digital Learning started to disseminate their research findings on EDCITE and CRO projects and yielded a series of high-quality publications on school-based research in top-tier journals such as *Educational Technology Research and Development, Distance Education, British Journal of Educational Technology*, and *Teaching and Teacher Education* (e.g., Kim, Xie, & Cheng, 2017; Xie, Kim, Cheng, & Luthy, 2017). Meanwhile, The Research Laboratory for Digital Learning welcomed another postdoctoral researcher, Dr. Vanessa Vongkulluksn (currently Assistant Professor at the University of Nevada—Las Vegas).

With expertise in educational psychology, Dr. Vongkulluksn brought unique insights into educational research. Dr. Xie and lab members started to examine the larger impacts of technology initiatives on students' social-emotional learning with educational technology in K–12 school settings (e.g., Xie, Di Tosto, Chen, & Vongkulluksn, 2018; Xie, Vongkulluksn, Lu, & Cheng, 2020). In addition, *translational research* became the core pillar of RLDL. Instead of formulating research questions among scholars first and collecting data in schools later, Dr. Xie and the lab members worked closely with stakeholders and teachers to generate research questions that were directly related to their school and student needs. They then disseminated the research findings to inform school policy. Each year, Dr. Xie and lab members would travel around the state of Ohio and visit school partners to share research findings that were relevant to stakeholders.

The deep connection with school partners transformed the perspectives of Dr. Xie and lab members on the definition of educational research. Educational research needs to be contextualized and relevant for school improvement in your local community. RLDL members were even more motivated than ever to engage in translational research and dissemination. From 2017 onward, RLDL's scholarly productivity reached double-digits, producing more than 10 publications every year in top-tier journals such as *Contemporary Educational Psychology, Computers & Education, Internet and Higher Education*, and *Teachers College Record*. In addition, RLDL received new grant awards from the Ohio Department of Higher Education and the Spencer Foundation, including projects such as *Algebra Ready, Scaffolding Students' Information Literacy Development in Science Classrooms,* and *The Influence of Contextual Features on Learning Engagement in Out-of-Classroom Settings for Academically At-Risk College Students,* to support his effort on translational research. In 2017, Dr. Xie received the Distinguished Research Award from the College of Education and Human Ecology at OSU.

Despite having tremendous support for external grants, Dr. Xie was aware that external funding was not always stable. Some of the partnering centers at The Ohio State University were closed down owing to budget cuts by the state government. It was clear to him that he needed to create additional funding sources to maintain lab activities, and most importantly, to support his graduate students. To this aim, Dr. Xie worked with the Office of Distance Education and eLearning at The Oho State University to create an online course—ELSTECH 2011: Keys to Academic Success to Online Learning—which introduces essential learning strategies and technologies to guide students to successful online learning experiences and ultimately academic success. Dr. Xie made a great effort to promote this course by sending out flyers and knocking on colleagues' doors to ask for help in disseminating the course information. As a result, about 350 students enroll in this course each year. In return, the course supports two teaching assistantship positions and provides his students with college teaching experience.

Reflecting on his academic journey, Dr. Xie felt that he had learned a great deal by giving everything a try. Prior to establishing RLDL, he saw himself more as an independent researcher, taking charge of every step of the research process. At that time, he did not have any idea on how to manage a research lab and coordinate members' effort. After having his own lab, Dr. Xie learned numerous new skills from managing finances, building connections with schools, and creating a cohesive and culturally inclusive working environment. "I am still learning each day with my role as a lab director," he enthusiastically commented. Dr. Xie's effort, perseverance, and complete dedication to improving schools through translational research have been recognized by his colleagues in the College of Education and Human Ecology at The Ohio State University. Dr. Xie was granted the title of full professor on June 3rd, 2020.

CROSS-CUTTING THEMES OF CHALLENGES AND STRATEGIES

Dr. Kui Xie's story has several cross-cutting themes that may be informative to early- and mid-career scholars. Although he met with various adversities, he was able to persevere and overcome those adversities to become a leading researcher in the educational technology field.

Adaptability

The first cross-cutting theme in Dr. Xie's professional life is adaptability. In each new institutional setting and changing role, he was met with new challenges and shifting expectations. Dr. Xie was able to regroup and re-strategize, finding new ways to adapt and turn obstacles into opportunities. Dr. Xie commented, "When you move to a place, you have to adapt … Instead of trying to be critical, try to improve the place and try to improve the program that you're in. When you put your heart in, you will shine." Dr. Xie saw clearly that every professional environment had its advantages and limitations. He was able to look for the advantages each environment offered to counter some of the difficulties he was facing. Further, he focused on making contributions to his professional environment and local community. His hard work and perseverance gained him respect from his colleagues and facilitated professional stakes to fall in place as they should.

Another area of adaptability was related to funding structures. As previously noted, Dr. Xie expressed that as an early career scholar, he was ambitious towards getting grant funding but was largely unsuccessful. He adapted and changed his tactics during his years at OSU. He collaborated with others at the university and beyond. He was then successful in receiving several large external grants, including from the Ohio Department of Education and Institute of Education Sciences. He continued to build a team that began with these funding sources. Currently, as he leads a thriving research laboratory, he is in the midst of yet another adaptation. He is looking to diversify funding strategies by looking for school-supported funds. Dr. Xie demonstrates the resiliency needed to work within the current system and gain needed resources to continue making impactful research and supporting graduate students.

In our conversation with Dr. Xie, he also expressed the importance of another concept related to adaptation: balance. We saw that in his early years, he had to balance a heavy teaching load with grant writing and research activities. Later, as a newly tenured faculty member, he also had to balance other commitments with building the learning technologies program at OSU. Dr. Xie expressed that he encountered some difficulties in balancing all of these professional activities, as well as "putting family into the equation." Ultimately, his advice to newer academic professionals is to set priorities. He commented, "You only have 24 hours a day and 7 days a week. You have to prioritize your tasks." Also, Dr. Xie reflected that he received much support from lab members and colleagues. He suggested that others may also find both social and professional support from those in their social networks. These two strategies helped Dr. Xie achieve the balance needed to continue being a productive scholar even with other professional and personal commitments.

Collaboration

Another consistent theme in Dr. Xie's story is that of collaboration. At OSU, Dr. Xie established the Research Laboratory of Digital Learning with a team of students and post-doctoral scholars. He reflected that working with this team is essential to his current success. Dr. Xie commented, "I want to build a larger scale impact with my work. I'm not going to achieve that alone. I need to have a team." Dr. Xie also expressed the importance of collaborating with colleagues. In his early years at Mississippi State, he discussed forming networks with scholars both within and outside his home university. This strategy helped him maintain research productivity while providing the social network needed to assimilate to a new position and professional environment. Similarly, in his years at OSU, he collaborated closely with experts in other fields to produce meaningful research and grant-funded projects. In his reflection, Dr. Xie expressed that cross-disciplinary collaborations are more attractive to grant-funding agencies. More importantly, working with experts in other fields helps generate more in-depth research questions that approach a problem from multiple, deeply-rooted angles. These collaborations produce new research ideas that move the field forward.

Mentorship

Dr. Xie considers mentorship an extremely important aspect in his professional practice. He observes that students normally come to the program with different career goals. One important job for mentors is to identify those goals and tailor mentoring strategies to support them. Based on years of experience, Dr. Xie has also found that some students may change their career goals in the middle of their academic journey. His strategy is to expose students to a variety of learning opportunities such as educational research, grant writing, teaching experience, data analysis, software development, and instructional design projects to broaden students' knowledge and skill base. These experiences greatly enhance students' professional profile and employability after graduation.

Dr. Xie sees mentees as his academic family members. That means paying attention not only to their professional needs but also personal needs. Each year, he will arrange 2–3 major social events in his lab to strengthen bonds between lab members and relieve the pressure and anxiety from research and coursework. Dr. Xie firmly believes that social support is essential to students' well-being and academic success in the program. Dr. Xie has been invited several times to serve as the mentor for graduate students and early career scholars by American Educational Research Association (AERA) and the Association for Educational Communications and Technology (AECT). Recently, Dr. Xie was named Faculty

Mentor of the Year 2019 by the Department of Educational Studies, College of Education and Human Ecology, at The Ohio State University.

From Dr. Xie's perspective, the goal of the lab team and academic family is not only to produce quality research, but to develop graduate students and mentees into thoughtful and successful scholars. Dr. Xie provides a simple illustration of how important the success of his mentees is to him: "Every conference we can talk about how excellent Shonn [one of his graduate students] is. We can talk about this for 20 years. It's still going to be a really interesting topic. However, I can't keep talking about my ETR&D paper for 20 years. I truly believe that the next generation of scholars will be my best scholarly products."

Impact

The final cross-cutting theme in Dr. Xie's professional story is related to impact. Dr. Xie reflected that his research impact has shifted as he moved from an early career scholar to a full professor. He began with small-scale classroom research on online learning. He discussed working in a hands-on manner in his earlier research, which allowed him to gain expertise in all areas of research and dissemination. As he gained grant funding, he then focused on fulfilling the goals of the grant related to evaluating teacher professional development and technology-related interventions. These works were larger in scale and involved many teachers and classrooms at a time. Currently, he is working on research on an even larger scale, often with school- and district-wide data collection efforts. These works have implications for practice on district-wide administration and school policies. Dr. Xie reflected that he was led to scale up his research activities not only because of opportunities afforded by grant-funding, but also because of the expertise of his graduate students and post-doctoral scholars. His team brought large-scale research to life through great collaborative effort. Dr. Xie also reiterated that his ability to engender higher-scale research is both through opportunity and effort: "We have great opportunities in the past several years. But, at the same time, we are making great effort in writing and generating funding to maintain this enterprise." His achievements reflect the research success that can occur when fortune and hard work are combined.

Dr. Xie's idea of "impactful" work has also shifted through the years. He has shifted his approach to research from idea-focused to practitioner-focused through his effort at *translational research*. He expressed that currently he is "shifting to the idea of working with practitioners not only in collecting data and analyzing data according to our own research questions, but also to really working with practitioners in generating research questions. [We are] getting questions from practitioners, translating them into scientific research questions, then designing research based on those." In addition to anchoring research within a concrete school context, this strategy gets at research questions that are timely and relevant for schools. Ultimately, Dr. Xie is looking to have an impact on schooling in his local community and beyond. He summed up that "publication is not the ultimate goal. Of course, we still pursue publications. But, I really put the school practice first, then my research second. I want to build a research program that works with the school, that helps the school, and at the same time advances our field." This generative strategy is the key to success as he defines it—to be a positive influence in his local and professional community.

CONCLUSION

Dr. Kui Xie is a standout example of resiliency and persistence. His story represents the often-untold side of academia: the strategic planning and adaptive thinking needed to become a leading research scholar. Discussions of this nature would counter the narrative that professional success is easy, and that scholars rise to success in academia solely because of some unknown innate ability. This chapter presents a real-life commentary on a successful minority scholar, which we hope will be helpful to other early- and mid-career scholars in their professional planning.

REFERENCES

Ke, F., & Xie, K. (2009). Toward deep learning for adult students in online courses. *Internet and Higher Education*, *12*(3–4), 136–145.

Kim, M. K., Xie, K., & Cheng, S. L. (2017). Building teacher competency for digital content evaluation. *Teaching and Teacher Education*, *66*, 309–324.

Xie, K., DeBacker, T. K., & Ferguson, C. (2006). Extending the traditional classroom through online discussion: The role of student motivation. *Journal of Educational Computing Research*, *34*(1), 67–89.

Xie, K., Di Tosto, G., Chen, S. B., & Vongkulluksn, V. (2018). A systematic review of design and technology components of educational digital resources. *Computers & Education*, *127*, 90–106.

Xie, K., Di Tosto, G., Lu, L., & Cho, Y. S. (2018). Detecting leadership in peer-moderated online collaborative learning through text mining and social network analysis. *Internet and Higher Education*, *38*, 9–17.

Xie, K., Durrington, V. A., & Yen, L. L. (2011). Relationship between students' motivation and their participation in asynchronous online discussions. *Journal of Online Learning and Teaching*, *7*(1), 17–29.

Xie, K., Heddy, B. C., & Greene, B. A. (2019). Affordances of using mobile technology to support experience sampling method in examining college students' engagement. *Computers & Education*, *128*, 183–198.

Xie, K., Heddy, B., & Vongkulluksn, V. (2019). Examining engagement in context using experience sampling method with mobile technology. *Contemporary Educational Psychology, 59*, 101788.

Xie, K., Hensley, L., Law, V., & Sun, Z. (2019). Self-regulation as a function of perceived leadership and cohesion in small group online collaborative learning. *British Journal of Educational Technology, 50*(1), 456–468.

Xie, K., & Ke, F. (2011). The role of students' motivation in peer-moderated asynchronous online discussions. *British Journal of Educational Technology, 42*(6), 916–930.

Xie, K., Kim, M. K., Cheng, S. L., & Luthy, N. C. (2017). Teacher professional development through digital content evaluation. *Educational Technology Research & Development, 65*(4), 1067–1103.

Xie, K., Lu, L., Cheng, S. L., & Izmirli, S. (2017). The interactions between facilitator identity, conflictual presence, and social presence in online collaborative learning. *Distance Education, 38*(2), 230–244.

Xie, K., Miller, N. C., & Allison, J. R. (2013). Toward a social conflict evolution model: Examining the adverse power of conflictual social interaction in online learning. *Computers & Education, 63*, 404–415.

Xie, K., Vongkulluksn, V., Lu, L., & Cheng, S. L. (2020). A person-centered approach to examining high-school students' motivation, engagement and academic performance. *Contemporary Educational Psychology, 62*, 101877.

Xie, K., Yu, C., & Bradshaw, A. C. (2014). Impacts of role assignment and participation in asynchronous discussions in college-level online classes. *Internet and Higher Education, 20*, 10–19.

CHAPTER SIXTEEN

Bridging East and West

Dr. Guofang Li's Success as a Transnational Scholar in Language and Literacy Education in North America

KONGJI QIN

Dr. Guofang Li is a Professor and Canada Research Chair (Tier 1) in Transnational/Global Perspectives of Language and Literacy Education of Children and Youth in the Department of Language and Literacy Education, Faculty of Education, University of British Columbia, Canada. Due to intersectional inequality (Crenshaw, 1991), it is still rare to see Asian female scholars in chair professor or endowed professor positions in the humanities and social sciences. Dr. Li achieved this distinction through her two decades of programmatic, influential research in the education of immigrant and minoritized learners. As one of the leading scholars in the field of language and literacy education, she has pioneered research in several important areas in the education of immigrant learners: immigrant children's bicultural and biliteracy development through educational systems, immigrant children's new literacies practices in and out of school, technology-infused ESL/EFL instructional approaches, diversity and equity issues, and teacher education and professional development for culturally and linguistically diverse children and youth. She has published 12 books and over 100 journal articles and book chapters on language and literacy education. The excellence of her scholarship and the rigor of her research have been recognized by several prestigious national and international awards, including the 2006 and 2013 Ed Fry Book Award from the Literary Research Association (LRA), the 2008 American Education Research Association (AERA) Division G Early Career Award, the 2010 AERA Early Career Award, the 2011 Publication Award from the Association of Chinese Professors of Social Sciences in the United States (ACPSS), and the 2016 AERA Second Language Education SIG Mid-Career Award.

Dr. Li's research and influence are as far-reaching as her collaborations. As a scholar with a transnational background, her journey to academia started in Wuhan, China, where she attended Wuhan University, one of the most prestigious universities in China, and earned a master's degree in applied linguistics in 1996. After graduation, she moved to Canada and began her doctoral studies in language and literacy education at the University of Saskatchewan. After her doctoral studies, she moved to Vancouver for a post-doctoral fellowship at the University of British Columbia (UBC), Canada. In 2001, she took a position as an Assistant Professor of Teaching English to Speakers of Other Languages (TESOL) at the State University of New York (SUNY) at Buffalo. In 2006, she accepted a position as an Associate Professor of Second Language and Literacy Education in the Department of Teacher Education at Michigan State University (MSU). In 2015, she returned to UBC as a Professor and Tier 1 Canada Research Chair.

During her tenure at universities across Canada and the United States, Dr. Li has led numerous research projects funded by national and federal agencies, collaborated with peers, and mentored many doctoral students who have gone on to become researchers and scholars in language and literacy education across the globe. Her scholarship, wisdom, and generosity have profoundly influenced the field and touched a generation of junior scholars. I am one such person who has had the opportunities to learn directly from and work with her. I met Dr. Li during my doctoral studies in MSU's Department of Teacher Education. My own research interest in the education of English language learners (ELLs), identity and culture in language education, and the preparation of culturally and linguistically responsive teachers for ELLs was influenced by her scholarship on the language and literacy development of immigrant and other minoritized learners and inspired by her steadfast pursuit for improving the schooling experience for these disadvantaged learners.

EARLY YEARS: UNIVERSITY OF SASKATCHEWAN AND UBC

Dr. Li's journey to academia started at the University of Saskatchewan, Canada, where in 1996 she began her doctoral studies in language and literacy education in the Department of Curriculum Studies, under the supervision of Dr. Sam Robinson. During her doctoral studies, she was exposed to critical theories that established the theoretical foundations of her research for years to come. In the introduction to her recent book, a collection of two decades of her major publications on language, literacy, culture, and identity, she wrote:

My views quickly changed after my first year of study, during which I studied critical theorists such as Jürgen Habermas, Michael Apple, Henry Giroux, Paulo Freire and Pierre Bourdieu who argue that educational practices are not neutral but ideological. I learned that schools as one of the key agencies of the social, economic, and political institutions are not educational equalizers but instead, they work to maintain if not produce the inequalities in the society (Li, 2018, p. 5)

Building on this critical understanding of education and schooling, Dr. Li centered her research on issues of language, literacy, identity, and culture in immigrant children's and families' literacy practices. This theoretical orientation was manifested in her first publication (Li, 2000), based on a pilot study that investigated a Filipino immigrant family's identity formation, and the intergenerational conflicts that arose during the process of acquiring a second language and assimilating into the mainstream society. This article was published in the *McGill Journal of Education* and received the "Best Article Award" from the Journal in 2001. This study paved the way for Dr. Li's dissertation research, which investigated the language learning experiences of Chinese Canadian children from different social class backgrounds. In her dissertation, she compared Chinese Canadian children whose parents were working within the university setting to those whose parents owned restaurants. She found vastly different approaches to and expectations of the educational system in Canada from these two groups; at the same time, they shared very similar Chinese cultural beliefs on how education should be approached. Her research demonstrated that cultural beliefs, along with other factors such as parental educational backgrounds, occupational choices and chances, and adaptation and integration into Canadian society, contributed to their children's ability to learn a second language.

In addition to critical theories, Dr. Li's scholarship in this area is anchored in sociocultural approaches to learning, with a focus on understanding how issues of culture, identity, and social class influence the language and literacy development of immigrant learners. As Dr. Li (2007) writes:

In this paper, I situated my understanding of the two children's experiences and their intersecting social relationships in the world of home and community, and the world of school. I looked at forces that sustain their continuous engagement with literacy and factors that deter their investment in learning. From a socioconstructivist perspective, I look at second language learning as a dynamic social process in which a learner is an active meaning maker (Vygotsky, 1978; Wells, 1986). A learner makes sense of self, home and school experiences, school practices, and her/his experiences in society at large (Wells, 1986). Therefore, this dynamic process involves complex social relationships that a learner forms with other co-constructors of knowledge in their everyday literacy activities and events. These co-constructors are members of the learners' particular sociocultural contexts — teachers, peers, parents, and community members. (p. 3)

Dr. Li's work on immigrant children and youths' literacy development not only provided empirical evidence on how literacy is situated in practice (Li, 2001), but also contributed significantly to the theory of language and literacy research. For instance, her research on overachieving and underachieving students provided important insights on the impact of the model minority myth on Asian immigrant learners, which furthered the field's theoretical discussion of the model minority discourse. For underachieving students, in her article "Other People's Success" (Li, 2005), Dr. Li argues that model minority images have become a "destructive myth" for Asian children who do not fit the stereotypes. For overachieving students, she draws particular attention to their social processes of learning by exploring their socio-emotional well-being in their acculturation experiences. In "Behind the 'Model Minority' Mask" (Li, 2009), Dr. Li explores how deep social isolation and multiple responsibilities in the home resulted in acute psychological stress for a Vietnamese youth who was trying to achieve a balance between school-home cultural conflicts and academic expectations. Dr. Li's work on the model minority myth is well known and oft cited. Her co-edited book (Li & Wang, 2008), *Model Minority Myths Revisited: An Interdisciplinary Approach to Demystifying Asian American Education Experiences*, won the 2011 ACPSS Publication Award.

Additionally, by looking at the linguistic and cultural discontinuity between the Chinese Canadian children's school and home language and literacy experiences, Dr. Li's work shed important light on the site of struggle which led to their potential failure at school. This body of research concludes that the dynamics and processes of different cultural models of literacy practices shape qualitatively different home literacy practices that were largely unknown to the West. To spotlight the role of culture and cultural models of learning, situated in children's lived experiences outside of schools, this body of work contributes to the effort to abandon a simple remedial approach to literacy instruction and promotes a culturally grounded approach that utilizes learners' personal and cultural knowledge as a scaffold for powerful academic learning.

By focusing on issues of immigrant and minority students' language and literacy practices and connections between home and school settings. Dr. Li's scholarship is situated in the same intellectual lineage of scholars such as Denny Taylor, Shirley Brice Heath, Luis Moll, James Paul Gee, David Barton, Mary Hamilton, and Guadalupe Valdes, each of whom challenged the traditional power relationships in language and literacy learning in school, especially deficit perspectives on minority children and families, by focusing on children's voices, experiences, and practices outside school. The work of these scholars revealed that language and literacy learning is not merely a linguistic issue, but a personal, social, cultural, and political phenomenon that extends beyond the confines of schools. Deeply situated in the new literacy tradition, Dr. Li's scholarship brought the education of immigrant learners to the center of the larger field of language and literacy education, with rigorous programs of research that contributed significantly to the field.

Upon receiving her doctorate from the University of Saskatchewan, Dr. Li received a post-doctoral fellowship from the Social Sciences and Humanities Research Council of Canada (SSHRC) to extend her research on Chinese immigrant children from the home contexts to the school settings. For her post-doctoral research, she examined the interaction of culture and social class on language learning by focusing on affluent immigrants and their children from Hong Kong, China, who were living in Vancouver. Her research revealed that this population held very strong ideas about education, and culturally valued education; and, their higher social and economic status afforded them more agency and social capital to provide the kind of education they wanted for their children outside of school. The teachers at the school she studied held very different values and did not agree with the Chinese parents' educational beliefs that prioritized academic achievement. This phase of research confirmed her earlier findings that cultural beliefs on achievement and education were consistent among Chinese immigrants, but it also showed the role social class played in immigrant children's educational experiences. The conflicts between school and parents were compounded by an absence of dialogue between families and schools, which could have allowed both groups to recognize each other's value systems.

MID-CAREER YEARS: SUNY BUFFALO AND MSU

In 2001, after completing one year of research as a post-doctoral fellow at the University of British Columbia, Dr. Li accepted a position as an Assistant Professor of TESOL at SUNY Buffalo. During her tenure there, she continued to pursue research on the literacy and language education of disadvantaged student populations, such as children from immigrant and refugee families and economically disadvantaged white families. While her scholarship during this period continued to focus on how cultural beliefs held by parents influenced their children's literacy learning, she broadened the field's understanding of these issues by situating language and literacy development of minoritized children within larger sociopolitical contexts, and by pointing to inequality in literacy education that resulted from structural and institutional discrimination and neglect. For instance, driven by this critical lens, Dr. Li conducted a new research project that focused on multi-ethnic, low socio-economic immigrants, referred to by the media as the "Rainbow Underclass," that included immigrant and refugee participants from Sudan, Vietnam, and Europe, and poor whites living in one U.S. inner-city. Similar to her previous findings, she discovered what influenced English language acquisition within this population were the cultural beliefs they brought from their home cultures, as well as the new challenges of being low-income minorities in an inner-city context. While they were grateful for the opportunities they had in America and were supportive of their children's learning at home, their children's schooling was significantly impacted by the larger social, institutional factors such as widespread racism and stereotypes against them in society, a hostile school environment with low student morale, a dangerous inner-city neighborhood, a lack of social and community support in the host society, and financial constraints due to their status as low-skilled laborers.

Extending her work on immigrant children's language and literacy learning, Dr. Li developed another program of research on immigrant parents, as her previous work had demonstrated the importance of understanding and supporting parents of these children: they are their children's first educators, and they are tasked with negotiating complex identities as immigrants, minorities, and language learners who are in the process of learning about Western educational systems and practices. These complex identities work together to influence their interactions with their children, the home language environment, the access to resources they can provide their children, and their ability to negotiate with mainstream schools at the same time they're working on their own language acquisition. Dr. Li's work illustrated that it is imperative to unpack the critical and overlooked lines of difference and cultural complexities between home and school. To this end, she proposed a "pedagogy of cultural reciprocity" advocating a reciprocal relationship between teachers and parents (Li, 2006, 2008). By emphasizing that *both* mainstream teachers and minority parents can become change agents, this pedagogical approach has moved the concept of culturally relevant/responsive teaching (by Gloria Ladson-Billings, Geneva Gay, and Kathy Au) forward, as the current literature tends to demand that *either* teachers adjust to parents' cultural backgrounds *or* parents accept mainstream school practices (both of these options have proven to be difficult or impossible to achieve). This important contribution, outlined in her two books *Culturally Contested Pedagogy* (Li, 2006) and *Culturally Contested Literacies* (Li, 2008), was recognized by the prestigious Ed Fry Book Award from the Literacy Research Association (formerly the National Reading Association) in 2006 and 2013, respectively.

In 2006, Dr. Li accepted a position as an Associate Professor of Second Language and Literacy Education in the Department of Teacher Education at MSU. Again, building upon her previous research on the education of immigrant learners, she began a new program of research to focus on supporting mainstream in- and pre-service teachers who often struggled to understand the needs of immigrant and refugee students, and to communicate with their parents about school programs. Dr. Li's important research concurred with other leading scholars (e.g., Gloria Ladson-Billings) that the old assumption of "just good teaching" is not enough to teach the immigrant student population. We must have well-trained teachers who have the cultural knowledge and pedagogical skills to support this particular population. Her research program at MSU, therefore, was devoted to supporting current teachers with innovative pedagogical models (e.g., pedagogy of cultural reciprocity), and how to better prepare pre-service teachers to teach English learners by examining teacher education instructors' beliefs, practices, and curriculum, and teacher candidates' perceptions and experiences.

In this area, Dr. Li launched a series of research projects and published several important articles that investigated the preparation of teachers for English language learners. In 2013 she edited a special issue in *Theory and Practice* on effective professional development for teachers of culturally and linguistically diverse students. In this special issue, she put forward a cultural approach to professional learning to empower pre- and in-service teachers to successfully address increasingly diverse student populations and become culturally responsive to students' diverse backgrounds. The professional learning approach outlined a 3-stage model: *cultural reconciliation, cultural translation*, and *cultural transformation*. This model aims at "building teachers' ability to recognize their own cultural practices and relate to those of their students, as well as enhancing their performance and action in empowering their students to work against cultural hegemony" (Li, 2013, p. 136). This special issue included articles written by leading researchers in the United States on the issue of EL teacher preparation, such as Tamara Lucas, Ana Maria Villegas, Okhee Lee, Deborah Short, Kip Téllez, Manka Varghese, Ester J. de Jong, Candace A. Harper, Maria R. Coady, Edmund T. Hamann, and Jenelle Reeves. Alongside these scholars, Dr. Li made a vital contribution to the field of teacher preparation for ELs, a field which had just started to gain momentum in both research and practice.

In this line of research on preparing teachers for culturally and linguistically diverse learners, Dr. Li chaired the ELL/ESL Task Force in the Department of Teacher Education at MSU from 2012 to 2013. Since little research has been conducted to understand how teachers are being prepared to teach immigrant and minority learners, Dr. Li's research in this area addresses this knowledge gap by first identifying pre-service teachers' learning needs from teacher educators' perspectives and practices as well as their own perspectives. Based on the important knowledge gaps identified from data collected from these perspectives, Dr. Li led a team of doctoral students to design online modules to support pre-service teachers' learning to teach English learners. Their findings have had a significant positive impact on the teacher education program under study and they have published a strong body of research that will impact other teacher education programs in the areas of curriculum revision, program reform, and professional development for teacher educators. This line of Dr. Li's work has addressed issues including how to prepare culturally and linguistically competent teachers for EIL education (Li, 2017a), using multimodal modules to support pre-service teachers in developing their knowledge for working with ELLs (Li et al., 2017), pre-service mainstream teachers' beliefs and perceptions about their preparation to teach ELLs (Li, Hinojosa, et al., 2018), TESOL pre-service teachers' perspectives on their professional preparation for working with ELLs (Li et al., 2019), and teacher educators' challenges in preparing teachers of ELLs (Li & Bian, 2022, in press).

SCHOLARSHIP ON ENGLISH AS A FOREIGN/INTERNATIONAL LANGUAGE EDUCATION

In addition to her research on immigrant and minoritized learners in the education systems in North America, Dr. Li has conducted, often collaborating with doctoral students and post-doctoral fellows, a series of studies on English language teaching in Asian countries (Li & Bian, 2022, in press). For example, she has conducted a program of research on how technology is taken up in EFL classrooms in China. Drawing on survey data, she and her colleague (Li & Ni, 2011) examined the patterns and perceptions of technology use by primary EFL teachers in China. They found that although Chinese EFL teachers held positive attitudes toward the value of technology for teaching and learning, their use of technology did not change the teacher-centered nature of instruction because they mainly used technology for teaching preparation and instructional delivery, and seldom utilized technology for student-centered activities. Drawing on videotaped technology-infused EFL lessons in China, she and her doctoral advisees conducted a conversational analysis of the classroom practice to examine the nature of technology-assisted practices and their influence on teacher-student interaction in the target language. The analysis confirmed the findings from her earlier survey studies that the technology-assisted practices mainly served as an alternative presentation tool to meet a range of traditional pedagogical goals and facilitated minimal spontaneous language use among the students. Her research in this area has significant implications, as technology has been increasingly promoted as a tool to enhance learning in China. Additionally, she and her doctoral advisee (Sah & Li, 2018) have published research on English Medium Instruction (EMI) in Nepal, pointing to the challenges of EMI instruction when it is promoted without adequate teacher preparation and infrastructure support in the school.

Dr. Li has also published articles and books, written either in English or Chinese, in China-based academic journals or by Chinese publishing houses. They cover a wide range of topics from learner agency in literacy instruction (Li, 2017b), to Chinese immigrant family language policies in Canada (Li & Sun, 2017), to family language attitudes of the Sibe (Xibo) ethnic group in China

(Yin & Li, 2019), to Chinese American mothers' perspectives on early child-hood education (Li & Zhang, 2015). These publications not only allow Dr. Li's scholarship to reach non-English readers, but also disrupt the normalcy of academic publishing that privileges English publications and journals based in the academic North.

CURRENT RESEARCH AS A CANADIAN RESEARCH CHAIR AT THE UNIVERSITY OF BRITISH COLUMBIA

In 2015, Dr. Li returned to the University of British Columbia as a Professor and Tier 1 Canada Research Chair in Transnational/Global Perspectives of Language and Literacy Education of Children and Youth in the Department of Language and Literacy Education, Faculty of Education. Building on her two decades of rigorous, influential research on the language and literacy development of immigrant and minoritized learners, she continues to expand her work to understand better the new generation of immigrant students' connective multiliteracies learning around new technology and social media, in and out of school, and to develop innovative pedagogical approaches for teachers to connect their in-school and out-of-school experiences. She continues to focus on Asian immigrant students, who have become one of the fastest growing populations in Canada and the U.S., and who now come with wealth. The large influx of Chinese children from wealthy families has generated new tensions between immigrant and mainstream groups, and between earlier generations of Asian immigrants and the wealthy newcomers. Explorations of how these new tensions around social class and cultural identity shape the Asian children's (and their peers') language and literacy development are particularly needed to better understand their processes of integration in schools and communities in these new globalized contexts.

Dr. Li's current research program takes a long view of immigrant students' language literacy development through a longitudinal research study (a five-year SSHRC Insight Grant project). The project aims to identify factors affecting Cantonese and Mandarin-speaking students' differential achievements in English and core academic subjects in the context of Vancouver. This is the first holistic study that examines whether and how differences in sociocultural characteristics (i.e., parental beliefs in education, family literacy practices, and socioeconomic status), the availability and type of English as a second language (ESL) programs and/or support, and Chinese language support at home and in community schools, intersect longitudinally to affect academic and English literacy achievements of the two groups of learners. Understanding these factors is essential for teachers, parents, and policymakers to better support immigrant students' language and literacy development in school.

In addition to taking a system's approach (a long view) to understanding immigrant students' language and literacy development, a second strand of Dr. Li's current work addresses how to prepare pre-service teachers to provide effective English language development support in school. She recently co-edited a special issue in the *Journal of Family Diversity Education* on the topic of supporting teachers with diversity-plus competencies for working with culturally, linguistically, and racially diverse students, families, and communities (Li et al., 2018). Her co-edited book, *Superdiversity and Teacher Education: Supporting Teachers in Working with Culturally, Linguistically, and Racially Diverse Students, Families, and Communities* (Li et al., 2021), further explores this topic by looking at issues of teacher preparation in the context of superdiversity. These new publications are a reflection of Dr. Li's unwavering commitment to the education of immigrant and minoritized learners through teacher education. She has contributed significantly to the field of ELL teacher preparation through her programmatic research and her pursuit of equity-based instruction for this disadvantaged student population.

Dr. Li's contributions to the field go beyond her research and scholarship. She has mentored a generation of students who have established their own careers as researchers and scholars. She has served, and continues to serve, leadership roles in professional associations such as AERA, LRA, TESOL, and IRA (International Reading Association). She serves on the advisory board for 20 journals in language and literacy education. Currently, she is serving as a co-editor of the *Journal of Literacy Research*, the flagship journal of the LRA.

I close this essay on a more personal note, for I have been both Dr. Li's student and collaborator. Over the years of following her work, and working alongside her, I have always been most taken by her humanity and generosity. Dr. Li has explored the issues of bicultural and biliteracy practices of immigrant and minoritized students, connections between home and school settings and in transnational contexts and spaces, and preparing teachers for culturally and linguistically diverse learners with passion and warmth, offering them to the field with an intellectual generosity, rigor, and wisdom that have enriched her writings and others. And her work and scholarship will continue to influence and shape the field, advocating for immigrant learners, a student population facing insurmountable challenges in the current context with the rise of nationalist, racist, and xenophobic rhetoric and ideologies we are currently witnessing across the globe.

REFERENCES

Crenshaw, K. W. (1991). Mapping the margins: Intersectionality, identity politics, and violence against women of color. *Stanford Law Review, 43*, 1241–1299. https://doi.org/10.2307/1229039

Li, G. (2000). Family literacy and cultural identity: An ethnographic study of a Filipino family in Canada. *McGill Journal of Education*, *35*(1), 9–29.

Li, G. (2001). Literacy as situated practice. *Canadian Journal of Education/Revue Canadienne de l'éducation*, *26*(1), 57–75. JSTOR. https://doi.org/10.2307/1602145

Li, G. (2005). Other people's success: Impact of the "model minority" myth on underachieving Asian students in North America. *KEDI Journal of Educational Policy*, *2*(1), 69–86.

Li, G. (2006). *Culturally contested pedagogy: Battles of literacy and schooling between mainstream teachers and Asian immigrant parents*. State University of New York Press. https://muse.jhu.edu/book/5000/

Li, G. (2007). Second language and literacy learning in school and at home: An ethnographic study of Chinese Canadian first graders' experiences. *Journal of Literacy Teaching and Learning*, *11*(1), 1–40.

Li, G. (2008). *Culturally contested literacies: America's "rainbow underclass" and urban schools*. Routledge.

Li, G. (2009). Behind the "model minority" mask: A cultural ecological perspective on a high achieving Vietnamese youth's identity and socio-emotional struggles. In C. Park, R. Endo, & X. L. Rong (Eds.), *New perspectives in Asian American parents, students, and teacher recruitment* (pp. 165–192). Information Age Publishing.

Li, G. (2013). Promoting teachers of culturally and linguistically diverse (CLD) students as change agents: A cultural approach to professional learning. *Theory Into Practice*, *52*(2), 136–143. https://doi.org/10.1080/00405841.2013.770331

Li, G. (2017a). Preparing culturally and linguistically competent teachers for English as an international language education. *TESOL Journal*, *8*(2), 250–276. https://doi.org/10.1002/tesj.322

Li, G. (2017b). Reading "the word" and "the world": Promoting learner agency through an engagement model of literacy instruction. 英语学习 (教师版) *[English Language Learning]*, *2*, 24–34.

Li, G. (2018). *Languages, identities, power, and cross- cultural pedagogies in transnational literacy education*. Shanghai Foreign Language Education Press.

Li, G., Anderson, J., Hare, J., & McTavish, M. (Eds.). (2021). *Superdiversity and teacher education: Supporting teachers in working with culturally, linguistically, and racially diverse students, families, and communities*. Routledge.

Li, G., Anderson, J., Hare, J., & McTavish, M. (Eds.). (2018). Supporting teachers with diversity-plus competencies for working with culturally, linguistically, and racially diverse students, families and communities [Special issue]. *Journal of Family Diversity Education*, *3*(1), 1–91.

Li, G., & Bian, Y. (2022, in press). Preparing all teachers for ELLs: Teacher educators' challenges and practices. In E. Rui & I. Lee (Eds.), *Becoming and being a TESOL teacher educator*. Routledge.

Li, G., Bian, Y., Martinez, J. M., Keengwe, S., & Onchwari, G. (2019). Learning to teach English Language learners as "a side note": TESOL pre-service teachers' perspectives of their professional preparation. In *Handbook of research on assessment practices and pedagogical models for immigrant students*. IGI Global.

Li, G., Hinojosa, D., & Wexler, L. (2018). Beliefs and perceptions about their preparation to teach English language learners: Voices of mainstream pre-service teachers. *International Journal of TESOL and Learning*, *7*(1 & 2), 1–21.

Li, G., Hinojosa, D., Wexler, L., Bian, Y., & Matinez, J. (2017). Using multimodal modules to address pre-service teachers' knowledge gap in learning to teach English language learners. *TAPESTRY*, *8*(1). https://stars.library.ucf.edu/tapestry/vol8/iss1/2

Li, G., Jee, Y., & Sun, Z. (2018). Technology as an educational equalizer for EFL learning in rural China? Evidence from the impact of technology-assisted practices on teacher-student interaction in primary classrooms. *Language and Literacy*, *20*(3), 159–184. https://doi.org/10.20360/langandlit29415

Li, G., & Ni, X. (2011). Primary EFL teachers' technology use in China: Patterns and perceptions. *RELC Journal*, *42*(1), 69–85. https://doi.org/10.1177/0033688210390783

Li, G., & Ni, X. (2013). Effects of a technology-enriched, task-based language teaching curriculum on Chinese elementary students' achievement in English as foreign language. *International Journal of Computer-Assisted Language Learning & Teaching*, *3*(1), 33–49.

Li, G., & Sun, Z. (2017). 加拿大华人家庭语言政策类型及成因 [Chinese immigrants' family language policies in Canada]. 语言战略研究 *[Chinese Journal of Language Policy and Planning]*, *2*(2), 46–56.

Li, G., & Wang, L. (Eds.). (2008). *Model minority myth revisited: An interdisciplinary approach to demystifying Asian American educational experiences*. Information Age Publishing.

Li, G., & Zhang, L. J. (2015). 玩比学重要:美国华裔妈妈教你快乐早教 [More play, less study: A Chinese American mother's advice on early education]. Beijing University Press.

Sah, P. K., & Li, G. (2018). English medium instruction (EMI) as linguistic capital in Nepal: Promises and realities. *International Multilingual Research Journal*, *12*(2), 109–123. https://doi.org/10.1080/19313152.2017.1401448

Vygotsky, L.S. (1978). *Mind in society*. Cambridge, MA: MIT Press.

Wells, G. (1986). *The meaning makers: Children learning language and using language to learn*. Portsmouth, NH: Heinemann.

Yin, X., & Li, G. (2019). 锡箔家庭语言态度的代际差异研究 [Family language attitudes of the Sibe (Xibo) ethnic group in Xinjiang, Northwestern of China]. 语言战略研究 *[Chinese Journal of Language Policy and Planning]*, *4*(2), 31–41.

Linking the Crossroads of Our Liberation

A Reflection of Joy in Academia, Mentorship, and Collective Action

CHRISTIAN D. CHAN

I find myself writing this reflection while in the midst of several crossroads. I was recently transitioning between institutions, battling with the throes of academic livelihood, and living with societal concerns about severe racism and xenophobia targeting several communities of color. It is a strange epoch of survival and living. Globally, we are collectively organizing to fight a pandemic known eminently as COVID-19. Beyond COVID-19, I want to highlight that we are fighting a persistent and pernicious virus known characteristically for decades as racism. While it has mutated over time, it still carries the same chronic and lasting effects interpersonally and systemically (An, 2020; Hayes & Hartlep, 2013; Matias, 2016; Museus et al., 2019). It is fitting that this text amplifies not only a personal story, but also stories of liberation.

As a queer brown second-generation Asian American of multiple ethnic heritages linked to Filipino, Chinese, and Malaysian communities, I write this reflection excavating an ancestry as the child of two immigrants who experienced economic hardship in transition to the United States of America. In their narratives of persistence, they were driven by generational history, community, and familial resilience. My parents shared those values with me to sustain my own privileges of living in a middle-class family with access to educational and career opportunities. They served as my inspiration for connecting to my own ancestry and ethnic heritages, but more so, they were pivotal in shaping my personal ties towards scholar-activism and pursuing a Doctor of Philosophy (Ph.D.). As

I reflect back on my upbringing, I attend to a deeper consciousness of the stories my family told me over years of implicit and explicit racism and racial violence. Although the stories may seem pessimistic, I also note the way in which my own family healed from racial violence through combining heart, community, and an ultimate responsibility for generations to come. My family members were my first teachers on activism. In this text, we are prominently paying homage to our ancestors, lineage, and legacy.

The structure of this text offers readers brilliant insights into the capacity for complex understandings of the academy and of our survival. Each story is different in its pathway to transformation. Each story links different values, worldviews, strengths, and heritages. Each story covers a primary relationship signifying our attachment to community as a means to thrive in the academy. It is a method to explore our intersections by noting the intersections interconnecting many of our social identities simultaneously with privilege and oppression (Chan et al., 2018; Jones, 2016; Wijeyesinghe & Strayhorn, 2017). As I share my reflections, *this reflection is a privilege, which means it has never only been about my story.* Thus, I intentionally organized my reflections into three themes to essentially cover the next steps in the journey: collective action, mentorship, and joy in academia.

COLLECTIVE ACTION

The timing of this edited volume is truly impeccable for personal, professional, and societal reasons. I am often tasked with teaching multicultural courses in counselor education at both the master's and doctoral levels while conducting a number of diversity-, equity-, and inclusion-focused trainings for academic units and consultations across institutions. Coincidentally, I am writing this reflection at the close of my advanced multicultural class, where I frequently dialog about resistance, community organizing, and collective action in the academy. In curating resources for the course, I shared Dr. Don T. Nakanishi's (1990) article poignantly titled "Why I Fought" as a message of resilience and hope, notably for students of color ultimately preparing themselves for academic careers in light of a broken system of racial inequities. In the article, Dr. Nakanishi, a renowned education and ethnic studies scholar credited for the visibility of Asian American Studies, documented his arduous three-year battle with seeking promotion and tenure at a prestigious institution. Assigning that article was not to elicit despair, but rather, to serve as the fuel to ignite collective action. It reminds me why I fight and why I stay in the academy. It reminds me of every narrative threading through this text. For Asian communities, our act of mobilization is a powerful tool for community and transformation (Manzano et al., 2017; Maramba et al., 2017). As Nakanishi saliently discussed, our collective action is not simply a horizontal act.

It is one that transcends time and generations by leaving a significant impact for students and faculty to enter this system (Koshino, 2016; Lee, 2019). Collective action reminds us of our capability to mobilize and use resistance work to transform the systems that continuously fail to see us (Museus et al., 2019). Seeing Asian American faculty and scholars in prominent leadership positions across academic institutions with this vision of resistance work. Given the crossroads of recent events, the timing of this text has raised the urgency for collective action in a time where Black, indigenous, and people of color (BIPOC) communities are subjugated to white supremacy and where Asian faculty, in particular, are typically erased or delegitimized from narratives of leadership. We cannot wait any longer.

MENTORSHIP

Linking the relationship between a department chair and a scholar, this text also serves as a testament to mentorship, which invited me to reflect on my lifelong journey of education. I remembered walking into an Asian American Psychology seminar curious about the content, without fully realizing that this class would serve as a pivotal moment in my journey. Dr. Irene Park's seminar brought forth a multitude of emotions that I had felt over my life, gave me language to contextualize my lived experiences, and named painful and resilient moments. This moment chartered a new motivation for me to locate points for racial equity and community organizing while sustaining efforts to dismantle racism and white supremacy. The course enhanced my ongoing commitment to social justice and activism as a lifelong career goal. Similarly, I reflect on my master's program and joining a research team under the supervision of Dr. Sara Cho Kim to research Asian American psychological issues, counseling experiences, and faculty experiences. Again, I revisited a moment of mentorship because I had never envisioned myself attaining a Ph.D. nor conducting research. As many years progressed, I continue to embrace the mentorship of my dissertation chair Dr. Sam Steen, whom I remember as the critical reason that I stayed in a doctoral program and received a Ph.D. Mentorship surfaces as a predominant catalyst as I reflect on stories of Asian American communities, scholars, faculty, and leaders.

Mentorship is reflected in this text through leadership, representation, and praxis, which have been cornerstones for contending with a racialized and white supremacist power structure (Chung, 2014; Kawahara et al., 2013; Maramba et al., 2017). The academy was ultimately constructed as a system devoted to white interests (An, 2020; Hayes & Hartlep, 2013). The importance of this text and its structure connect to meaningful stories about leadership that rarely feature Asian American leaders. Because of cultural values associated with a plethora of

Asian American communities, academics rarely perceive Asian American scholars and faculty as leaders (Lee, 2019). Rather than highlighting their strengths in community, harmony, and collectivism, Asian American scholars are overlooked for leadership roles or, in worse circumstances, denied promotion and tenure (Chin, 2013; Lee, 2019). In response, leadership offers a significant impetus to increase the pipeline and to share stories of success that dismantle barriers created by whiteness (Hayes & Hartlep, 2013; Matias, 2016). Representation of Asian American leadership lays the foundation for opportunities and generations of mentorship (Liang et al., 2018; Mac et al., 2019). For me, it has served as a reminder of paving the path forward for mentorship as a mechanism of transformation (Kawahara et al., 2013; Kodama & Dugan, 2019). As a timely and informative vehicle of storytelling, this text brings forth a personal connection to trials and possibilities of leadership that illuminate the promise of mentorship (Chin, 2013; Hartlep & Hensley, 2015). It serves as a reminder of our strengths as Asian American communities founded upon our kinship, hope, and joy (Kodama & Dugan, 2019).

A COLLECTION OF JOY

As I fully digested the heart of this text, I hold it close not only for me personally, but to share with the students I teach as an academic. I can recall the consistent message I share with students that the best part of my job is the opportunity to work with our students. As faculty and, particularly, for department chairs, we find joy in the academy through transgenerational work with students. We forage into an uncertain future that is ripe with the effects of racism, white supremacy, spirit murdering, xenophobia, and racial inequities (Williams, 1987). After reviewing this illuminating text, my hope for you is to find persistence and joy in your work. I hope that you find energy from and cherish your relationships that will transcend time and decades to come. We are living the dreams of our ancestors. We are dreaming of new possibilities. We are reimagining the future.

One day, I know this text will serve as the lifeline to a scholar's narrative of survival and resilience—one in which we are not only surviving, but also thriving. Let these stories speak to you. Let these stories forge your path as a catalyst for hope. Let these stories deepen your connection with your communities. In this collective, I see a vision of Grace Lee Boggs, a prominent Asian American activist, feminist, and Civil Rights revolutionary, who poignantly invoked the work of Margaret Wheatley, "We never know how our small activities will affect others through the invisible fabric of our connectedness. In this exquisitely connected world, it's never a question of 'critical mass.' It's always about critical connections" (Wheatley, 2008, p. 45) Thank you again to the editors and contributors for this text in addition to the scholar-activists who cultivate a path of generational fidelity and transformation. I will forever carry gratitude to the generations before me and the legacy to arrive after me.

REFERENCES

An, S. (2020). AsianCrit as a theoretical lens to trouble and transform white supremacy. In A. Hawkman & S. Shear (Eds.), *Marking the invisible: Articulating whiteness in social studies education* (pp. 3–28). Information Age Publishing.

Chan, C. D., Cor, D. N., & Band, M. P. (2018). Privilege and oppression in counselor education and supervision: An intersectionality framework. *The Journal of Multicultural Counseling and Development, 46*(1), 58–73. https://doi.org/10.1002/jmcd.12092

Chin, J. L. (2013). Introduction: Special section on Asian American leadership. *Asian American Journal of Psychology, 4*(4), 235–239. https://doi.org/10.1037/a0035144

Chung, J. Y. (2014). Racism and Asian American student leadership. *Equity & Excellence in Education, 47*(2), 117–132. https://doi.org/10.1080/10665684.2014.900392

Hartlep, N. D., & Hensley, B. O. (Eds.). (2015). *Critical storytelling in uncritical times: Stories disclosed in a Cultural Foundations of Education Course.* Sense Publishers.

Hayes, C., & Hartlep, N. D. (2013). *Unhooking from whiteness: The key to dismantling racism in the United States.* Sense Publishers.

Jones, S. R. (2016). Authenticity in leadership: Intersectionality of identities. *New Directions for Student Leadership, 2016*(152), 23–34. https://doi.org/10.1002/yd.20206

Kawahara, D. M., Pal, M. S., & Chin, J. L. (2013). The leadership experiences of Asian Americans. *Asian American Journal of Psychology, 4*(4), 240–248. https://doi.org/10.1037/a0035196

Kodama, C. M., & Dugan, J. P. (2019). Understanding the role of collective racial esteem and resilience in the development of Asian American leadership self-efficacy. *Journal of Diversity in Higher Education,* 1–13. https://doi.org/10.1037/dhe0000137

Koshino, K. (2016). Campus racial climate and experiences of students of color in a midwestern college. In F. Tuitt, C. Haynes, & S. Stewart (Eds.), *Race, equity, and the learning environment: The global relevance of critical and inclusive pedagogies in higher education* (pp. 98–111). Stylus.

Lee, F. (2019). Asian American and Pacific Islander faculty and the bamboo ceiling: Barriers to leadership and implications for leadership development. *New Directions for Higher Education, 2019*(186), 93–102. https://doi.org/10.1002/he.20326

Wheatley, M. J. (2008). Leadership and the new science. Berrett-Koehler.

Liang, J. G., Sottile, J., & Peters, A. L. (2018). Understanding Asian American women's pathways to school leadership. *Gender & Education, 30*(5), 623–641. https://doi.org/10.1080/09540253.2016.1265645

Mac, J., Sarreal, A. D., Wang, A. C., & Museus, S. D. (2019). Conditions that catalyze the emergence of Asian American and Native American Pacific Islander Serving institutions. *New Directions for Higher Education, 186,* 67–77. https://doi.org/10.1002/he.20324

Manzano, L. J., Poon, O. A., & Na, V. S. (2017). Asian American student engagement in student leadership and activism. *New Directions for Student Services, 2017*(160), 65–79. https://doi.org/10.1002/ss.20244

Maramba, D. C., Kodama, C. M., Manzano, L. J., Poon, O. Y. A., & Vanessa, S. (2017). Asian American student engagement in student leadership and activism: Asian American student engagement in student leadership and activism. *New Directions for Student Services, 2017*(160), 65–79. https://doi.org/10.1002/ss.20244

Matias, C. E. (2016). *Feeling white: Whiteness, emotionality, and education.* Sense Publishers.

Museus, S. D., Wang, A. C., Hyun White, H., & Na, V. S. (2019). A critical analysis of media discourse on affirmative action and Asian Americans. *New Directions for Higher Education, 2019*(186), 11–24. https://doi.org/10.1002/he.20320

Nakanishi, D. T. (1990). Why I fought. *Amerasia, 16*(1), 139–158.

Wijeyesinghe, C. L., & Strayhorn, T. L. (2017). Using intersectionality in student affairs research: Using intersectionality in student affairs research. *New Directions for Student Services, 2017*(157), 57–67. https://doi.org/10.1002/ss.20209

Williams, P. (1987). Spirit-murdering the messenger: The discourse of finger pointing as the law's response to racism. *University of Miami Law Review, 42*, 127–157.

About the Editors

Daisy Ball (Ph.D., Virginia Tech) is Associate Professor and Coordinator of the Criminal Justice Program in the Department of Public Affairs at Roanoke College (Salem, VA). Her research focuses on the intersection of race and the criminal justice system, with an emphasis on the criminal justice contact of Asian Americans. Recent publications have appeared in *Sociological Spectrum* and *Deviant Behavior*.

Nicholas D. Hartlep (Ph.D., University of Wisconsin, Milwaukee) is the Robert Charles Billings Endowed Chair in Education at Berea College where he Chairs the Department of Education Studies. Before coming to Berea College Dr. Hartlep Chaired the Department of Early Childhood and Elementary Education at Metropolitan State University, an Asian American and Native American Pacific Islander-Serving Institution (AANAPISI) in St. Paul, Minnesota. While there he also served as the Graduate Program Coordinator. Dr. Hartlep has published 23 books, the most recent being (2020) *Racial Battle Fatigue in Faculty: Perspectives and Lessons from Higher Education* which was published by Routledge. His book *The Neoliberal Agenda and the Student Debt Crisis in U.S. Higher Education*, with Lucille L. T. Eckrich and Brandon O. Hensley (2017) was named an Outstanding Book by the Society of Professors of Education. In 2020 he received three national awards: (1) *Diverse: Issues in Higher Education* named him an Emerging

Scholar, (2) the American Association for Access, Equity & Diversity (AAAED) granted him the first, Emerging Scholar Award, and (3) the Global Forum for Education and Learning (GFEL) named him a "Top 100 Leaders in Education." In 2018, the Association of State Colleges and Universities (AASCU) granted Dr. Hartlep the John Saltmarsh Award for Emerging Leaders in Civic Engagement Award. In 2017, Metropolitan State University presented him with both the 2017 Community Engaged Scholarship Award and the President's Circle of Engagement Award. In 2016, the University of Wisconsin, Milwaukee presented him with a Graduate of the Last Decade Award for his prolific writing. In 2015, he received the University Research Initiative Award from Illinois State University and a Distinguished Young Alumni Award from Winona State University. Follow his work on Twitter at @nhartlep or at his website, www.nicholashartlep.com or on his YouTube Channel www.youtube.com/nicholashartlep.

Kevin E. Wells (Ph.D., Baylor University) is Assistant Professor of Research and Educational Foundations at The University of Southern Mississippi. His research focuses on quantitative research methodology with emphases in structural equation modeling and non-linear longitudinal growth. He has recently authored or coauthored a series of articles dealing with temporal psychology that have appeared in a variety of journals, including, *Psychological Assessment*, *Psychiatry Research*, *Journal of Adolescence*, and *International Journal of Behavioral Development*. He is currently teaching courses in research methodology, educational statistics, and missing data.

About the Chapter Contributors

Charlotte Achieng-Evensen is a Kenyan-American poet, learner, and academic. Her scholarly work is centered in the intersections of Indigenous Philosophies and colonization, culturally responsive research methodologies, and professional learning for teaching practice within secondary schools. As well as presenting at multiple conferences on issues surrounding education, Dr. Achieng-Evensen has been a practitioner within the K–12 system for the past 18 years. In addition to her work as an adjunct professor, she currently serves her school district in the curriculum, instruction, and assessment office.

Cynthia Maribel Alcantar is a Visiting Professor of Sociology at Pitzer College and Postdoctoral Scholar for the Institute for Global-Local Action & Study (IGLAS). She is also a Research Associate for the Institute for Immigration, Globalization, & Education at the University of California, Los Angeles. Her research focuses on issues of college access and completion for first-generation college students, undocumented students, racial/ethnic minority students, and the impact of minority-serving institutions and community colleges. She has extensive experience working in K–12 and higher education settings, including Norco Community College, Claremont Graduate University, Mount St. Mary's College, and at John Adams Elementary in Riverside. Her research and practice have culminated in publications in *The Review of Higher Education, Teachers College Record, Harvard Educational Review,* and *Journal of Hispanic Higher Education.*

She received her B.A. from the University of California, Riverside in Psychology with a minor in Sociology, M.A. in Higher Education from Claremont Graduate University, and Ph.D. from the University of California, Los Angeles in Social Science and Comparative Education.

Timothy Bolin is an adjunct faculty member at Chapman University whose research explores educational, theoretical, and policy interventions that may promote social change. Specifically, his work demonstrates what role contemporary leaderless democratic movements and community/university partnerships may play in transforming society. Applying his research, he explores the ways that researchers can ethically, equitably, and democratically engage with the community.

Christian D. Chan (he, him, his), Ph.D., NCC is an Assistant Professor in the Department of Counseling and Educational Development at The University of North Carolina at Greensboro, President of the Association for Adult Development and Aging (AADA), and a proud Queer Person of Color. As a scholar-activist, his interests revolve around intersectionality; multiculturalism in counseling practice, supervision, and counselor education; social justice and activism; career development; critical research methodologies; and couple, family, and group modalities with socialization/communication of cultural factors. Dedicated to mentorship for leaders and scholars, he has actively contributed to over 43 peer-reviewed publications in journals, books, and edited volumes and has conducted over 120 refereed presentations at the national, regional, and state levels. He currently serves on the editorial boards of *Journal of Counseling & Development*, *Counselor Education and Supervision*, *Journal of Multicultural Counseling and Development*, *Journal of LGBT Issues in Counseling*, *Adultspan*, *Journal of Counseling Sexology & Sexual Wellness: Research, Practice, and Education*, and *Asia Pacific Career Development Journal*.

Gaowei Chen is an Associate Professor in the Faculty of Education at the University of Hong Kong. He received a B.S. in Information Engineering from Xi'an Jiaotong University, and an M.S. in Educational Technology from Peking University. He received his Ph.D. in Educational Psychology from the Chinese University of Hong Kong. Before joining the University of Hong Kong, he spent three years as a postdoctoral associate in the Learning Research and Development Center at the University of Pittsburgh. His research interests include computer supported collaborative learning, classroom dialogue, technology-enhanced teacher education, STEM education, learning analytics, and educational assessment.

Crystal Chen Lee is an Assistant Professor of Literacy and English Language Arts in the Department of Teacher Education and Learning Sciences at North Carolina State University in Raleigh, NC. Her work examines the intersections among literacy, teacher education, and community-based organizations in urban and multicultural communities. She received her Ed.D. from Teachers College, Columbia University and her B.A. and M.Ed. from Rutgers University. Crystal began her teaching career as a high school English teacher in New Jersey.

Sheng-Lun Cheng (Ph.D., Ohio State University) is an Assistant Professor of Instructional Systems Design and Technology (ISDT) in the Department of Library Science and Technology at Sam Houston State University. Dr. Cheng earned his Ph.D. in Learning Technologies from the College of Education and Human Ecology at Ohio State University. At Ohio State University, Dr. Cheng worked as a research associate at The Research Laboratory for Digital Learning on state-wide funded projects related to technology initiatives in K–12 settings and found his passion for improving students' learning in technology-enhanced environments. Before joining the faculty at Sam Houston State University, Dr. Cheng pursued his postdoctoral training at Virginia Commonwealth University where he worked with faculty members in the School of Education on planning, designing, and implementing research to examine the well-being of at-risk students in public schools. Dr. Cheng's current research focuses on college students' motivation and self-regulation in online courses and in-service teachers' technology integration in K–12 settings with an aim to help at-risk students learn better in technology-enhanced environments.

Kate Dooley is currently an Assistant Professor of Special Education at the University of Saint Joseph in West Hartford, CT. She is a doctoral candidate in Educational Psychology in the Department of Special Education at the Neag School of Education at the University of Connecticut (UCONN). Her research foci are School-Wide Positive Behavior Intervention and Supports (SWPBIS) and self-management for adolescents with behavioral challenges. She received her master of arts in Education and her bachelor of science in Special Education from the University of Saint Joseph in West Hartford, CT.

Jennifer Freeman is an Assistant Professor in the Department of Educational Psychology and is a research scientist for the Center for Behavioral Education Research (CBER) at the University of Connecticut. Dr. Freeman studies the effects of Positive Behavior Interventions and Supports (PBIS) on outcomes at the high school level for high-risk student groups including students with disabilities. She is particularly interested in improving graduation rates across and within student groups. She also studies professional development methods for improving teachers' use of evidence based classroom management strategies. She currently teaches undergraduate and graduate courses in the special education program. Prior to joining the faculty at the University of Connecticut, she had 10 years of special education teaching experience across grades K–8 in both urban and rural school settings and had served as a K–12 district level consultant working to implement PBIS and Response to Intervention (RtI) strategies.

Brandon O. Hensley (Ph.D., Illinois State University) is an independent scholar and award-winning educator who lives in Michigan and continues his research in bullying, whiteness studies, and student loan debt. In addition to co-editing *Critical Storytelling in 2020: Issues, Elections and Beyond* with Brill Publishers (Hensley, Hartlep, & Novak, 2020), his most recent single-authored work is a public speaking textbook titled *Building Your Voice: Powerful Public Speaking in the 21st Century* (2018, Great River Learning). You can find Brandon's work at https://wayne.academia.edu/BrandonHensley.

Xinye Hu is a doctoral student in the Higher Education program at Florida State University (FSU). She earned her M.S. in Education Policy and Evaluation from the same department in 2016. She has been working as a graduate assistant in the quantitative team of the Center for Postsecondary Success at FSU since August 2016. Before that she interned in the Dean's Office in the College of Education at FSU for two semesters to assist with data organizing, statistical analyses, and information reporting. She is interested in college access and student success.

Ed Kame'enui is the Dean-Knight Professor Emeritus in the College of Education, Founding Director of the Center on Teaching and Learning (CTL) and Associate Dean for Research and Faculty Development at the University of Oregon (UO), where he has been since 1987. Prior to the UO, Ed was a faculty member at the University of Montana and Purdue University. From 2005 to 2007, Ed took leave from the University of Oregon and moved to Washington, DC to accept an appointment as the Founding Commissioner of the National Center for Special Education Research (NCSER) in the Institute of Education Sciences (IES), the research, evaluation and statistical arm of the U.S. Department of Education. Ed has spoken at the White House, participated in presentations with First Lady Laura Bush at UNESCO in Paris, and represented the U.S. Department of Education in Doha, Qatar. He has directed several national federal research initiatives and also served on the original advisory boards for the PBS television shows "Between the Lions" and WETA's "Reading Rockets." Dr. Kame'enui has co-authored 20 college textbooks and has more than 200 publications, mostly refereed research articles and book chapters. He has served as Principal Investigator (PI) or Co-Principal Investigator (Co-PI) for more than $70 million federal and private research and training grant awards. In 2006, Dr. Kame'enui was awarded the Distinguished Special Education Researcher Award from the American Educational Research Association (AERA). In 2015, he received the award for Outstanding Alumni from the College of Education at the University of Oregon where he received his Ph.D. in 1980.

Laura Kern is currently a Postdoctoral Research Scholar at the University of South Florida. She is finishing her doctorate in Educational Psychology with a focus on Special Education at the University of Connecticut's Neag School of Education and is interested in the intersection of policy with educational practice, the reduction of aggressive behaviors in schools, and the implementation of multi-tiered systems of support. She practiced law for over 10 years before studying special education, receiving her J.D. from Quinnipiac University. She also received her master of arts in special education from the University of Connecticut.

Brian C. Kim is a research technician in the Department of Radiation Oncology at the Perelman School of Medicine. His research focuses on investigating mechanisms of radiation resistance in cancer and methods to enhance current immunotherapy treatments. He earned both his M.S. in Chemistry and B.A. in Biochemistry at the University of Pennsylvania in 2017. He will pursue a combined M.D./Ph.D. program starting in the fall of 2018.

David Wesley Lausch holds a doctorate in Educational Administration from the University of Wyoming's College of Education. He studies Adult and Postsecondary Education. David has taught instructional technology, introduction to research, and multicultural international education for undergraduate and masters students. Formerly a K–12 humanities teacher in Japan, Kuwait, United Arab Emirates, and California, he has also recently worked on developing statewide systems of support for K–12 administrators in Wyoming, the ECHO Network. David's research interests include the academic retention, graduation, support, acculturation, and experiences of international students in U.S. higher education.

Amy E. Lein is currently an Assistant Professor of Special Education at Bellarmine University in Louisville, Kentucky. Before moving to Louisville, she worked as a Master Coach for Minnesota Math Corps and adjunct faculty at the University of Minnesota in Minneapolis where she earned her Ph.D. in Educational Psychology and received the Balow Dissertation Award. Dr. Lein also has a Master's degree in Special Education from Lesley University in Cambridge, Massachusetts. As a former public school teacher, she taught special education and general education mathematics at the high school and middle school levels in both the Boston metro area and in Charlotte, Michigan.

Yanli Ma is currently Institutional Research and Assessment Specialist at Elmhurst College. He received his Ph.D. in Higher Education from Florida State University and his M.A. in Linguistics from the University of Georgia. His research examines college student retention and success, assessment of student learning outcomes, and practice in the field of institutional research. He has published articles in journals such as *Innovative Higher Education, Journal of College Student Retention*, and *New Directions for Institutional Research.*

Bethany D. Merillat (M.S., Ohio University, M.Ed., Cleveland State University) is a health and education research psychologist focused on helping individuals in all stages and walks of life live happier, healthier, and more productive lives. Her research has focused on better understanding the factors that influence and impact educational outcomes, and interventions to help individuals make better choices about the foods they eat, and how they live. She has eight peer-reviewed publications and has contributed to a number of poster and educational presentations.

Bach Mai Dolly Nguyen is an assistant professor of education at Oregon State University. Her research examines the relationship between social categorization and inequality in education, with particular attention to racial and organizational classifications. These foci have manifested in studies on minority serving institutions (MSIs), ethnic stratification, and organizational behavior. Her research has been published in *American Educational Research Journal, Review of Research in Education* and *Review of Higher Education* and is currently supported by the Bill & Melinda Gates Foundation and Spencer Foundation. Dolly is currently writing her first book (under contract with University of Chicago Press) on how higher education organizations at the intersection of two MSI designations navigate racialized tensions, enact widespread cultural ideals, or "myths," and give life to unique organizational frames of racial equity.

Rita Poimbeauf is an educator with nearly 50 years of service to the education field; she recently retired. She began her career as a teacher's aide in Ohio and concluded her career teaching prospective teachers and aspiring principals at the University of Houston in Houston and Victoria, Texas. Dr. Poimbeauf worked for 31 years in public schools, and as a principal of elementary and secondary schools for 27 of those years. During that time, she became a proponent of year-round education and started the first year-round school in Texas. Dr. Poimbeauf became the state president for the Texas Association of Year-Round Education and later was a member of the Board of Directors for the National Association for Year-Round Education (NAYRE). After completion of her Ed.D. in Administration and Supervision at the University of Houston (UH) where she studied teacher training and in-service practices, she remained on campus teaching and became intensely interested in Asian studies. That led to a research position in the Asian American Studies Center (UH) under the direction of Dr. Yali Zou. In all, Dr. Poimbeauf has made eight trips to China for pleasure and research. Dr. Poimbeauf's research has resulted in papers, publications and presentations. Written with two associates, a selection of her work includes: *Three Images of the Principalship: One Narrative Account of Schooling in China* (2014); *Journal Writing as a Way to Know Culture: Insights from a Travel Study Abroad Program* (2015); *Narrative Inquiry as a Travel Study Method: Affordances and Constraints* (2013); *China Study Trips: Expanding Teaching and Leadership Horizons* (2014); and *What the West Could Learn from the East: Retrospective Analysis of a Research Project Conducted in a Chinese School* (2016). Dr. Poimbeauf also in 2014 edited for Tianjin University in Tianjin, China a book on Chinese culture titled, *Knowing China by Learning Chinese Culture*. Although now retired, Dr. Poimbeauf hopes to continue writing about her passion for China.

Kongji Qin (Ph.D., New York University) is an Assistant Professor of TESOL, Bilingual, and Foreign Language Education in the Department of Teaching and Learning at New York University. His research centers on the language and literacy education of emergent bilingual students in K–12 classrooms. One line of his research focuses on understanding the relationship between racialized masculinity and language learning of adolescent immigrant boys. Another line of his research examines issues related to preparing linguistically responsive teachers for English learners, particularly on the development of language-related knowledge for subject area teachers. In this area of research, Dr. Qin's work has been supported by the Spencer Foundation and the Research Challenge Grant at New York University. His work has been published in prominent peer-reviewed journals such as *Research in the Teaching of English, International Multilingual Research Journal, Reading Research Quarterly*, and *The Modern Language Journal*.

Brandi Simonsen (Ph.D., University of Oregon) is a professor of Special Education with tenure in the Department of Educational Psychology at the Neag School of Education and a co-director of the Center for Behavioral Education and Research (CBER) at the University of Connecticut. She is a partner of the National Technical Assistance Center on Positive Behavior Interventions and Supports (PBIS). Dr. Simonsen conducts research, publishes, teaches, and provides training/technical assistance in the areas of (a) school- and class-wide PBIS, (b) positive and proactive professional development supports for teachers, and (c) applications of PBIS in alternative settings. In addition, Dr. Simonsen coordinates UConn's Graduate Certificate Program in School-Wide Positive Behavior Support. Before joining the faculty at University of Connecticut in 2005, Dr. Simonsen was the director of a non-public (alternative) school for students with disabilities who presented with challenging educational and behavioral needs.

Sheetal Sood (Ph.D., Lehigh University) is currently the Chair of the Department of Education and an Associate Professor of Special Education at the University of Hartford, where she teaches both undergraduate and graduate courses in Special Education. She helps pre-service teachers develop and differentiate between wide ranges of instructional strategies to ensure that their students can reach their highest academic potential. Dr. Sood's research interests focus on investigating methods to improve mathematics instruction for pre–K through elementary school students who are at risk of, or are identified with, a disability. In addition, she is also interested in early intervention, instructional design, textbook analysis, and curriculum-based assessment. Her most recent research focuses on the impact of Number Sense instruction on mathematics competence of elementary school students.

Kevin Stockbridge (Ph.D., Chapman University) received his doctorate in Education from Chapman University with an emphasis in Curriculum and Culture Studies. He is a critical scholar of sexuality and gender, focusing on the construction of queer identities within Catholic educational contexts. Kevin currently teaches as an adjunct professor at Chapman University in Education and the Humanities. He hopes to embody some of the transformative lessons that he continues to learn from his mentor, Dr. Suzanne SooHoo, in his work as educator, activist, and scholar.

Vanessa W. Vongkulluksn (Ph.D., University of Southern California) is an Assistant Professor for the Learning Sciences Program in the Department of Educational Psychology and Higher Education at the University of Nevada, Las Vegas (UNLV). She earned her Ph.D. in Education with a concentration in Educational Psychology and Quantitative Methods from Rossier School of Education, University of Southern California. Before joining the faculty at UNLV, Dr. Vongkulluksn was a school-based researcher and postdoctoral scholar at The Ohio State University, during which time she found her passion for research-community partnerships. Dr. Vongkulluksn's research utilizes a variety of statistical methods to examine factors associated with student learning and motivation in technology-integrated contexts, particularly the influence of digital and information literacy skills on student learning. Through her work, she is committed to find specific, actionable changes for the design of learning environments that match the needs and affordances of modern classrooms. She is driven to help diverse students develops digital and twenty-first century skills they need to become effectual learners and well-informed future citizens.

Jonathan Wai (Ph.D., Vanderbilt University) is Assistant Professor of Education Policy and Psychology, the twenty-first century Endowed Chair in Education Policy in the Department of Education Reform at the University of Arkansas, and also holds a joint (courtesy) appointment in the Department of Psychology. He was a Von Brock Postdoctoral Fellow and Research Scientist at Duke University, Visiting Scholar in the Department of Psychology at Case Western Reserve University, and Research Fellow at Geisinger. His work has been cited over 3,000 times on Google Scholar, and has appeared in *Journal of Educational Psychology, Contemporary Educational Psychology, British Journal of Educational Psychology, Policy Insights from the Behavioral and Brain Sciences, Current Directions in Psychological Science*, and *Perspectives on Psychological Science*, among others. He has received multiple international Mensa Awards for Research Excellence, the AERA Michael Pyryt Collaboration Award, and his work has been funded by the American Psychological Foundation and the Walton Family Foundation. He serves as "member at large" for the AERA Research on Giftedness, Creativity, and Talent Development group, on the Board of Directors of the International Society for Intelligence Research, and on the editorial boards of *Intelligence, Journal of Expertise, Journal for the Education of the Gifted*, and *Gifted Child Quarterly*. His work has been featured multiple times in *The New York Times, The Wall Street Journal, The Washington Post, The Economist, Scientific American, Nature*, and *Science*. He has served on the board of directors of the MATHCOUNTS foundation. Broadly, he studies education policy through the lens of psychology. Twitter: @JonathanLWai. Website: jonathanwai.net.

Yurou Wang (Ph.D., University of Kansas) is a Clinical Assistant Professor of Educational Studies in Psychology at the University of Alabama. Her research agenda coalesces around motivation, emotion, and the usage of advanced quantitative statistical modeling, specifically how students internalize learning motivations and beliefs to influence their persistence and self-regulation, particularly within different cultural contexts. She endeavors to uncover cultural differences among Western and East Asian student's learning motivation, as well as the degree to which students internalize different learning motivations. Her current research agenda encompasses experiments on students' learning persistence, social-emotional competence, self-regulated learning, and achievement emotion. Her Micro-Facial Expression Tracking (MET) Lab seeks to understand students' emotions and persistence while they are conducting various learning tasks. Website: https://yurouwang.people.ua.edu/

Chanjin Zheng (Ph.D., University of Illinois at Urbana-Champaign) is an associate professor of the Department of Educational Psychology, Faculty of Education, East China Normal University (ECNU), Shanghai, China. His research interests mainly include educational and psychological assessment, cognitive diagnostic modeling, computerized adaptive testing, and applied statistics. He has published over 20 articles in peer-reviewed journals including *Journal of Applied Psychology*, *Journal of Educational Measurement*, *Applied Psychological Measurement*, and *International Journal of Testing*. Follow his work at his webpage, http://www.dep.ecnu.edu.cn/b6/db/c16533a177883/page.htm.

Author Index

Subject Index

EDUCATION and STRUGGLE

Narrative, Dialogue,
and the Political
Production
of Meaning

Michael A. Peters
Peter McLaren
Series Editors

To submit a
manuscript or
proposal for editorial
consideration,
please contact:

Dr. Peter McLaren
Chapman University
College of Educa-
tional Studies
Reeves Hall 205
Orange, CA 92866

Dr. Michael A. Peters
University of Waikato
P.O. Box 3105
Faculty of Education
Hamilton 3240
New Zealand

WE ARE THE STORIES WE TELL. The book series Education and Struggle focuses on conflict as a discursive process where people struggle for legitimacy and the narrative process becomes a political struggle for meaning. But this series will also include the voices of authors and activists who are involved in conflicts over material necessities in their communities, schools, places of worship, and public squares as part of an ongoing search for dignity, self-determination, and autonomy. This series focuses on conflict and struggle within the realm of educational politics based around a series of interrelated themes: indigenous struggles; Western-Islamic conflicts; globalization and the clash of worldviews; neoliberalism as the war within; colonization and neocolonization; the coloniality of power and decolonial pedagogy; war and conflict; and the struggle for liberation. It publishes narrative accounts of specific struggles as well as theorizing "conflict narratives" and the political production of meaning in educational studies. During this time of global conflict and the crisis of capitalism, Education and Struggle promises to be on the cutting edge of social, cultural, educational, and political transformation.

Central to the series is the idea that language is a process of social, cultural, and class conflict. The aim is to focus on key semiotic, literary, and political concepts as a basis for a philosophy of language and culture where the underlying materialist philosophy of language and culture serves as the basis for the larger project that we might call dialogism (after Bakhtin's usage). As the late V. N. Volosinov suggests "Without signs there is no ideology," "Everything ideological possesses semiotic value," and "individual consciousness is a socio-ideological fact." It is a small step to claim, therefore, "consciousness itself can arise and become a viable fact only in the material embodiment of signs." This series is a vehicle for materialist semiotics in the narrative and dialogue of education and struggle.

To order other books in this series, please contact our Customer Service Department:

peterlang@presswarehouse.com (within the U.S.)
orders@peterlang.com (outside the U.S.)

Or browse online by series:

www.peterlang.com

www.ingramcontent.com/pod-product-compliance
Lightning Source LLC
Chambersburg PA
CBHW070937050326
40689CB00014B/3244